Gender and Generation

YOUTH QUESTIONS

Series Editors: PHILIP COHEN and ANGELA McROBBIE

This series sets out to question the ways in which youth has traditionally been defined by social scientists and policy-makers, by the caring professions and the mass media, as well as in 'common-sense' ideology. It explores some of the new directions in research and practice which are beginning to challenge existing patterns of knowledge and provision. Each book examines a particular aspect of the youth question in depth. All of them seek to connect their concerns to the major political and intellectual debates that are now taking place about the present crisis and future shape of our society. The series will be of interest to those who deal professionally with young people, especially those concerned with the development of socialist, feminist and anti-racist perspectives. But it is also aimed at students and general readers who want a lively and accessible introduction to some of the most awkward but important issues of our time.

Published

Inge Bates, John Clarke, Philip Cohen, Dan Finn, Robert Moore and Paul Willis
SCHOOLING FOR THE DOLE?
The New Vocationalism

Angela McRobbie and Mica Nava (eds)
GENDER AND GENERATION

Forthcoming

Philip Cohen and Harwant Bains (eds)
MULTI-RACIST BRITAIN

Philip Cohen and Graham Murdock (eds)
THE MAKING OF THE YOUTH QUESTION

Andrew Dewdney and Martin Lister
YOUTH PHOTOGRAPHY

Dan Finn
TRAINING WITHOUT JOBS:
From the Raising of the School-Leaving Age to the New Training Initiative

Gender and Generation

Edited by
Angela McRobbie and Mica Nava

MACMILLAN

First published 1984 by
Higher and Further Educaton Division
MACMILLAN PUBLISHERS LTD
Houndmills, Basingstoke, Hampshire, RG21 2XS, and London
Companies and representatives
throughout the world

Typeset by
Wessex Typesetters Ltd
Frome, Somerset

Printed in Great Britain by
The Pitman Press,
Bath

British Library Cataloguing in Publication Data
Gender and generation.
1. Youth—Sexual behaviour
I. McRobbie, Angela   II. Nava, Mica
306.7′088055   HQ27
ISBN 0–333–33251–2
ISBN 0–333–33252–0 Pbk

Contents

Acknowledgements

Many people have contributed directly and indirectly to the ideas expressed in this book. We would particularly like to thank the following for their interest, support and constructive criticism: Lucy Bland; Peter Chalk; Hanna Chalmers; Martin Chalmers; Phil Cohen; Simon Frith; Phil Jones; Matthew Jones; Steven Kennedy; Clara Mulhern; Jake Nava; Orson Nava; Zadoc Nava; Michelle Stanworth.

ANGELA McROBBIE
MICA NAVA

Contributors

Erica Carter is completing her thesis at the Centre for Contemporary Cultural Studies, University of Birmingham.

Adrian Chappell works in the Cultural Studies Department, ILEA Cockpit Arts Workshop.

Barbara Hudson is at present researching into juvenile justice. The article published here is based on work done while at Essex University.

Angela McRobbie teaches Complementary Studies at St Martin's School of Art.

Mica Nava is a lecturer in Cultural Studies at North East London Polytechnic.

Valerie Walkerdine is a lecturer at the University of London Institute of Education.

Julian Wood is completing his research on disruptive units.

Introduction

Angela McRobbie and Mica Nava

When we first began to think about assembling this collection we were very conscious of the fact that certain youth questions had been dealt with exhaustively while others remained quite unexplored. Our objective was then clear from the start. It was to move away from a preoccupation with youth as deviant, youth as spectacular, youth as a peculiarly and unproblematically male genus – involved in the culture of the street, playground and shop floor but absent from the domestic sphere and from personal and inter-generational relationships. We wanted to focus upon the ordinary. We wanted to find articles which looked at relations *between* boys and girls; at age relations; at the everyday leisure activities and at the regulation of young people. And above all we wanted to centrestage the question of gender. The fundamental impulse for this book, then, was the desire to expose the ways in which commonplace relations, experiences and representations of youth are quite crucially related to questions of the masculine and the feminine.

This theoretical paradigm is broad and important absences remain, as inevitably they will. But as editors we also felt that in the present climate of youth politics we wanted to address questions of current practice. Thus in a context in which girls' projects are proliferating throughout the country, in which anti-sexist learning materials are being produced in schools and in which political education initiatives are being established for school-leavers, in which a feminist critique of sexual harrassment is daily gaining common assent, and (finally) in which the impact of feminism on popular cultural forms like television is growing, we need to be constantly vigilant about the quality of these interventions and about the analysis that underpins them. A number of articles in this book concern themselves with precisely these areas of feminist influence.

These then are the themes which reappear throughout *Gender and Generation* and which connect the articles in it to each other. Thus Mica Nava's piece, 'Youth Service Provision, Social Order and the Question of Girls' starts off by looking at the history of the youth service and at its contribution to the social policing of young people, particularly in urban areas. This is in order to highlight the striking failure of the youth service to provide amenities for girls; Nava argues that this failure is related to the fact that girls do not constitute a street problem in the way in which boys do. She then goes on to examine some of the distinctive ways in which girls are regulated, and in a detailed concluding section, assesses recent feminist attempts to compensate for the historical marginalisation of girls in the youth club movement by demanding for them extra and special provision – by creating girls' projects.

Barbara Hudson is also concerned with the regulation of girls and in 'Femininity and Adolescence' she examines the ways in which the institutional definitions that operate in social work and schooling have effects upon them. She argues that among social workers the dominant expectation is for girls to conform to conventions of femininity, whereas among teachers the expectation is that girls will behave as adolescents – as unruly and immature. The connotations of adolescence and femininity thus generate conflicting standards; indeed the discourse of adolescence often subverts that of femininity. Barbara Hudson gives further substance to her assertion by drawing attention to the appearance of these contradictions in popular magazines for teenage girls.

Julian Wood's piece 'Groping Towards Sexism' is the result of several months intensive research in a secondary school disruptive unit. It is an unusual contribution to the field of youth studies in that it critically examines sexual power relations between boys and girls in a way which combines a recognition of the importance of the feminist critique with a personal and masculine perspective. Wood describes how much adolescent male heterosexuality operates in a collective fashion both at the level of fantasy and in its overt daily enactment in and out of the classroom. These expressions of boys' sexuality are frequently aggressive, constraining and depersonalising for girls. Mica Nava, in her second piece 'Drawing the Line' also focuses upon the power component in sexual relations, this time in the context of an encounter between a male teacher and a fourteen-year-old boy pupil. Her particular concerns in this article are, on the one hand, to analyse the theoretical, moral and practical dilemmas such relationships raise for feminists, and on the other, to draw attention to the limitations of the existing institutional procedures designed to deal with circumstances of this nature.

In 'Family Fortunes' Adrian Chappell describes an innovatory photography project in which an eighteen-year-old girl constructs and uses a series of photomontage panels with accompanying text to explore some of her growing reservations about her anticipated place in the world of wives and mothers. Her work, most of which is reproduced here, serves at once as a private reflection of her new family (she has moved in with her boyfriend and his parents) and also as a document of some features of contemporary working-class femininity.

Visuality and representation are key terms in the final three contributions to the book. Angela McRobbie, in 'Dance and Social Fantasy', provides an analysis of dance and disco culture. She shows the special place it has within women's and girls' leisure, and she suggests that its popularity is carried as much in texts and images as in direct experience. To justify this claim she considers, briefly, schoolgirl ballet books, and in more detail, the television programme *Fame* and the film *Flashdance*. Following on from this Valerie Walkerdine takes up fantasy in its more precise psychoanalytical meaning and shows how it functions in the context of little girls' comics and magazines. She suggests that for those engaged in developing alternative practices of representation, and for those interested in challenging the hegemony of official femininity as defined in the pages of *Bunty*, *Tracey*, *Jackie* and *My Guy*, it is not enough simply to replace 'weak' with 'strong' images, passivity with action or fantasy with realism.

Finally Erica Carter takes up some of the other stubborn pleasures of popular culture which have escaped the notice of mainstream sociologists. In her examination of teenage experience in post-war West Germany she sheds light on the importance of shopping and consumerism in the development of 'appropriate' modes of youthful femininity. But these are, she claims, still contradictory processes, as much open to subversion as to absolute conformity. Carter locates consumerism as the missing link in the chain which connects the products of popular culture, especially fashion, with the body and thus with the self. She shows more generally how buying is a vital part of our orientation towards the modern world.

In all of these articles the construction and contradictions of gender and generation constitute a central axis around which other more detailed preoccupations revolve. Since this is one of a series of books addressed to questions of youth it covers only a relatively narrow range of concerns. We hope however that the particular selection we have made will expand the conceptual field of inquiry and inform as well as provoke a reconsideration of some current political phenomena.

1

Youth Service Provision, Social Order and the Question of Girls

Mica Nava

> Mixed provision is . . . in reality predominantly male . . . but is
> described as mixed . . . as no one actually excludes the girls.
> (Camden Area Youth Committee, 1982, p. 7)

In this article I look at the development of the youth service in
Britain as a form of provided leisure and at the historical marginalisation of girls within this. An examination of these issues illumi-
nates both the part played by youth work provision in the social
policing of young people and the distinctive mode in which girls are
regulated. I also look at the consequences of these phenomena for
contemporary youth work, and draw out some of the implications of
the different kinds of politics and practice embedded in feminist
youth work with girls. However, I shall start off by making some
general observations about the study of youth and about the
shifting and sometimes contradictory definitions, relations and
location of young people.

As is well known, during the last fifteen years an enormous
amount of work has been done in order to refine our understanding
and analysis of the social position of women, and a study of the
specific attributes of girlhood has been included in this project.
Over the same period, the field of youth studies has also expanded
and a considerable amount of research has been done into the
particularities of the situation of young people. It is by now a
commonplace to point out that this second body of work has been
predominantly about boys – usually white urban working-class boys
– and that girls are rendered visible only where they are pertinent to
the experience and perceptions of the boys.[1] In these studies a
critical analysis of the relationship *between* boys and girls rarely

1

appears. But much feminist work has also failed to address this terrain: it has concerned itself either with the culture and circumstances of girls only, or – as has generally been the case in sociological and psychological studies of childhood, youth and schooling – it has compared boys and girls. The different educational performances, the different positions of boys and girls as subjects in an adult world, have been contrasted. But the power relations which connect and define boys and girls as distinct categories, and which vary according to the context or discourse in which they are situated, have tended to be neglected. Yet the relationships *between* boys and girls and *between* masculinity and femininity are of considerable importance. In this article I draw attention to the way in which aspects of these relationships become apparent in the course of a more general examination of the provision of leisure facilities for young people.

Another common absence in the study of youth is an analysis of gender difference in the relationship of young people to adulthood. Distinctions between girlhood and adulthood and the transition from one to the other have been presumed to be the same as those between boyhood and adulthood. Youth *in relation to adulthood* has been understood as a category undivided by differences of sex, race and class, that is to say by all those differences we immediately look for *within* the categories of youth and adulthood. Yet these are issues which cannot be taken for granted. Differences of age and class may not have the same significance for women as they do for men; class, for example, has been a more significant divider of women at some historical conjunctures than at others. These are questions which again are pertinent in a study of the youth service and also have particular implications for feminist youth work with girls.

Historically youth has been an enormously variable category, and of course still is. Not only, for example, is there no agreement about which age group constitutes 'youth' (manifested in the fluctuating age of entitlement to half-fares, educational grants, marriage and the vote), over recent years young people have contradictorily been defined as the mainstay of industries such as music and fashion (both as consumers and producers) and simultaneously as in need of supervision, control and training. Dominant preoccupations and perceptions about young people are neither constant nor coherent. They shift, as do institutional definitions and the structural location of youth, in relation to other changes. Thus in a period of recession and unemployment a number of new attributes of youth are produced and exposed to scrutiny. One of the most striking of these is that young people who are unemployed or on government training schemes (and who tend to be working-class) are dependent upon the income of their family of origin for an unprecedented length of time. With the raising of the school-leaving age in the early seventies and the youth opportunity programmes and unemployment of more recent years, there has in effect been a prolongation of the period of childhood – of young people's dependency and of parental responsibility and control.[2] The decline in the material power of young people has led to a decline in their importance as consumers. Since so few jobs are available, 'adult' comportment and 'respectable' appearance become increasingly irrrelevant. The possibilities of moving away from home, of travelling (even to the centre of town) recede. Not only are young people increasingly disassociated from the culture of employment and from financial resources of their own, they are confined to the local street and family culture of their schooldays.

This process of infantilisation which has occurred over recent years has increased the relative importance of the informal activities and relations of the street, of leisure, the youth club and the domestic sphere.[3] These are contexts which are differently structured from those of employment, consumption and schooling, and which when examined can illuminate aspects of gender and generational relations not immediately visible in studies of the economy and education. Youth culture of the street and club is relatively unshaped and unsupervised by adults; it thus both transforms and exposes relationships within the category of youth. The current economic climate then, when combined with the feminist critique which, as well as stressing the need to focus upon girls, has always emphasised the importance of the domestic sphere, indicates also the need for a much closer examination of the activities and regulation of boys and girls within the *home*. As a subject, the domestic lives of young people has rarely been considered of significance either in studies of the family or in studies of youth. In contrast however, urban street culture has featured prominently in the sociology of youth for some time now.[4] It would therefore be misleading to imply that the contemporary context of unemployment, riots and recession is alone responsible for the current focus upon young people and their 'leisure' – this preoccupation has a very long history. Nevertheless present-day political circumstances both centrestage these issues and offer new ways of looking at them; it becomes possible to postulate theoretical links between youth on the streets, youth service provision, and the regulation of young people within the family. An examination of gender differences in these domains will be the project of this article.

The development of the youth service as a form of provided leisure

It is of course no longer new to draw attention to the fact that anxiety about the visible presence of youth on the streets has been not about youth in general, but about working-class male youth. Concerns expressed about dirty and unruly children during the period of rapid urbanisation and social dislocation prior to the imposition of compulsory education in the nineteenth century, in which insurrection appeared a constant possibility, were mainly concerns about boys (Mayhew, 1968; Stedman Jones, 1976; Gillis, 1974; Walvin, 1982; Pearson, 1983). Late nineteenth-century and early twentieth-century attempts to regulate the leisure time and supervise the moral development of disorderly working-class youth, were on the whole directed towards young males (Blanch, 1979; Gillis, 1974; Thompson, 1975). In nineteenth-century representations of youth subcultures, youth unemployment, youth as rioter, youth in opposition–in the imagery of youth as a problem – girls were usually invisible. As Blanch has said, '"youth" [is a] term with strongly masculine and delinquent connotations' (1979, p. 103; see also Hebdige, 1982).

The development of the present youth service and the creation of special provision for young people outside formal schooling can be interpreted largely as a response to these 'masculine and delinquent connotations' of youth. Torwards the end of the nineteenth century, with the advent of compulsory education, working-class children were displaced as a problematic and disruptive genus by post elementary school 'youth'. Gillis (1974) has suggested that this was the period of the emergence of the social category of 'adolescence'. The period also saw the emergence and consolidation of voluntary youth organisations and clubs which acted as a complement to schooling; in addition to religious and moral guidance they offered a form of out-of-school surveillance and social policing by members of the Church and middle classes. A founder of the Working Boys' Clubs wrote in 1890 that the clubs provided 'wholesome recreation' to those who would otherwise be likely to have only 'vicious and degrading pleasures' (quoted in Simon, 1974, p. 70). The objectives of the Boys' Brigade were stated in 1883 to be 'The Advancement of Christ's Kingdom among Boys, the promotion of habits of Obedience, Reverence, Discipline, Self-Respect and all that tends towards a true Christian manliness' (quoted in Simon, p. 64). Blanch (1979) has argued that during this period coercive measures were increasingly used to suppress street subcultures and control the spare time of young people by directing them into 'provided leisure forms'. Most of these provided activities were not only moral and religious in content, they were also unquestionably militaristic, and had the aim of cultivating the *esprit de corps* considered to be lamentably lacking in the poor – that is to say, patriotism and discipline. Underlying the provision was an attempt to contain street problems and delinquency among mainly working-class boys; an additional objective however, was to combat the seditious influence of workers' social and political clubs. Youth provision was thus part of a much wider attempt to create moral and social cohesion, to win consent. Brian Simon (1974) has concluded that the youth movement initiated in the latter part of the nineteenth century was a 'reaction to the problems of a particular period, to a particular and a menacing social crisis' (p. 71). Its aim was predominantly to 'preserve the established order in Church and State by educating the masses in manners and morals and up to political responsibility, which meant, of course, acquiescence'. (McG. Eager, 1953, p. 149, quoted in Simon, 1974, p. 61). It attempted to capture and regulate boys and young men both physically and morally.

Under these circumstances youth provision in the late nineteenth century was directed towards girls only when it was considered that they lacked domestic and moral surveillance and instruction. This would arise either when they were away from home, as domestic servants, which was very frequently the case, or when their own homes were considered inadequate for the purpose, and it was felt that they required not only training but protection from the 'temptation' that their 'precocious' financial independence could expose them to (Dyhouse, 1981, p. 105). Girls were also singled out for special educational and youth service provision where it was felt that they could in consequence contribute to the enterprise of 'civilising' the working class by transmitting back into their 'demoralised' and 'deficient' familial environments their newly-acquired bourgeois domestic and religious values (Nava, 1984; Dyhouse, 1981). In the early part of the twentieth century, a period in which bad mothering was often held responsible for the decline of the British race and empire (Davin, 1978) the emphasis in girls' clubs was on developing the maternal skills considered so inadequate (Dyhouse, 1981; Davin, 1978; Blanch, 1979). Overall however, provision for girls was minimal compared with that for boys. For example, Blanch has estimated that in Birmingham in 1913, the number of girls attending Street Children's Union clubs amounted to only 1 per cent (1979, p. 117). Although there was a considerable increase in these figures subsequently, on the eve of the First World War it was still considered inappropriate for girls and women to spend their leisure time outside the confines of the domestic sphere.

Since its inception during the latter part of the nineteenth century and the early twentieth century, youth work has continued to aim at exercising some form of supervision over the leisure time of poor and working-class youth, particularly in urban areas, and at coping with oppositional culture and potential delinquency. 'In the 1920s and 1930s . . . the youth service . . . was seen as offering some defence against poverty, depression and disease, and as helping to bring some cohesion into a society whose values were widely thought to be under threat' (HMSO, 1982, p. 4). That is not to say that the objective of recruiting the 'deprived' has always been successful. Blanch (1979) points out that in the early part of the century, although 'the children of unskilled and semi-skilled parents were thought to be more in need' (p. 116) it was predominantly children from the more prosperous and respectable sectors of the working and lower middle-class who attended clubs. And Pearl Jephcott in 1954 (pp. 110–11) bemoaned the inability of youth organisations to attract the 'below-average' child from the 'below-average' home.[5]

In this respect the authors of the Albermarle Report (HMSO, 1960) distinguished themselves by insisting that the youth service was 'not a negative, a means of "keeping them [youth] off the streets" or "out of trouble"' (p. 35). They argued that the state should provide facilities for young people who did not benefit from the amenities available to those in full-time further and higher education – that it should in effect equalise the distribution of resources. Nevertheless, these progressive claims were backed up by drawing attention to the growing rates of delinquency – 'the crime problem is very much a youth problem' (p. 17) – and to the increase in the numbers of young people in the population, particularly male young people, because of the post-war 'bulge' and the abolition of National Service (p. 13). Thus it too envisaged the youth service as a means of combating the effects of 'disadvantage' and of coping with the entry of '200 000 young men between the ages of 18 and 20 [into] civilian life' (p. 13). In 1969 the HMSO report *Youth and Community Work in the Seventies* also presented an argument against the custodial tradition in youth work, yet all the same emphasised the need to establish contact with 'young people at risk' as well as to 'integrate immigrant adolescents'.[6]

Thus although wide variations exist in the style of provision available in the 1980s, from highly traditional boys' clubs and uniformed voluntary organisations[7] to informal youth and community centres, on the whole the youth service today continues to act as a non-compulsory extension of formal schooling which attempts to deal with some of the problems generated by unemployment, failure and disaffection in school, 'inadequate' homes and potential insurrection. Much of the more progressive youth provision of the last decade has been quite successful in exerting a counter-attraction to the freedom of the streets. Many young people have benefited through the provision of facilities, excursions, camps, the presence of often sympathetic adults in a less structured environment than the school, the provision of space for meeting friends away from the constraints of the family and off the streets. All of these are concrete gains. Nevertheless this kind of softer practice remains predicated upon a welfarist cultural-deficit model which conceptualises certain sectors of youth as in need of supervision, protection and 'life skills'; which, in short, tends to hang on to the notion of certain sectors of youth as a problem.

The recognition of the ways in which youth work is still directed at winning young people who would otherwise – or do – constitute a problem, points to the part youth work continues to play in the maintenance of control and consent. The massive increase in expenditure over the last few years on Youth Opportunity Programmes (YOPs) and more recently on the Youth Training Scheme (YTS) at a time of general cut-backs in the public sector serves to endorse this perspective. According to documents drawn up by the Conservative Government's Central Policy Review Staff in February 1981 (before the riots) and leaked to *Time Out*, YTS has among its purposes the removal of unemployed young people from the street in order to minimise the possibility of disorder and dissent. It is stated that 'The effect [of long-term unemployment upon young people] in terms of attitudes to work and opportunties for crime and other forms of social disruption is undoubtedly a matter for justifiable concern'. (*Time Out*, 20–26 May 1983). The most recent evidence in support of this proposition is contained in government plans to withdraw supplementary benefit from those young people unwilling to participate in YTS (*Guardian* 6 Aug. 1983). In drawing attention to some of the considerations underlying the creation of government youth schemes, I do not wish to suggest that the youth service constitutes a monolithic united apparatus which has as a sole and conscious objective, class and generational control. However it is being proposed that the youth service be made a more cohesive institution and be more tightly linked to YTS (HMSO, 1982). The Thompson report also points out that in the last decade four private members' bills in Parliament have attempted to make the youth service both more comprehensive and mandatory (HMSO, 1982, p. 7). Nevertheless to suggest that youth work is only, or principally, about the policing of young people is to conceptualise it too narrowly and to fail to take account of its multiple aims, and of the diverse and sometimes conflicting politics and practice of different regions, agencies and individuals. For example the resistance of some youth workers to the constraints under which they operate, their participation in struggles to organise politically, to improve provision and to win social and political enfranchisement for youth, has been considerable and cannot be categorised in such a way. All the same, in the context of this argument it is necessary to emphasise the fundamentally regulatory and coercive features of state provision for young people in order to be able to illuminate the particular position of girls both inside and outside the youth service.

Gender differentiation in the youth service and the regulation of girls

So how do girls fit into this kind of analysis of the objectives and effects of youth service provision – or indeed into the category of youth? First of all it is necessary to emphasise the *marginality* of girls and women in today's youth service. As could perhaps be predicted, national provision for girls is far below that of boys. The Thompson Report says:

> As regards . . . young people aged 14 and over, the evidence suggests that, in terms of membership of youth groups of all kinds, the boys outnumber the girls by about 3:2, and that in terms of their participation in activities and the use of facilities, the boys are much more conspicuous than this proportion would suggest. (HMSO, 1982, p. 63)

A recent ILEA report, *Youth Service Provision for Girls* (1981) shows that girls' membership in voluntary and statutory clubs averages about one third that of boys.[8] This does not include the 24 000 membership of the London Federation of Boys' Clubs, of which there is no girls' equivalent. The report also points to the 50 per cent decline in membership among girls over fourteen, as well as to the slight increase among boys of the same age. But, as the quote from the 1982 Thompson Report suggests, membership figures give no indication of attendance, participation in activities and use and distribution of resources. In some 'mixed' London clubs, even those with a positive policy towards girls, attendance ratios are often as low as twelve boys to one girl. Indeed, as the Camden Area Youth Committee Report *Out of Sight* (1982) on provision for girls suggests 'Mixed provision is the term used to describe what in reality is either predominantly male, or sometimes all male work, but is described as "mixed work or mixed provision" as no-one actually excludes the girls' (p. 7). In fact girls' access to activities and facilities is so limited in most clubs, it seems not unreasonable to speculate that a primary reason for establishing or converting to mixed clubs in the first place, was to increase their attractiveness to *boys*. As one male youth worker told me, 'the boys are so much easier to handle when there are girls present'. In terms of resources, the ILEA report (1981) calculated that some boroughs were spending an astonishing five times as much on boys as on girls (p. 9).

More remarkable still are the 1982–83 figures for resources grants paid to registered youth organisations in Islington, an inner London borough with a reputation for being progressive. These indicate that only 2 per cent of the total amount was allocated to girls-only groups (this includes organisations such as the Girl Guides), 32 per cent went to boys-only groups, and the remaining 66 per cent was allocated to mixed groups, which as we have already seen, are predominantly male. Women as workers are also marginal in the youth service. It has been estimated that only 25 per cent of full-time paid staff are women, and that at officer level the figure declines to less than 10 per cent (HMSO, 1982). Most youth and community training courses pay little attention to the issue of work with girls (*Working with Girls*, issue 14, 1983, p. 2), and the recent Thompson Report (HMSO, 1982) while devoting a small section to work with girls, has been criticised for failing in the rest of the report 'to reflect in any substantive way the views, or specific needs of women and girls . . . the Review Group – a predominantly male group – produced a document which reflected a very male view of what the Youth Service . . . is or could be' (Janet Paraskeva Hunt, quoted in *Working With Girls*, issue 14, 1983, p. 15).

Certain questions and conclusions emerge when this evidence, about the under-representation of girls and women and the paucity of resources available for them, is combined with the analysis of the development of the youth service which was made earlier. If youth provision is indeed largely a response to the 'delinquent connotations' of 'youth', then the implication is that girls are not in need of the same kind of regulation as boys. From this it follows that nor are girls properly 'youth'. These are distinct points which will be developed separately.

Historically girls have presented far less of a street problem than boys. Delinquency figures have always been far lower than for boys. Girls are less likely to be involved in gangs and riots, and confrontations between them and the formal state apparatus of law and order occur less often. They are also less likely to be politically militant, to take part in industrial action and demonstrations.[9] As Wilmott (1966) naïvely stated on page one of his study *Adolescent Boys of East London*, 'In general girls pose less of a problem to adult society; partly for this reason, partly because resources were limited, we decided to confine the study to boys'. This association between boys as a problem and the unequal distribution of resources and attention is echoed in Jephcott (1954, p. 116) when she protests that girls' club activities are often jettisoned in favour of activities for boys because 'girls are less delinquent' and do not need to be kept out of trouble. It reappears in the Thompson Report (HMSO, 1982) in its minimal coverage of discrimination against girls, and indeed in its assertion that the term 'work with girls' is misleading in that it might convey the impression that girls were a 'problem' for the youth service (p. 62), a comment made without any apparent consciousness of the way it serves paradoxically to justify and confirm girls' marginality. This approach must be compared with the substantial concern shown throughout the same report about racism in Britain, and about the need to nurture multi-culturalism. Since girls are not considered a problem, whereas black youth is, they get less attention in the report and fewer recommendations are made to increase provision for them.

However it is not only that girls are less insurrectionary than boys, they simply do not occupy public spaces to the same extent. Girls are less of a problem on the streets because they are predominantly and more scrupulously regulated in the home. On the whole parental policing over behaviour, time, labour and sexuality of girls has not only been more efficient than over boys, it has been different. For girls, unlike for boys, the *principal* site and source for the operation of control has been the family. These are very general assertions and of course the form of this control has not been uniform. Class and cultural variations even within Britain are very substantial. However on the whole working-class girls (the sisters of the boys to whom youth provision is most often directed) spend far more time at home than their brothers, whether still at school, on the dole, at work or on a youth training scheme. Their leisure time is far more likely to be spent in their own house or their friend's (McRobbie, 1978), in contrast to the boys whose spare time is more likely to be spent in public places – the street, the club, the local café – doing nothing (Corrigan, 1979). Working-class girls are also expected to take on a larger share of the labour and responsibility in the domestic sphere. As a detached London youth worker has observed:

> An aspect of girls' lives which was noticeable is the isolation in which some girls live and the amount of domestic chores they have to do. Many girls were only to be seen on their way home

from school, on errands to the shops, in laundrettes or minding younger siblings during holidays or evenings. One activity almost *all* girls do is babysitting, paid and unpaid, for friends, neighbours and relatives. It appears that for girls there are few social outlets. (ILEA, 1981, p. 65)

Girls' sexuality is subjected to far greater parental scrutiny and vigilance, and they are frequently just not allowed out, not even to youth clubs. Indeed a recent survey of girls aged 14–15 in several north London schools (ILEA, 1981, p. 71) showed that 16 per cent never went out in the evenings without their parents, and that 33 per cent went out only once a week. Where moral panics about girls have arisen, and social service intervention into the terrain of the familial considered justifiable, this has usually been (as in the nineteenth century) because parental authority over domesticity and sexuality has appeared inadequate. These claims are confirmed by Annie Hudson's recent research on the relationship between girls and welfare service professionals (1983). She points out that whereas boys in trouble are likely to be referred to social services 'by the formal agents of social control (predominantly the police) the behaviour of girls is often . . . the source of consternation for families. The processes of control are more subtle, hidden and diffuse' (p. 6).

However, these processes of regulation are not only in operation within the family; they also occur in schools, in clubs and on the streets. In the public and less structured context of the youth centre, the regulation of girls is enforced largely by *boys* through reference to a notion of femininity which incorporates particular modes of sexual behaviour, deference and compliance (Wood, this volume; Cowie and Lees, 1981). In this culture outside the home, girls are observers of boys' activity and boys are observers and *guardians* of girls' passivity. The ability to exercise this control does not usually reside within the individual boy. Such power is located in groups of boys (and girls) who, through reference to certain discourses and categories – like 'slag' and 'poof' – are able to ensure 'appropriate' masculine and feminine behaviour. It is therefore not only through the family, but also through the interaction of girls with boys outside it, that the femininity and thus the policing of girls is assured.

In this way we can begin to see that the lack of equal youth service provision for girls cannot merely be attributed to oversight, partiality or tradition. A substantial part of the explanation must lie in the fact that, since girls have not constituted a street problem to the extent that boys have, a need to devise informal ways of containing and supervising them has simply not arisen on the same scale.

Conflict and difference within the category of youth

This differential regulation of boys and girls both inside and outside the family (reflected in differences in youth provision) is one of a range of phenomena which point to the inadequacy of the conceptualisation of youth as a unitary category. As I have already said, it is not new to point to the failure of most 'youth' studies to take any account of girls. But it is not only that in examinations of 'youth' and 'children', girls are invisible or marginalised. In these studies girls are simply unproblematically subsumed under the general category that defines one group of people to another, that is to say youth to adults. This approach obscures differences within the category. Emphasis on youth as a period situated between childhood and adulthood has resulted in the neglect of gender as a *relational* concept – of power relations *between* boys and girls.[10]

Thus, to refer again to the case of youth work, it is not just that (male) administrators fail to provide equal resources for girls, or provide resources which reinforce traditional gender roles; that parents demand the presence of their daughter in the home; that most male workers (and many female workers) encourage or tolerate the subordination of girls in their clubs. It is also, very importantly, that *boys* lay claim to the territory of the club, and inhibit attempts by girls to assert their independence from them, to speak, to act, to disrupt conventional forms of femininity and masculinity. The manner in which this inhibition and control is exercised by boys over girls is quite complex. Paradoxically girls on the streets and in clubs are less likely than most boys to become victims of physical attack by (other) boys, precisely because they are *girls*, precisely in order to preserve definitions and boundaries of masculinity and femininity. These observations do not undermine the notion that power relations are structured into sexual difference, but suggest that in a public context it is not necessarily physical violence which enforces sexual dominance and control over youth club territory.[11] Of course boys often physically disturb girls' activities, physically appropriate facilities and exercise power through their ability to project the *threat* of physical assault, both over girls and women workers; and it is this kind of rough 'masculine' behaviour which effectively excludes most girls (and quite a number of boys) from youth clubs. But actual physical assault and the most violent threats experienced in the public sphere by the boys and girls I have talked to has come from within their own gender category. And because boys, in their expression of physical violence, do not transgress the boundaries of what constitutes acceptable gendered behaviour, as girls would, and are therefore violent more often, it is actually *boys* who are ironically most regularly vulnerable on the streets to attacks by other boys (and for similar reasons, to being picked up by the police). The dominance exercised by boys over girls is rooted rather in their ability to enforce the boundaries between femininity and masculinity, which in a context of violent physical engagement would be in danger of erosion. These boundaries are secured by them through harassment, through the policing of sexuality – to maintain a double standard – and through the branding of gender unorthodoxy (of activity, initiative and independence) as unfeminine and undesirable.[12]

These different forms of regulation which exist for boys and girls within the category of youth, which are lived out through their relationships to each other, have an immediacy that often structures the experience of youth quite as significantly as class does (McRobbie, 1982b, p. 48). However it is not only that boys and girls are placed differently in relation to each other, they are also placed differently in relation to their adulthood. I would like to suggest that there are systematic differences which exist between the ways in which most males and females experience generational boundaries and the process of becoming adult. Given the present state of research this is a largely unsubstantiable claim, but one which I think is worth making in the context of this argument, since implications of political importance emerge from it. Thus, to return to the proposition, it is customary to conceptualise masculine youth as a temporal phenomenon. Manhood (defined in relation to women, to children, to labour) and its concomitant social power in this society, is significantly different from boyhood. It is marked off from it. One could speculate that the recognition by young men of the provisional nature of their subordination as youth is what prompts them to struggle against it and in this fashion to accelerate the process of their transition into adulthood. This accentuated differentiation between manhood and boyhood has a long history. It is apparent in traditional labour hierarchy (Cohen, 1982). A recurring phenomenon in many cultures, it echoes (to enter other levels of analysis and speculation) the distinctive infantile rupture between boys and mothers, the commonplace absence of fathers from the domestic domain, and may well signal a key aspect of masculinity as a problematic and ambivalent construct. The details of the distinct nature of boys' transition into manhood are beyond the scope of this discussion, but the process is certainly not unchanging and is currently being postponed and reconstituted by high rates of unemployment. (And of course one way for boys to occupy and mitigate this prolonged moment of youthful powerlessness, of joblessness, compulsory schooling and economic dependence, is to acquire practice in the relations of domination and exclusion *vis-à-vis* other groups – girls and immigrants for example.)

The situation for young women is different. Boundaries between girlhood and womanhood are far less accentuated, and the confined and permanent status of womanhood cannot be easily distinguished from girls' transient subordination as youth. The apparent inevitability of subordination is perhaps one of the factors responsible for girls' lesser propensity to resist the specific social constraints imposed upon them as young people. Where they do rebel against the confines of girlhood, this is likely to take the form of overt expression of sexuality and can include pregnancy and motherhood. In a context in which sexuality is considered appropriate for adults only, girls' expression of it amounts to a form of subversive behaviour which unlike other forms of adolescent resistance does not jeopardise femininity. However, as a strategy of resistance it is limited in its effectivity for precisely this reason. Although constituting a challenge to parental and school authority, it does not free girls from the regulation of boys (unless of course it is lesbian sexuality[13]). Ultimately and paradoxically, girls' most common form of rebellion serves only to bind them more tightly to their subordination as women. But on the whole girls appear less inclined than boys to struggle against their status as youth. Labouring in the home, pleasing and serving others, their girlhood merges into womanhood. This state of prolonged dependency and infantilisation – of femininity – may be disturbed in early adulthood only to be recomposed at the moment of marriage. This may appear a bleak and pessimistic portrayal, and it is important not to underestimate the authority of women *within* the home, nevertheless both compared to men and because of their relations with men, most women never really acquire 'adult' status and the social power that accompanies it. Perhaps in compensation, though also because their lives more closely resemble those of the adults of their sex, girls are more likely to be awarded the social designation 'mature'.[14] This position of subordination which women and girls hold in common, and the distinctive nature of their relation to each other which results from it, suggests that generational difference does not contain the same meanings for them as it does for men and boys. These assertions remain largely speculative and a great deal of work would need to be done in order to give them proper substance. But however insubstantial they may be at this point, they seem worth making, since to question the common-sense assumption that the transition into adulthood is a process unmodified by sexual difference has political as well as theoretical consequences.

Also relevant to the discussion about girls and the youth service are those arguments which suggest that class boundaries, like generational boundaries, tend to be anomalous in the case of women. The location of women in class categories has never been a straightforward matter (Delphy, 1981) and differences between them have their own historical fluctuations which do not necessarily reflect the class position and relations of their husbands. For example, since the beginning of this century a number of factors have contributed to a diminution of difference in the experience of middle and working-class women and girls. In the domestic sphere, the decline in the number of servants, the emphasis on the importance of mothering and household management for women of all classes (Davin, 1978) and the similarity of structural relations between women and their husbands, regardless of their standards of living, are among these.[15] The conventional focus on income differences between male 'heads' of families can obscure the social position held in common by women whose labour in the home is unremunerated. A further factor which has contributed to a levelling of difference between women of different class origins has been the rise in the rate of marriage breakdown and the concomitant increase in the number of women-headed households. Class differences in educational provision are no longer as acute as they once were, in spite of the fact that middle-class girls are still far more likely to continue to higher education. In the labour market discrimination against employed women does not operate in a predictable manner in class terms. Studies in recent years have shown that working-class women quite often have higher status jobs than their husbands (Garnsey, 1978) (that is to say, according to the registrar general's classifications; however, these skilled non-manual women's jobs are not necessarily better paid) whereas middle-class women, with some exceptions, are likely to have less prestigious and less well paid jobs than the men of their class origin. They are under-represented in positions of power and responsibility, even in predominantly female areas like teaching and social work. Thus the work of women of all class origins tends to cluster round the low status white-collar occupations, and here too it would be an error to assume that women were as polarised by class as men are. Heath (1981) has summed up his research on this issue in the following way: (p. 135) 'Womanhood is a leveller. The restrictions on women's job prospects mean that they are much less divided by their social origins than are men. Class discrimination divides men, but sexual discrimination brings women together.'

The politics and practice of youth work with girls

The proposition that class and generational distinctions are of less significance for women than for men has implications for youth work,[16] in that men and women youth workers are placed differently in relation to the young people that they work with. For example, the demand by women youth workers for better work conditions and opportunities for themselves is an integral part of the demand for an improvement in the general level of youth service provision for girl users. The lesser significance of class and generational difference is enhanced by the unstructured 'integrated'[17] and informal nature of the youth work context, as well as by the less 'professionalised' status of the youth worker (compared with the school teacher). A consequence of these particular combinations offer the potential for women and girls associated with the youth service to construct alliances and to provide for each other a degree of egalitarian support which might well not be available to men workers whose common terrain with working-class boys is far more circumscribed. Relations with boys are limited not only by the usual style of intervention employed by many male workers, but also because (whatever their origins and political affiliations) men employed in the youth service are more likely to be 'adult', 'middle-class' and hold senior positions in the youth service.

These potential alliances have not always been recognised by radical women youth workers. Socialist analyses which prioritise class, assume that class operates uniformly across gender divisions and conceptualise youth work as one form of class (and generational) control, have tended to predominate. Emphasis on class, and therefore on class and cultural *difference* have often been demoralising and have also helped to obscure the degree of homogeneity which exists between women youth workers and working-class girls.

However, over the last few years, things have started to change. An increasing number of women youth workers are organising in order to create for themselves a stronger base, to improve both their own conditions of work and the quantity and quality of youth service provision for girls. *Working With Girls Newsletter* has recently won permanent funding from the National Association of Youth Clubs, a step which, as the editorial points out 'hopefully signals the recognition of work with girls and young women as a valued and validated central part of mainstream youth work' (*Working With Girls Newsletter*, 15, 1983). Pressure has been put on training institutions to take the issue of work with girls more seriously, to provide more flexible conditions for 'mature' women students, and to increase the proportion of women teaching staff. The different emphases in these demands – on organisation and better conditions for women workers on the one hand, and on improved provision for girls on the other – are linked and complement each other. As one worker in the Camden Report (1982) points out, 'It is . . . vital for girls to see alternative images of women, exercising authority and power in decision-making, dealing with difficult and . . . troublesome situations' (p. 28). Although the presence of women in senior posts is no guarantee that the needs of girls will be attended to, the Camden study found that where this was the case, work with girls was indeed more likely (1982, p. 6). However the nature of these interventions in youth work and the

political perspectives underlying them are not uniform and remain to be examined and evaluated.

The London Youth Committee Report on *Youth Service Provision for Girls* (ILEA, 1981), which was referred to earlier, is an interesting document in this respect in that it highlights some of these different perspectives. Of course it must be remembered that the sometimes contradictory ways in which the arguments in it are couched reflect not only the general political context and the different positions of the individual authors, but also their common recognition of the need to convince the authority to increase its expenditure on facilities for girls. It is nevertheless worth looking at the theoretical differences which co-exist within the report.

The perspective which predominates is liberal. It is declared that the main aims of youth work should be 'to enable each individual to fulfil his or her potential as an individual and as a member of society' (p. 5) and to provide 'choice' for girls as well as boys, both in the youth service and in the selection of adult roles.[18] In the conclusion it is stated that the main issue is one of unequal opportunities for girls; sex discrimination in the youth service is both illegal and unfair; appeals are made for a change of attitude among workers, management committees and youth officers. These kinds of statements fall into the social democratic 'equal access' tradition[19] and are fundamentally liberal in that, in spite of a relatively benevolent emphasis on choice and equal opportunities, they make no reference to the limitations of these, and slide over the existing power relations and resource distribution which underlie inequalities.

Simultaneously present in the report is a second, conservative, strand, evident in that appeals for more provision are justified by referring to the ways in which girls are increasingly a *problem*:

> Because of the changing patterns in society – rising unemployment, increased crime rate among girls, the rise in the number of teenage and unsupported mothers, etc. – in the future – it will be even more important for the Youth Service to address itself to the needs of girls and young women. (p. 18)

This is one of the key statements in the concluding section and it expresses notions which, as we have seen, have recurred throughout the history of leisure provision for young people. Reference to them in this instance may have been considered an appropriate tactic in order to gain maximum resources for girls. Nevertheless, whether used with tongue in cheek or not, the insertion of such arguments into the report indicates a recognition of the appeal that ideas of this kind continue to possess, and clearly substantiates the kind of analysis which suggests that an important purpose of the youth service is to contribute to the control of young people. It is ironic that an examination of the way in which girls have been marginalised in the youth service and have on the whole not constituted a problem on the streets, is ultimately able to illuminate the way in which the youth service has operated as a regulating device for boys.

But the report also contains a third more radical perspective in which it calls for an increase in provision for girls *only*. It draws attention to the fact that 'mixed' clubs are in practice predominantly boys' clubs; that in such clubs, facilities are normally monopolised by boys and that boys frequently intimidate girls. It points to resistance from administrative levels, male workers and boys to positive discrimination and the expansion of provision for girls only. Implicit in the report are arguments which are more clearly articulated in subsequent publications (like *Working With Girls*). These suggest that separate provision enables girls to develop more independence, self-esteem and confidence; that it can provide a context for them to discuss their experiences and feelings; that it offers the opportunity to girls of acquiring expertise in activities and skills traditionally considered masculine. The report refers to a girls' project in which it is claimed that 'girls have broadened their understanding of their own situation *as girls*' (p. 57).

Sections of the report then, clearly embody certain basic feminist principles about the need for the disruption of traditional patterns of masculinity and femininity, for 'consciousness raising', and for autonomous organisation. The report thus implicitly recognises the political and agitational potential of work with girls. This recognition marks a departure not only from traditional, hierarchically organised types of youth work, it is also to be distinguished from much socialist provision. The Labour Party of the post-war period has been criticised for not recognising the political and agitational possibilities in education. Finn, Grant and Johnson (1977) have argued that the Labour Party's focus on access to secondary schooling and on opportunities was at the cost of attention to the content and form of education. In that it failed to develop a concept of socialist education it 'remained an educational *provider* for the popular classes, not an educational *agency of* and *within* them' (p. 153). These arguments can be extended to youth service provision, and indeed Gillis (1974) has pointed out that during the 1930s, the membership of the socialist youth movements in Britain was small in comparison with that of the various bourgeois organisations. 'The low overall enrolments reflected the fact that neither the Labour Party nor the powerful trade unions had taken much interest in youth mobilisations' (p. 148). Feminism of recent years has been unique in this respect, both in relation to schooling and to youth work. One of its most significant contributions is that it has usually gone beyond the question of more provision and a broader curriculum, to a scrutiny of the content, quality and implementation of these. The kinds of changes that have been demanded by feminists in the areas of knowledge, organisation and participation, demonstrate quite clearly a commitment to the agitational and recruiting potential of schooling and of youth work.

However, as is to be expected, views about what counts as a valid feminist intervention are not uniform. Differences of opinion and approach (which are only loosely related to the range of political positions within feminism) are not always clearly defined and their implications both for and beyond youth work are not always considered. I want to identify and draw out some of these contradictions and different styles in youth work practice with girls.

Youth work with girls only is not of course inherently feminist, as the ILEA report indicates (1982). There are large numbers of girls' church groups, friendly societies, brigades, Guides and such like, which had among their initial objectives the protection of girls from sexual contact with boys, and which continue to have the aim of preparing girls for their future roles as wives and mothers. (Dyhouse, 1981, pp. 104–14; ILEA, 1981, p. 46). These will not be considered here. In this section the focus will be upon the kind of provision which has developed over the past few years largely as a consequence of feminist pressure and persuasion. Although constituting a very small proportion of youth work nationally, it is all the same a sector which is expanding very rapidly and implies either an absolute increase in resources, or a re-allocation of funds from boys to girls. There are various types of work with girls and girls' projects, and although differences between them are not clear-cut, it is possible all the same to distinguish three broad categories of provision. It is important to point out not only that a substantial overlap exists between categories, but also that individual feminists may well support aspects of each type. This does not obviate the need to draw attention to the differences and their implications.

First, then, there is the type of work in which the focus is upon *access* and *interaction*. The priority here is to compensate girls for their marginalisation in the youth service, to single them out, establish contact and value their interests, whatever these may be. Thus quite traditional feminine concerns like nutrition and beauty are considered appropriate by some feminists if they are popular among girls and able to recruit them to the clubs.[20] Although activities of this kind, and some girls-only outings and camps, seem quite traditional in their apparent endorsement of femininity and domesticity, this type of provision is often defended by feminists on the grounds that what counts is to attract girls to the youth service and to provide them with resources and a context in which to develop confidence, become independent of the approval and control of boys,[21] and enhance their solidarity with other girls. The continuous and personal interaction between women youth workers and girls is an integral aspect of this process.

In the second type of provision, which occupies a centreground between the other two, the focus goes beyond access and interaction. It includes providing a context for girls to explore and devlop expertise in activities, such as motorcycling, football, music-making and pool, which are normally monopolised by boys. Since this type of provision constitutes an entrance into the domain of male activity it implies, and frequently entails, a challenge to traditional assumptions about the nature of masculinity and femininity, and thence to an understanding of gender as a social construct. However it must be kept in mind that it is not impossible to imagine an instance in which girls ride motorcycles, play football,[22] and have the run of all the facilities in a club, yet nevertheless fail to address the question of gender relations and women's subordinate status.

A systematic examination of gender relations is one of the principal objectives of the third category of provision. This type of project is likely to consist of a series of social and political education evenings which focus upon specific subjects (like employment and unemployment, sexuality and the family) include the use of resources (like film and visiting speakers) and involve girls in discussion as well as in more informal workshops and activities.[23] (In this respect they embody those principles articulated by youth service policy-makers which propose that youth work should offer not only leisure activities, but also a 'social and political education' (Davies, 1981; HMSO, 1982)). Within such provision the quality of personal interaction among girls, and between girls and women workers, although important, is not as vital an aspect of the intervention. Indeed these projects rely least upon a girls-only context in order to be effective. It may very well be the case that this kind of provision in a single-sex environment proves to be a more productive and gratifying experience for girls; however, the focus upon content – upon knowledge and consciousness raising – means that it does not *depend* upon the exclusion of boys in order to be feminist. The characteristic which defines this type of project as feminist is not, as it is with the other two kinds, its compensatory nature (the provision of access) and its girls-only context (the quality of interaction). Instead it is the fact of understanding and challenging social inequalities based on gender.

It is essential to reiterate that these are crude delineations of the different feminist approaches to youth work. Although provision will vary in the extent to which the main emphasis is upon recruitment or upon questions of sexual politics, in reality most interventions contain aspects of each of the three models. It is, all the same, worth constructing these examples – or 'ideal types' – in order to identify some of their limitations. However, first I want to draw attention to certain factors which distinguish youth work from formal education and which must be taken into consideration when evaluating the issues of access and single-sex provision. The most significant among these is the *compulsory* nature of schooling. It is this which inhibits the gross marginalisation of girls from taking place in education in the way in which it does within the youth service. Obligatory attendance and the institutionalisation of the transmission of knowledge in schools, pre-empts the extreme discriminatory practices which are possible in the less structured context of youth work.[24] It is precisely the non-compulsory unstructured nature of the youth service which permits such an unequal distribution of resources and the effective exclusion of girls. But it is not only that boys monopolise facilities, that girls are uninterested in the available provision or are made to feel unwelcome; it is also that parents are able to forbid the attendance of their daughters at clubs and insist that they stay at home. The voluntary nature of youth service provision thus not only reveals discrimination against girls, paradoxically it actually produces and reinforces it. This structural difference between youth work and schooling and the effects which it has, helps to provide an explanation for the greater unanimity among women youth workers than among women teachers for separate and special provision for girls.[25]

Under the circumstances I have described it is not surprising that the question of expanding youth work access for girls (of affirmative action) should be given priority, and that feminists should argue for special and separate provision for girls in order to attract them to youth service premises and to achieve a more just distribution of resources. However it is important that these demands be kept in perspective. There is a danger that the question of access can supersede all others; that too great a focus upon it can lead (as it did in post-Second World War Labour Party policy) to a neglect of the *content* of education (whether at school or in a youth club) and of the agitational potential of *knowledge*. When the traditional activity orientation of much youth work is combined with a certain feminist celebration of experience,[26] it is not surprising that the kinds of pedagogic girls' projects which offer a systematic study of the position of women in society are a relatively infrequent phenomenon. Yet these have proved popular even with girls for whom school has ceased to provide anything of interest,[27] and to ignore this aspect of work with girls is to risk shearing it of its radical potential. Demands for a more equal distribution of youth service resources and for provision for girls-only (for greater and separate access) are in themselves relatively modest. The fact that they are so vociferously – and indeed often violently – opposed, although extremely significant, must not blind us to their intrinsically liberal nature. I shall return to this point later.

There are also certain problems which arise from the feminist concentration upon single-sex provision in the youth service. Although, as is clear from what has already been written, girls-only nights and projects are often the only means of ensuring that girls get more than a merely nominal share of youth service resources, there are all the same certain dangers associated with the demand for separate provision. Implicit in the politics and practice of youth work with girls only, there is a definition of girls' needs as distinct from those of boys. One of the risks to which I refer lies therefore in the possible conceptual slippage which can occur between an analysis which perceives girls' needs and interests as different from boys *now* (because of a range of historical and social factors) and one which asserts a more fundamental and essential difference between boys and girls and men and women. A consequence of an assertion such as the latter by feminists could be to reaffirm a separate feminine sphere within which women become confined – to confirm rather than to attenuate gender as an organising social category.[28] Such a consolidation of gender difference is ultimately self-perpetuating in that it tends to construct masculinity not only as an attribute of all males and undesirable, but also as immutable. In addition, although a feminist approach of this kind may (inconsistently) not assume an essential femininity for girls to parallel its notion of masculinity, it does all the same serve to confirm girls as different, as in some sense victims and in need of protection.[29]

A second risk in the establishment of separate provision for girls is that girls-only nights and girls-only projects fail to challenge or to offer possibilities to boys and men, except in so far as they feel excluded by them. There is a danger that questions of gender become once again hived off, and sexual politics a matter of concern for women only. This kind of scenario could inhibit a consideration by boys of the ways in which they are implicated in the perpetuation of gender difference and of the ways in which many of them are simultaneously disadvantaged by it. Masculinity and femininity as social constructs present problems for boys as well as girls. Yet the withdrawal of girls and women youth workers from mixed provision and their examination of these issues in a single-sex context relies upon a small number of committed men in the youth service to initiate discussion about sexual divisions with boys.[30] Although I consider that single-sex meetings are a vital aspect of the development of girls' confidence and consciousness, ultimately shifts in ideas and power relations can be accomplished only through dialogue and engagement *with* boys and men.

Nevertheless, it is extremely important not to minimise the political impact that work with girls only has already had. Paradoxically, it is precisely the fact of boys' exclusion and the association of girls on their own, regardless of the content of such gatherings, which have generated attention and contestation over questions of gender throughout the youth service. Opposition and resistance to separate provision for girls and to a redistribution of funding has been widespread and often very bitterly expressed, not only by boys but also by men at all levels of youth service staffing and administration. In some instances the hostility has been so intense and menacing that it has resulted in the closure of girls-only nights; this in itself has been a remarkably politicising experience for the girls and women involved. There are numerous examples of aggression and prevarication which can be cited by women youth workers.[31] The conflict surrounding youth work with girls only is an obvious indicator of its contentiousness and of its ability to disturb existing relations, but care must be taken not to misrecognise the situation. Violent opposition to such interventions cannot *alone* be used as evidence of their radical nature and effectivity, nor can it be used to justify their existence.

We are witnessing during the present period an expansion of government expenditure on the youth sector, primarily of course on YTS, in spite of widespread cuts in most areas of the social services. This is comprehensible only when perceived as part of a broader strategy designed to cope with youth unemployment and the problem of social order. At such a time it is of course vital to ensure that girls receive their just share of new as well as existing youth service resources. Contact must be made with girls before they are swallowed up into the domestic sphere, facilities must be provided in order to attract them to clubs and to enable them to enhance their leisure time. But if youth work is ultimately to do more than cope with young people as a problem, if the object of work with girls is also to disturb existing relations between the sexes, then it will not be sufficient to focus upon questions of access and upon the provision of a female environment. It will not be sufficient that girls-only youth work has proved threatening to many boys and men merely as a consequence of their exclusion from it. Feminist youth work is uniquely placed to modify barriers between adults and young people and to nurture the formation of alliances between women and girls. Its unstructured and informal nature creates the ideal context in which to conduct a social and political education. If the radical potential of youth work is to be exploited, it must maintain at the forefront the question of sexual politics; and in the long term men and boys must be included in the debate.

Notes

1. In many instances girls have been completely ignored: see for example Wilmott (1966); Robins and Cohen (1978); Corrigan (1979). See also Goldthorpe's study of social mobility (1980) and Halsey *et al.* on educational opportunity (1980). For a critical discussion of the invisibility of girls in youth studies, with particular reference to Willis (1977) and Hebdige (1979), see McRobbie (1980).

2. Studies of the new government training schemes have on the whole failed to examine the impact that these are having upon family organisation and budgeting.

3. Attention has been drawn to this by Simon Frith (1981).

4. Since the work of the Chicago school in the early part of this century. More contemporary examples include Willis (1977) and Hall and Jefferson (1976).

5. She goes on to describe these children as 'scruffily dressed', the 'mental dullards', the 'emotionally unstable', the 'undisciplined' and 'semi-criminal' whom, she says, come from 'insecure' and 'cheerless' homes where no-one bothers to do anything with any regularity. (Jephcott, 1954, pp. 110–11). It comes as a surprise to note that sexual precocity and immorality are not included among her colourful epithets.

6. However in the most recent government report on the youth service (HMSO 1982, pp. 60–1), 'cultural diversity' and 'the needs of the community' are given greater weight than 'integration', most probably as a result of pressure from ethnic minority organisations.

7. Large numbers continue to exist and were described by John Cunningham in the *Guardian* (27 Oct. 1980) as still representing 'a big old-fashioned chunk of Victorian missionary zeal, based on Christian ethics and wholesome pursuits', they claim today to 'offer sound leadership, a disciplined atmosphere' and are 'very much against the more trendy places'.

8. This was also the case in the early fifties (Jephcott, 1954).

9. The recent peace movement is of course an honourable exception.

10. The sociology of education has of course recognised gender *differences* and the way in which these are reinforced by schooling, but has not usually focused upon power relations between boys and girls, though see Shaw (1978). Julian Wood (this volume) is an exception among male commentators in that both gender and power are central concerns in his study.

11. The domestic context is of course a different matter, as are romantic sexual relations; both are frequently considered a legitimate arena for inter-gender violence.

12. For graphic accounts of this process, see again Julian Wood (this volume).
13. For a further discussion of these issues, see 'Everybody's Views Were Just Broadened: A Girls' Project and Some Responses to Lesbianism' (Nava, 1982).
14. Single mothers, although usually materially the least well off, are likely to be the exception here. Responsible for themselves and for their children, they are perhaps the most 'adult'.
15. These points are made and developed in Christine Delphy and Diana Leonard's paper 'The Family as an Economic System', presented at a conference on *The Institutionalisation of Sex Differences*, University of Kent, 1980.
16. A number of youth workers have told me that girls' nights are more likely to be racially mixed than 'mixed' nights. It is possible that women in Britain are also, on the whole, less divided by race than men are.
17. Basil Bernstein in his article 'On the Classification and Framing of Educational Knowledge' (in Bernstein, 1977) suggests that a shift from collection to integrated codes in schooling is likely to weaken the 'boundary between staff, especially junior staff and students/pupils . . . and may well bring about a disturbance in the structure and distribution of power . . . and in existing educational identities . . . It involves a change in what counts as . . . knowledge' (p. 104). This is of particular interest here because, although not specified by Bernstein, junior staff are of course most likely to be women.
18. The work of Eileen Byrne is quoted in the report in this context. For a discussion of the limitations of her liberal analysis, see Nava (1980).
19. Exemplified by post-war Labour policy which argued for 'equal opporunity' both as a principle of social justice and in order to avoid 'human wastage', but tended to overlook fundamental inequalities of condition. This dualism in Labour Party policy, and its commitment to gradualism, are discussed in Finn, Grant and Johnson (1977).
20. See for example the activities included in the Cheshire and Wirral Federation of Youth Clubs Girls Work Project, reported in *Working With Girls Newsletter*, issue 14 1983, (p. 20).
21. A male youth worker with obvious reservations about girls-only work made the following astonishing comment to the author of the Camden Report (1982, p. 30), 'I am not happy at the idea of encouraging girls to see themselves capable of enjoying their leisure without being dependent on boys'.
22. Football is a popular sport among women in Mexico.
23. There is a more detailed description of one of these in Nava (1982). The Mode III CSE Women's Studies Course at Starcross School,

described in *Schools Council Sex Role Differentiation Newsletter 3* in some respects also fits into this category.

24. The proposal to introduce an obligatory core curriculum in schools, although apparently reducing choice, actually increases the likelihood of girls receiving the same education as their brothers.

25. Although there are differences between socialist and radical feminists over the issue of separate provision, this alone cannot explain why in ILEA (for example) a number of teachers, parents and girls are demanding *mixed* PE and games in schools at precisely the same moment that their counterparts in the youth service are demanding *separate* facilities, which, given the non-compulsory nature of the youth service, appears to be the only way of ensuring that girls get any sports at all. The defence of single-sex schooling for girls has been most persuasively put by Shaw (1980), however recent research by Bone (1983) indicates that such a defence cannot be made on academic grounds.

26. This sometimes goes hand in hand with an anti-intellectualism – a denial of the power and usefulness of analysis and research to the feminist project. For a discussion of this see McRobbie (1982b). These issues are also raised in the correspondence published in *Feminist Review*, no. 13 (1983) regarding my 1982 article.

27. This was the case with Jo at the girls' project described in Nava (1982).

28. There are of course many instances of such occurrences in the past. Delamont (1978) has identified two kinds of feminist educationalist in the nineteenth century, the 'separatists' and the 'uncompromising'. The 'separatists' argued for a serious education for girls composed of a curriculum which although demanding should suit their needs as future wives and mothers. The 'uncompromising' on the other hand, insisted that girls have exactly the same school curriculum, however inappropriate, since anything else could be construed as pandering to a softer, inferior intellect, and could be used as justification for the continued exclusion of women from other spheres. Similarly in the early part of the twentieth century, the focus upon motherhood, and the new ideologies surrounding it, were on the one hand to benefit women (through the improvement of welfare services) and on the other, to confine them within the domestic sphere, to define yet again the boundaries between men and women, between masculinity and femininity.

29. Differences within feminism with regard to this matter are discussed in Nava, ('Drawing the Line', this volume) and Gordon and Dubois (1983).

30. This is being done with growing frequency. See for example Smith and Taylor (1983). Men and women staff at Hackney Downs Boys School

(ILEA) have designed a course for junior boys entitled 'Skills for Living' of which a central component is the interrogation of sexism. See also p. 23 of the Camden Report (1982).

31. There are several instances of this in the Camden Report (1982) and *Working With Girls Newsletter*. For example a male youth worker reports that 'Due to harrassment by the boys during the girls' night provision, damage to premises was caused, so the whole thing was stopped' (Camden Report, 1982, p. 29). The report also shows evidence of resistance from male workers. Another instance of opposition is the resignation in 1980 of the chairman of the London Youth Committee from the working party on provision for girls because he considered their report (ILEA, 1981) insufficiently moderate. In addition, requests to Area Youth Committees for the funding of work with girls are regularly subjected to more rigorous scrutiny, in spite of the fact that they are almost invariably also for smaller sums, than similar requests from traditional boys-only organisations.

Sections of this article have been taken from an earlier piece entitled 'Girls Aren't Really a Problem . . . ' published in *Schooling and Culture*, 9 (1981) and subsequently presented in a slightly altered form as a paper at the 1981 British Sociological Association Annual Conference.

2

Femininity and Adolescence

Barbara Hudson

Whatever we do, it's always wrong.

This comment, made to me by a particular 15-year old girl, but echoing the general complaint of countless teenage girls down many generations, is the main theme of this article. I want to show that such a comment comes not from adolescent sulkiness or youthful paranoia, but that it reflects a real dilemma stemming from the fact that teenage girls are confronted by conflicting sets of expectations, which I shall characterise as expectations arising from the connotations we attach to *femininity* and to *adolescence*. I shall suggest that by understanding femininity and adolescence as *discourses*, we may begin to uncover some of the traps we constantly set for teenage girls; and we may also throw some light on the difficulties and disappointments experienced by those who seek to work with teenage girls as, for instance, teachers and social workers. As well as showing some of the contradictory standards generated by these discourses, and the consequences of judging girls' behaviour by the terms of one rather than the other, I shall explore femininity and adolescence as discourses with structured sets of relationships between speakers and actors who occupy positions in them. Also, I shall demonstrate that these discourses have both 'professional' and 'public' variants, using the expressions of teachers and social workers as examples of the professional aspect of the discourses and drawing upon teenage magazines to illustrate the discourses in their public variant. It is a central argument of this article that femininity and adolescence are *subversive* of one another, and in particular, that adolescence is subversive of femininity; young girls' attempts to be accepted as 'young women' are always liable to be undermined (subverted) by perceptions of them as childish, immature, or any other of the terms by which we define the status 'adolescent'.

This work is based on interviews with fifty 15-year old girls in an East Anglian comprehensive school, interviews with teachers in the same school and social workers in the same town, and my reading of *Jackie*, *Mates* and *My Guy*, the magazines most frequently read by the girls in the study, during the autumn and winter of 1979–80. I asked the interview subjects for their views on a wide spectrum of behaviour, including shoplifting and vandalism, sexual behaviour, relationships with parents and friends; as well as seeking their views on girls' clothes and general presentation of self. Teenage magazines were studied for their attitudes and messages concerning the clusters of topics covered by the interviews. The aim of the research was not so much to see the relative influence on teenagers of different groups of adults, nor to look for intergenerational value differences, but to reveal the different modes of talking about the behaviour of teenage girls, and to give some structure to the perspectives revealed – the people who would be likely to use them, the occasions on which they would be likely to be used, and the import in terms of consequences for girls of the use of alternative perspectives on their behaviour.

Adolescence and femininity as discourses

Adult replies to my interview questions soon revealed the evidence of two dominant themes to which their judgements of girls' behaviour were related: the themes of 'normal adolescence' and 'maladjustment to femininity'. These two themes can most illuminatingly be seen as 'master concepts' in the two discourses of femininity and adolescence. The replies to questions about vandalism, breaking and entering, fighting, shoplifting etc., as well as replies to more general questions about what they would expect a 'nice teenage girl' to be like, revealed the subjects' orientation to a set of stereotypes either of adolescence or of femininity, which yielded replies of the form: 'that's a phase most go through in the adolescent stage'; 'childish, but they grow out of it', and so on, on the one hand, or: 'much more aggressive behaviour than you expect to find in girls'; 'that would worry me in a girl, it's denying their femininity', on the other hand. These two kinds of replies show judgements being made from within either femininity or adolescence perspectives, and orientation to one or the other of these discourses is prior to the expression of value judgements about the seriousness or otherwise of whatever behaviour was being discussed. Subjects' views seemed not to be related to their own gender, their age, their educational background, nor to their own expressed values concerning feminism, party politics, religion etc., so much as they seemed to be related to access to these dominant themes of normal adolescence or maladjustment to femininity, and the conceptualisation and terminology clustering around these themes. We shall see that different professional relationships with teenage girls, and different training backgrounds, contribute to knowledge of, and likelihood of use of, these orientations, concepts and terms. Further, we shall see that judgements of behaviour in terms of adolescence allow for more tolerance than judgements in terms of femininity, and that while some questions were generally discussed in terms of age and some in terms of gender, some groups of adults were more likely to use an adolescence perspective, some a femininity perspective.

By *discourse*, I intend a meaning similar to that given to the term by Foucault (1972): not just a unity of themes, or a grouping of objects of knowledge, a professional terminology, or a set of concepts; but an interrelationship of themes, statements, forms of knowledge, and (very importantly) positions held by individuals in relation to these. The discourse of adolescence, for instance, comprises not just our social connotations of the term 'adolescence': what makes it feasible to speak of adolescence as a 'discourse' in this sense is that there are professional positions, such as teacher and psychiatrist, which concern themselves not only with the control of adolescents themselves, but also with the definition of what adolescence, as a social role, *is*, what are the typical problems associated with adolescence, what are the remedies, and what are the images in which adolescence is viewed and the terms in which it is spoken about. These professional positions involve a structured hierarchy of authority, such that if a developmental psychologist makes a pronouncement about a new image or theory of adolescence, this will be admitted as scientific, authoritative, whereas teachers learn the formulations and theories of people such as psychologists and interpret their own dealings with adolescents in the light of these theories rather than proposing new 'scientific knowledge' about adolescents themselves. This concept of discourse is empirically useful rather than being rigorously theoretically derived. In his own works, Foucault's postulation of various discourses (to do with, for instance, medicine (1973), penology (1977), sexuality (1978)), while being arbitrary at the outset, enables him to make connections between ideas, positions and practices as they mesh together to mediate people's lives. It is the connections between ideas and practices which Foucault depicts vividly, with an immediacy not possible with more uni-dimensional approaches concerned with just the ideological level, or with the history of developing state practices, for instance. What the concept of 'discourse' in this meaning allows is not a history of the development of particular concepts, but a snapshot of the matrix of ideas, terminology and practices surrounding an area of social life at a particular time.

The existence of adolescence as discourse is well-established. 'Adolescence' is a term of relatively recent origin, in fact: 'The adolescent was invented at the same time as the steam engine' (Musgrove, 1964, p. 33). With the growth of pedagogy, paediatrics and psychiatry as professions, the terminology of a professional discourse of adolescence proliferated. The extension of schooling beyond the age of puberty meant the 'creation' of a period of life when young people, demonstrably no longer children, were nevertheless not yet adults and could therefore be subject to the discipline of their teachers and of their parents on whom they must remain financially dependent. Psychiatry, of course, has found a vein of gold in theorisation and treatment on the 'difficult transition period' between childhood and adulthood.

The 'popular mythology' of adolescence reflects the preeminence of psychiatric professionals in the positions of authority in the discourse of adolescence:

> If you were to walk up to the average man on the street, grab him by the arm and utter the word 'adolescence', it is highly probable – assuming he refrains from punching you in the nose – that his associations to this term will include references to storm-and-stress, tension, rebellion, dependency conflicts, peer-group conformity, black leather jackets, and the like. If you abandoned your informal street corner experiment and consulted the profes-

sional and popular literature on adolescence, you would quickly become impressed with the prevalence of the belief that adolescence is, indeed, a unique and stormy developmental period.

The adolescent is presumably engaged in a struggle to emancipate himself from his parents. He, therefore, resists any dependence upon them for their guidance, approval or company, and rebels against any restriction or controls that they impose upon his behaviour. To facilitate the process of emancipation, he transfers his dependency to the peer group whose values are typically in conflict with those of his parent. . . . (Bandura, 1964, p. 224)

I apologise here for reproducing the sexist language of this quotation, but it illustrates one of the most intractable problems faced by teenage girls: adolescence is a 'masculine' construct. All our images of the adolescent – those in the quotation above; the restless, searching youth, the Hamlet figure; the sower of wild oats, the tester of growing powers – these are *masculine* images. This is the basis of many of the conflicts posed by the coexistence of adolescence and femininity: if adolescence is characterised by masculine constructs, then any attempts by girls to satisfy society's demands of them *qua* adolescence, are bound to involve them in displaying not only lack of maturity (since adolescence is dichotomised with maturity), but also lack of femininity. Thus, the girl playing a lot of sport is doing something which is still conceived of as essentially masculine. Girls playing football, for instance, are often accorded headlines in the popular press such as 'playing the boys at their own game'; girls displaying competitiveness, or 'adolescent' aggression, will be displaying qualities thought of as masculine.

The ideas expressed in the quotation do not correspond to findings of studies which examine conflict between adolescents and their parents. Most studies (for example Bandura, 1964; Eppel and Eppel, 1966; Kitwood, 1981) find in fact that teenagers generally choose friends whose values echo rather than oppose those of their parents; and certainly my own research found most of the girls interviewed saying that they agreed with their parents on important issues and if they had disagreements, these were generally on trivial matters. Nonetheless, the existence of a discourse of adolescence framed in these concepts of trouble and conflict, with its highest-status expressions spoken in psychiatric and psychoanalytic terms, means that teachers, social workers, the media and parents are constantly expecting trouble.

The *problem* of adolescence as defined by adult society is that it is a time of uncontrolled appetites, a time when teenagers need protecting against themselves if they are not to damage their chances of reaching respectable adulthood; the problem of adolescence for teenagers is that they must demonstrate maturity and responsibility if they are to move out of this stigmatised status, and yet because adolescence is conceived as a time of irresponsibility and lack of maturity, they are given few opportunities to demonstrate these qualities which are essential for their admission as adults. Musgrove has claimed that the 'problem' of adolescence is not a problem at the level of values, but a power problem, arguing that:

Adolescence has been a 'protectorate' administered by adults for the past two centuries. Our contemporary conflict has the character of a colonial revolt. The subordination of the adolescent – like the subordination of the African – was first justified by the claim to protect him. His subordinate status was a 'protected status' – honourable and generally accepted when protection was apparently needed. Adolescence was justified by society's corruption. (Musgrove, 1969, p. 43)

This attitude towards adolescence was certainly present among my research subjects. For instance:

in an overcrowded, liberated world the dangers are so massive you couldn't rest easy and say she'd learn. She may profit enormously if she comes through without damage by what she has learnt, but you can't leave them to it. (Probation officer, female)

Femininity has been less well established as 'discourse', but the growth of feminist sociology has contributed much to revealing the ideological nature of the construct 'femininity' (see Women's Studies Group, 1978). This 'ideology of femininity' which has been demonstrated is now being shown to be operating in the reproduction of the female social role through education (see, for instance, Spender and Sarah, 1980) and in the continuance of traditional female domestic roles (for example in Ann Oakley's work, see Oakley 1972, 1977). The importance of the notion of the 'normal woman', derived from a set of stereotypical constructions of 'femininity' in the social control of females has also recently been explored (see, importantly, Hutter and Williams, 1981).

'Femininity', like 'adolescence', is a discourse whose highest status expressions are in psychoanalytic terminology. The description of female psychology offered by Freud has been so influential that even professed non-Freudians, or people who may be quite unaware of the formal theory of psychoanalysis, formulate their ideas about female personality, and particularly female sexuality, in Freudian concepts and Freudian imagery. Psychoanalysis has, as Lee and Stewart say, 'attempted to formulate general laws of the interaction between gender anatomy and individual psychosexual development' (Lee and Stewart, 1976, p. 27) so that lack of aggression, passivity-conformity and lack of striving for achievement are posited as universal feminine traits, arising out of the nature of female sexuality as the passive, receptive vehicle, gaining satisfaction through giving pleasure to a man. Freud's ideas on female sexuality were first systematically presented in his 'Three Essays on the Theory of Sexuality', originally published in 1905, but the difficulties of the resolution of the Oediapal complex in his account of 'parallel' development of male and female sexuality led him to revise his ideas on female sexuality. In his 1925 paper 'Some Psychic Consequences of the Anatomical Distinction between the Sexes', he thus relates female sexuality not to the Oedipal problem, but to the discovery by the girl that she lacks a penis. Once girls become aware of this 'anatomical distinction' they must, according to Freud, begin the process whereby sexuality is transferred from the clitoris, which they now realise is not a penis, to the vagina, a transfer which is only possible if the female accepts the feminine sexual role of receptivity.

The psychoanalytic emphasis on anatomical *difference* is paralleled in the set of stereotypes in which the dichotomised constructs of masculinity and femininity are formulated. Attributes of femininity/masculinity are generally seen as dichotomised, either/or conceptions. For instance, Kay Deaux and others report studies revealing male stereotypes as objective, independent, competitive, adventurous, self-confident and ambitious, with the stereotypical female being seen as dependent, passive, subjective, not competitive, not adventurous, not self-confident, not ambitious, and also as tactful, gentle, aware of the feelings of others, and able to express tenderness and emotion easily (Deaux, 1976). (The literature on the research into attributions of different character traits to males and females is well summarised by Oakley, 1972.)

These familiar stereotypes of femininity were well represented among my adult interview subjects. 'Femininity', first of all meant feminine appearance:

> They look better if they look feminine. Soft, female, womanly, not denying one's sex. I like girls to look female, one can look like that in jeans, but you should be able to say, 'there goes a female.' African women, I always think of that as femininity, with their round bottoms and big legs.

> I like them to look feminine, but that doesn't necessarily mean skirts. I don't know what feminine is, but I wouldn't like to see them aping boys, they should allow themselves some curves.

> Long hair, good looking, smart clothes.

> I like girls to be feminine. To dress nicely, they can look good in jeans, if they're worn nicely, with a bit of make-up. I don't like the heavy leather, lots of badges, greasy hair, . . . A good figure.

To these adults, who were both male and female, femininity as far as appearance is concerned is to do with prettiness, and also an attitude of mind: the feminine girl *allows* herself some curves, she is the one who wears jeans provocatively, making sure they fit well, and that her hair and make-up confirm that she is wearing jeans to show off her feminine shape rather than to signal her readiness for practical activity or her lack of interest in fashion; the femininity is in her and not in her clothes. The quotations above come from social workers, and the last one is a social work trained youth worker. In contrast, for the teachers and for most of the girls I talked to, 'femininity' in appearance meant the wearing of certain types of clothes:

> There should be an element of femininity, they should come out in a dress;

> I like to see them wearing skirts and dresses, not stick in jeans all the time,

were teachers' comments, whilst girls' own ideas of femininity in appearance were:

> It's right for girls to look feminine. Most girls wear trousers all the time, it's nice to see them in a dress sometimes, especially if they're going somewhere in the evenings,

and

> You should wear feminine clothes sometimes, not trousers all the time. There's a time and a place for looking feminine. You should wear dresses sometimes, when you're going out for discos. Not for school, you come to school to learn, not to dress up.

Obviously, the relationships of these groups of people to teenage girls' femininity are different. Social workers are generally trying to help girls accept and be confident in their femininity; teachers are more concerned with 'managing' femininity; whereas girls themselves are concerned to be accorded the status 'feminine', a judgement which they cannot bestow on themselves, but must have confirmed by adults and, of course, by boys.

Whilst, according to classroom observation studies (see Wolpe, 1977) teachers respond positively to 'feminine' girls, whilst they like to encourage the development of feminine traits; nevertheless, the school is not regarded as an appropriate arena for the display of unbounded femininity. The idea that femininity can be taken on and off by changing clothes explains a form of behaviour that is common amongst teachers: if femininity is bestowed by dress then teachers can keep displays of femininity within bounds by insisting on a plain, de-individualised dress. Even in schools where there is not a uniform, there will usually be suggested a repertoire of 'approved clothing', which does not include the pretty or the fashionable. By their emphasis on dress, teachers deny girls' success in maintaining this feminine appearance: one of the perennial battles in schools is over girls trying to sexualise their appearance by altering the way in which uniform is worn (changing the length of the school skirt, the heel height of plain lace-up shoes, the type of stockings) as well as by wearing make-up and jewellery to look provocative despite drab, regulation clothes. This is a battle also carried on in boys' schools of course, where unbounded machismo is also a problem for teachers.

Paul Willis (1977) describes the regular altercations taking place between teachers and disaffected pupils over dress. Dress, of course, is important to teenagers not just because of its potentiality for enhancing the sexuality of one's appearance. As the recent British series of writings on youth cultures have told us, since in a capitalist society one is bounded by one's position as producer or consumer, for teenagers who have not yet entered the labour market the only possible resistance or rebellion is through the adoption of particular styles of consumption, of which dress is the most easily accessible and the most noticeable.

Angela McRobbie points out that some girls assert their opposition to the de-individualised and class-oppressive school culture by exaggerating the femininity that is tacitly encouraged by teachers, in an account that at this point is parallel to Willis' account of his Hammertown boys:

> one way in which girls combat the class-based and oppressive features of the school is to assert their 'femaleness', to introduce into the classroom their sexuality and their physical maturity in such a way as to force the teachers to take notice. A class instinct finds expression at the level of jettisoning the official ideology for girls in the school (neatness, diligence, femininity, passivity etc.) and replacing it with a more feminine, even sexual one. Thus the girls took great pleasure in wearing make-up to school, spent vast amounts of time discussing boyfriends in loud voices in class, and used these interests to disrupt the class. (McRobbie, 1978, p. 104)

Schools, therefore, whilst not denying femininity, must also keep it within bounds, must 'manage it'. Wolpe reports teachers encouraging femininity, McRobbie tells of classes being disrupted by it: what both these observations reveal is that teachers' orientation to femininity is that of encouraging a modest and traditional feminine development, and having a 'group management' relationship with girls which will be threatened by inappropriate degrees of femininity, and especially by a markedly sexualised femininity.

Social workers, on the other hand, are on the lookout for any signs of lack of stereotypical femininity, as is particularly evident in their intolerance of aggression in girls. The statistics on children in local authority residential care, for instance, show that whilst girls appear in court for criminal offences in comparison with boys in the ratio of about 1:10, the ratio of girls to boys in residential care is about 1:1 nationally. Girls are disproportionately admitted to residential care because of aggressive behaviour of a fairly minor nature which is dealt with by way of 'Beyond Control' and 'Place of Safety' civil proceedings, and which would not justify a Care Order under criminal proceedings.

Girls themselves are faced with the problem of how far to display femininity, and assessing in what social situations it is appropriate to be feminine, and to what degree. The situational difficulties for girls of knowing how to behave according to the expectations of femininity exist, even though the cultural notion of what femininity 'is' may be clear and consistent.

As well as appearance, the connotation of femininity relates to stereotypical personality characteristics, and these were again well illustrated by the replies of my adult interview subjects. When asked about feminine characteristics, both teachers and social workers mentioned the usual traits of gentleness, caring for others, quietness and dependence:

> Being dependent, whilst at the same time confident and outgoing

(an impossible combination, surely);

> Feminine traits, I think I cling to the gentleness one:

> Despite my protestations, I still see feminine qualities as the nurturing kind;

> Pretty. Kind to other people, brains and beauty. She should have charity. . . . There's one I deal with who's 18, she's attractive because she's not hard-boiled. . . . Not strident, I like girls to be feminine.

> One who has feminine characteristics. Gentleness and kindness and compassion, rather than masculine traits of brutality, physical strength.

The difference between social workers and teachers was not that they had any different ideas of what feminine traits were, but that social workers when talking of 'a nice teenage girl' talked only of feminine appearance and feminine character traits, whereas teachers did also talk in terms of age-related characteristics. For instance, teachers did mention that they thought a girl *in her teens* should be becoming less dependent on her family and spending more time outside the home, should be making plans for a career, working towards examinations, taking an interest in the wider social and political world. The problem is then, of course, that what they are asking for is for teenage girls *qua teenagers* to develop 'masculine' characteristics of independence, political and career interests, whilst at the same time expecting them to develop a personality style of caring for others, looking after children, being gentle and unassertive.

Differential use of 'adolescence' and 'femininity': discourses as professional vocabularies

Some of the questions I asked were answered by all respondents in terms of femininity: they were spoken about always as to whether the behaviour concerned was worse for boys than for girls or – more usually – vice versa, rather than being talked about in relation to whether it would be worse for younger or older teenagers. For instance, with fighting, all subjects spontaneously addressed themselves to the difference between girls and boys fighting:

I'm old fashioned. It strikes me as unladylike. It would shock me more than boys fighting, because I'm old fashioned. I think girls shouldn't, I've got a slightly romantic view of ladies. If a man fights, I think there's a bit of the old west in him, it's the manly image. Girls fighting is terribly degrading. (a social worker)

It's less attractive for girls than boys. Ugly. Boys fight more than girls do. Girls use violence a lot less than boys do, girls do other things to be nasty to each other. (a teacher)

Some questions, on the other hand, concerning different types of behaviour, were all answered by relating ideas to age rather than gender differences; interview subjects in some cases would speak in terms of 'they ought to have grown out of it by that age', rather than in terms of 'it's far worse for girls'. Going to pubs, for example, was seen as age-related behaviour, by girls as well as by adults, and of course since the law relating to presence in pubs is defined by age rather than by gender, being served without being challenged in pubs is one of the principal means adolescents use to test their ability to 'pass' as adults.

With other behaviour, however, adults questioned were definitely divided over whether they would talk from within the adolescence or the femininity perspective, and their answers revealed not their personal values, but the nature of their concern with girls, and the professional vocabulary they have at their disposal to talk about this concern.

Vandalism, to take one prominent example, was regarded by teachers as a sign of boredom, of the lack of an ability – attributed to maturity – to find constructive things to do with one's time; while social workers were apt to talk of vandalism as 'unfeminine' aggression. Similarly, with breaking and entering, teachers envisaged a scenario of younger girls being taken along by older brothers, sisters or friends, and not having the mature moral sense to realise the wrongness of the action, and having insufficient mature concern for the rights of private property. Social workers were concerned with whether the girl would be acting as lookout for a boyfriend, which they would regard as obviously wrong and illegal, but not as a sign of emotional disturbance or role incongruence; or whether on the other hand a girl might be breaking and entering on her own account, in which case they saw it as: 'much more aggressive, anti-social behaviour than you normally expect from girls. She might be one of those very rare things, a female psychopath.' Setting fire to property, too, was envisaged by teachers as being a piece of minor vandalism which could get out of hand, and they imagined a girl being frightened of the enormity of her action and not doing it again, whereas to social workers any behaviour involving fire was: 'a sign of very deep disturbance'. Several social workers' views were typified by the probation officer who said that: 'It's a very significant sign of sickness. I wouldn't look for the Freudian explanation, but she must be very emotionally disturbed, it's the sexual thing', illustrating my earlier point that the Freudian imagery pervades the judgement even of those who deny any allegiance to his theories.

Whether the illegal behaviours covered by these interviews were seen in terms of femininity or of adolescence made a considerable difference to the seriousness with which they were regarded. If something can be seen as a 'phase', as normal albeit undesirable youthful behaviour, then the expectation is that increasing maturity will bring about its end; but if a form of behaviour is regarded as gender-inappropriate then there are fears that a girl is seriously disturbed, that she is not following the pattern of normal social and emotional development, and the behaviour comes to be judged not by its own seriousness in terms of consequences, social harm done, degree of delinquent motivation, or any other common-sense notion of seriousness, but it comes to be overblown as a predictor of future, more serious trouble. Adolescence is, after all, the status a teenager is moving out of, so that adolescent failings can be tolerated; but femininity is what a girl is supposed to be acquiring, so that any signs that she is rejecting rather than embracing the culturally-defined femininity are treated (by those whose professional vocabulary enables them to read the signs and offer such interpretations) as necessitating active intervention and urgent resocialisation.

For most of the behaviours discussed, there were explanations possible – possible, that is, in terms of being within the range of currently accepted explanations of behaviour – that drew on ideas of thoughtlessness and youthfulness, or that made reference to psychological disturbance and used psychoanalytic imagery. There was a noticeable tendency for teachers to use the first kind of explanation, and social workers the second.

Running away from home was one type of behaviour discussed in the interviews that illustrates these alternative forms of explanation. Running away could be seen as a consequence of immaturity, with girls likely to exaggerate problems in the home, and was seen least seriously when viewed as part of the 'storm and stress' of normal adolescence:

> That's not very serious. Most very soon come back. I'd think in terms of the trouble caused to parents trying to find her, the stress on the parents. They use it as a threat.

> . . . not a very heinous crime in itself. The majority do come back. In itself, any girl might get uptight, run off, come back the next day.

The scenario depicted here is a row between parents and their teenage daughter, a row that is within the scale of the 'normal', a breach of relations that can soon be healed. Social workers, however, saw a much more dramatic situation, feeling that girls exaggerate tensions because of their feminine emotionality or because of their rampant sexuality which makes them rush to a boyfriend, away from their parents, although, sometimes they are seen as fleeing from an emergent sexuality which they cannot cope with:

> A cry for help, if they run away they think the situation will cease to exist, they're scared of something. It depends on the age of the girl. If someone is teenage or older then they've been unable to face up to quite a major situation; quite a minor flare-up could cause a young girl to run away. She would be taken advantage of, she might get into the situation where she couldn't face her parents again, even if the original incident was resolvable, it could seem easier not to go back.

The view of female sexuality as passive, open to abuse and exploitation colours the social workers' emphasis on what happens to the girl when she runs away, whereas the teachers' general professional concern with adult-adolescent authority relationships leads to a particular focus on the stresses for parents of living with teenagers, which are, of course, analagous to the stresses for teachers of coping with teenagers in school.

This nature of the professional concerns of teachers and social workers means that with most of the interview topics, the range of answers given reflects constructions of the questions as dealing with different problems, there then being a range of views on the seriousness of the problem specified, and how it should be dealt with. To put it simply, to most questions there were what might be called liberal and authoritarian teachers' views, liberal and authoritarian social workers' views, but the problem defined in each pair of views would be seen as the same. For instance, with running away or staying out overnight, a liberal teacher's view would be that all girls stay away from home some time, they do not mean any harm, and sensible parents will not make too much fuss about it; whereas the authoritarian teacher would offer pronouncements about the thoughtlessness of adolescents, the flouting of parental authority, the need for firmer discipline in the home. Nonetheless, both views are representative of the teachers' perspective of adolescents' reactions to adult authority. A liberal social worker might say that girls could get pregnant just as easily before nine o'clock as after midnight so why fuss about their being out overnight; an authoritarian social worker would say that girls who are out all night or very late must be falling in with bad company and are probably being led into drugtaking, or prostitution. Again, though, with the social workers as with the teachers, there is a 'professional problem' – just as teachers problematise relationships within the home, so social workers problematise behaviour outside the home, and particularly sexual behaviour. Teachers will want to know how the parents respond and what stresses are caused for parents; social workers will want to know who the girls are keeping company with outside the home, and will be particularly on the lookout of evidence that a girl is spending her time with older men or older boys. What is particularly dangerous about this social work preoccupation with teenage girls' sexuality, of course, is that their concern is recognised in the legal specifications of 'In Moral Danger' and 'Beyond Control' as reasons for removing girls from home and placing them in local authority residential care.

On the topic of promiscuity, the teachers' group management concern with femininity again contrasted with the social workers' concern with the development of 'normal' feminine personality. Teachers were concerned that girls should not engage in sexual relations before receiving sex education, that they should not have to leave school because of pregnancy; but they did not, generally, feel it their place to make moral judgements, even when they themselves held strong personal views:

I would hope they get themselves on the pill;

The ignorance of some girls over pregnancy and VD is really staggering,

were teachers' views. In contrast, the social workers responded in terms of the relationship between sexuality and femininity, whereby sexuality is not something to be enjoyed for its own sake, but an indicator of the feminine skill of forming caring relationships. One social worker who described herself as a feminist and generally opposed to marriage, told me:

It's the coldness that worries me. There are two now I deal with, they seem so cold, they never seem to care. I would try to cut down the numbers and encourage some feeling.

The promiscuous girl was seen by social workers in stereotypical terms of 'seeking affection where she can find it', of loneliness and dependency, being led into promiscuity or delinquency in the manner described by Thomas (1928) in a formulation that has been little modified over the years. Promiscuity was seen as an indication of failure to form relationships, a lack of self-confidence which leads girls to offer sex as a way of trying to keep the one boy they can get or to try to attract more, of having no faith in the drawing power of one's own personality, so that sex has to be offered as well as the pleasure of one's company. The girl who was promiscuous because of thinking sex was fun was not imagined by any of the social workers I talked to. In matters of sexuality the discourse of adolescence is clearly at variance with the discourse of femininity: according to the terms of the adolescence discourse, adolescence is a time of shifting allegiances, rapidly changing friendships; whereas femininity involves the skill to make lasting relationships, with the ability to care very deeply for very few people. Thus the teenage girl has to tread a narrow line between 'getting too serious too soon', and being regarded as promiscuous by her elders and as 'a slag' by her peers. This contradiction in the social work variant of the two discourses is illustrated by Marchant and Smith (1977), who in establishing criteria for selecting girls as 'at risk' for their action-research project, specify both girls who change partners frequently, and girls who stick permanently to one boy or have no boyfriends. Having an older boyfriend is considered a danger signal by most adults; yet since the expectations of adolescence would lead a boy – for whom there are no expectations of femininity to be undermined by behaving according to the adolescence standards! – to change girlfriends frequently, having a boyfriend of her own age would, presumably, therefore not afford the girl the opportunity of demonstrating her developing feminine skills of making deep and lasting relationships.

Sources of differential involvement in femininity and adolescence discourses

Teachers and social workers use these different frameworks for talking about girls' behaviour for two principal reasons. First, as has already been suggested, the nature of their concerns with girls are different. For teachers, their contact with teenagers is organised on the basis of age rather than gender most of the time, and their aim is to facilitate age-appropriate cognitive development in large numbers of young people. In order to present lessons at all and to interact in the ways prescribed by the organisation of schools, teachers must emphasise the similarities between young people rather than their differences, or dealing with people in groups rather than individually would not be possible.

Their concern is the 'normal' youngster, manifestations of abnormality are dealt with outside the classroom either by teachers with specialist pastoral skills or by referral to social workers and psychologists. Social workers, on the other hand, are oriented to the help of the individual in trouble. Their contact is with young people who are distinguished by their differences from the normal, and even where their conduct is so widespread as to approximate at least statistically to normality (for instance involvement in shoplifting), the ethos of social work is to individuate in the treatment of clients. Where a client is absolutely conformist over most of her behaviour, it is the small part of her range of conduct which is deviant which will be the focus of the social workers' attention. This individuation, or 'individual pathology' approach as it is often termed, by social workers has been challenged in the small but growing body of critical literature devoted to social work practice (for instance, Bailey and Brake, 1975), but it remains the orientation of most present-day social work.

There is a second reason why teachers speak mostly within the adolescence discourse and social workers within that of femininity, and this relates to the terminology to which each profession has access. Teachers during their training take courses in developmental psychology, and are conversant with stage theories of personality development such as Erikson's formulations of emotional stages, and the linear-stage cognitive development theories of Piaget and Kohlberg. They therefore have at their disposal terms such as 'normal development' and 'adolescent phase'. With social workers, the developmental psychology studied during training is over-shadowed by the inputs of psychoanalytic theory and abnormal psychology. They will also study, generally in a rather sketchy, interdisciplinary way, criminology and deviance, where of course the treatment of females is still addressed overwhelmingly from a psychiatric perspective in terms of individual pathology. As training meshes with professional experience, developing expertise involves the deployment of the language of the accredited body of knowledge available, so that the 'expert' teacher will use more and more of the developmental psychology of the adolescence discourse while the 'specialist' social worker will become well versed in the psychoanalytic-based discourse of femininity.

Adolescence and femininity as public discourses

The professional forms of these two discourses generate sets of stereotypical, generalised ideas which operate as public discourses, and which at several points are contradictory and mutually subversive. Teenage magazines provide rich examples of the public variants of these discourses, and illustrate the way in which the accredited terms of discourses must be adhered to by low-status participants. It is the stated aim of these magazines to 'talk to girls in their own language', yet they reiterate the terminology appropriate to the generalised adult talking to the impersonal teenager. If girls write to the magazines, their letters, their concerns are not addressed directly in their own terms, but are refracted back to them in the appropriate language, correcting their unique anxieties into the trivial worries that are 'common to girls of your age'.

Several commentators have drawn attention to the ideological construct of teenage femininity presented in the fiction and advertising pages of these magazines (most notably Alderson, 1968; McRobbie, 1982a). The emphasis on leisure and fun as opposed to work and study; the preoccupation with romance; the conspicuous consumption and prominence of gossip, the lack of comment on the hard work necessary for success, in the sections on pop stars; the discouragement of enlarged social, geographical or occupational horizons; the stereotypical white, bland prettiness of the models; the telegraphed, slangy language, have all been well documented by Alderson and more recently by McRobbie, and while I would not wish to quarrel in any way with the findings of these studies or with their formulation of the ideological nature of this construction of a consumer product which is teenage femininity, I would point out that there is another discourse present in these magazines – the discourse of adolescence. As well as stereotypical images of femininity, teenage magazines are suffused with equally bland, stereotypical images of what it is to be in one's mid-teens. The magazines are aimed not just at a gender-specific audience but also at an age-specific audience, and so they are as concerned to appeal to the *teenager* as to the *girl*.

If one turns from the fiction to the allegedly non-fiction parts of these magazines, one finds a striking non-congruence. Just as the stereotypical images of desexualised romance pursued relentlessly by carefree, apparently parentless and friendless girls untroubled by overweight, acne or dandruff, pervade the fiction pages; in the 'agony columns' and 'problem features' we find the equally stereotypical problems of adolescence: shyness, parents who could never understand teenage anxieties and heartaches, worries over school and work, personality defects and unsatisfactory physical appearance. While on the fiction pages all girls are longing for the romantic date, the big goodnight clinch and a love that lasts for ever, on the problem pages 'all girls of your age' are shy the first time they go out with a boy, have problems in telling whether a boy cares about them or not, and dread the moment of the goodnight kiss (or even worse!) In the stories, parents never appear and other girls are rivals to be ruthlessly eliminated; in the non-fiction sections parents are always right, and readers are warned not to neglect girlfriends for boyfriends. *Jackie*, *Mates* and *My Guy* all run page-length 'problem features', in which boyfriend characters are used to support the message that parents know best, dropping their girl if she turns out to be deceiving her parents or lying about her age; and girls who neglect their girl friends or steal their best friend's boy are condemned to loneliness, deserted by both boyfriends and girl-friends.

Because magazines have only 'lay' status in the discourse of adolescence (they are not doctors, teachers, psychiatrists or any kind of expert in teenage problems) they voice only the most general terms of the adolescence discourse. Teenage magazines adopt – must adopt – the voice of any adult speaking to any teenager. They do not know the personal circumstances of the girls who write in, and in any case have to depersonalise the messages so that they appeal to a general teenage girl audience and are not tied to the specific biography of an individual inquirer. Thus, the combination of lack of status in the discourse and the need to appeal to a general audience rather than speaking directly to someone personally known, means that the magazines will only reproduce the most widely acceptable, bland and generally known terms of the adolescence discourse. This means that they appear to be purveying a crude, old-fashioned moralism. For instance, they are very conservative on sexual questions, they frequently point out the legal age of consent, and they respond to the most unreasonable sounding parental behaviour with the message that parents always have good reasons of care and concern for the things they do and the rules they make. The position of these magazines is the same in respect to both discourses. With femininity and with adolescence, they are helping keep in circulation established, stereotypical and uncontroversial notions of what it is to be feminine and teenaged.

The existence simultaneously of two discourses does not by any means mean that girls are free to choose whether to orient their behaviour to a femininity standard or to an adolescence standard. Their position in both discourses is that they must expect their behaviour to be judged by adults in terms of adults' own, rather than girls', invocations of one or the other of the discourses. Girls' claims to femininity are constantly open to subversion by judgements of their behaviour as adolescent, whilst at the same time if they are too demonstrable acquiring a mature femininity they are told to have more fun, to be the zany, thoughtless, selfish person we see as the 'typical teenager'. Since femininity is the 'master discourse' in the sense that it is the status of femininity that teenage girls are aspiring towards and the status of adolescence that they are aiming to leave behind, being dismissed as 'adolescent' is more dangerously subversive of femininity than being 'womanly' is of adolescence. Indeed, a constant preoccupation of the girls I interviewed was with whether or not their behaviour would seem childish. Behaviour such as making hoax fire calls or minor acts of vandalism brought forth much stronger condemnation from them than more seriously anti-social or personally harmful behaviour, not because of defective

value systems in teenagers or inter-generational value differences,
but because, I believe, these manifestations of adolescence are,
because of teachers' positions *vis-à-vis* the discourse of adolescence,
the behaviours against which they are constantly being warned, and
because they are the types of behaviour most likely to make adults
think of them as still being in the 'adolescent phase'. Because adults
talk about these types of behaviour when talking to and about
teenagers, not only are they uppermost in the minds of teenagers,
but adults are thereby giving teenagers the language in which to talk
themselves about these things. Some behaviours, such as drugtaking, brought forth very little comment from the girls, not because
teenage girls condone drugtaking, but because the girls had not
been given access to the terms in which they are commonly talked
about. They did not know, for instance, which drugs are generally
considered 'hard' and which 'soft'; they did not know the names of
many drugs; they do not use the medical terminology in which
debate about drugs is generally conducted. This is a possible
interpretation of the finding by McRobbie (1978) and Prendergast and Prout (1980) that even when girls have experiential
knowledge that contradicts the normative evaluation of marriage
and motherhood as desirable states, they still express the culturally
expected aspirations towards them, rather than rejecting them on
the grounds of their personal knowledge of mothers, older sister, etc.
for whom these have been unhappy experiences. I suggest that girls
do not so much discount personal, experiential knowledge on this
and other topics, as have no vocabulary in which to put it forward.
The public terms of the discourse of femininity precludes the
expression of such deviant views of marriage and motherhood, and
the public terms are the only ones to which girls have access. Part of
the task of feminist work with girls is thus, I would suggest, giving
girls terms in which to express their experiential knowledge rather
than having to fall back into the stereotyped expressions of
normatively defined 'femininity' in order to say anything at all
about areas of life which vitally concern them.

I have proposed here two principal discourses in which judgements about the behaviour of teenage girls can be spoken:
femininity and adolescence. Further, I have proposed that each of
these discourses has a public and a professional form, and that the
professional versions filter through to girls via the public versions as
sets of stereotyped images of femininity and adolescence, which

impinge on their lives as two, often conflicting, sets of expectations. Because they cannot perceive these statements about femininity and adolescence as *discourses*, they perceive only contradictory, generalised statements from adult society, contradictory to the extent that teenage girls find it difficult to know what adults *really* want of them. They experience the fact of being judged by two, incongruent, sets of expectations as the feeling that whatever they do, it is always wrong; a correct impression since so often if they are fulfilling the expectations of femininity they will be disappointing those of adolescence, and vice versa.

3

Groping towards sexism: boys' sex talk

Julian Wood

O, what men dare do! What men may do!
What men daily do not knowing what they do.
Much Ado About Nothing, IV, 1, 18–19

The centre

Sexuality is a 'notoriously elusive subject' (Barrett 1980, p. 42). It is suffused in everyday life: ever present yet, somehow, ever absent. It is not always possible to say what is sexual about a particular experience. For these reasons it would be wrong to laden sexuality in itself with the responsibility of explaining all our motivations. Sexuality has no essence, nor can it be put in a field all of its own. Rather, in our society, it is channelled into many areas, into leisure, consumption and work. It may be possible to investigate how this channelling contributes to the moral regulation of people if we pay close attention, first, to the actual practice of genders.

The chance to gather the information on which this article is based came from an individual research project that I did in a school 'sin bin'. The centre was a small on-site unit for 'disruptives' in a London, co-educational, secondary school. It may well be that there were specific features of the institution that helped to facilitate the behaviour described, and so I will sketch in the salient features of the place. It was set up, mainly on the initiative of the head, essentially to remove 'problem' children from the school and re-educate them into a position where they could once more 'benefit from what the school had to offer' (as well as re-introducing into them the habit of attendance). The staff (one male head of centre, one male assistant teacher and one female assistant teacher) saw their brief as more pastoral than academic. They wanted to help the kids *individually* to overcome what the staff defined as a rejection of adults and the adult world. The curriculum consisted mostly of basic maths and English with some craftwork and lots of recreation time. The centre was quite like the school it served except that some of the more rigid controls on movement, posture and language had been relaxed in order to avoid excessive conflict. Nevertheless, there was a constant struggle by the staff to stop the older kids using the centre as what the staff termed a 'day-time youth club'. It was important for the overall work of the centre, and especially for the elusive goal of re-integration, that the kids should be subject to definite, if not authoritarian, adult restraint.

The centre was located in an old terraced house next to the school grounds. At times, I confess, it reminded me of nothing so much as a primary school classroom with its school-like smell, its painting-covered walls, its rows of textbooks and its tiny, plywood chairs. There was one organisational feature that contributed to differentiating the centre from the main school and that was the lack of strict age divisions or 'years'. The centre took kids from twelve up to the school-leaving-age (no one would stay on as a sixth former) and usually they took the same lessons together. It is a feature of such centres that the numbers attending fluctuate, with lots of kids coming and leaving, around a core group. Although the average stay was two to three years this is not a very useful statistic because the long-term kids, who usually became informal leaders, could be there for their whole secondary careers. (The staff recognised that this made nonsense of the ostensible purpose of re-integration.) Because of these patterns of fluctuation around stability the centre went through various different phases.

One of the most important dimensions along which the state of the centre could be measured was the overall balance of power between the genders. In terms of friendship groups, particularly outside school, and in terms of unspoken understandings, the boys related primarily to the boys and the girls to the girls. For convenience I shall write *as if* the boys formed one cultural grouping and the girls formed another. However, this stresses the cultural separateness of the genders in a way which does oversimplify lived relations. What needs to be captured here is a series of *moods* present in the centre about relations between the genders. For example, there would be certain periods when the girls would become more united and acquire more collective confidence, they would complain that the boys were getting most of the attention, choice of lessons and so on. In these periods great emphasis would be put, by both genders, on the real, and imagined, social separateness of the genders. This contrasted sharply with times of inter-gender harmony when the more confident girls would join in with the boys on practical jokes ('wind ups') on the staff, sit close to the boys in lessons and so on. (Incidentally, there is a common staffroom notion that girls – who, in ideology, are characterised as being naturally more docile than boys – are more difficult when they *are* 'troublemakers'). Times of inter-gender conflict were worrying to the centre staff not just because there was more likelihood of rows and even pitched battles occurring, but because trouble with the main school and more 'disruption' generally were associated with such periods. Sometimes it seemed the kids could only fluctuate between a strained rebelliousness and a listless quiescence.

It was the issue of sexual attraction and sexual 'awakening' (as ideology would have it) that provided the axis for one of the centre's most interesting periods as far as inter-gender relations were concerned. There had often been a flirtatious tinge to relations between the genders: on school trips for example. In this particular period there was an apparent upsurge in (for the want of a better term) 'sexiness' in the centre. This produced some new forms of behaviour culminating in fairly boisterous groping sessions, as I shall describe later. It was from this phase, too, that most of the quotations from the kids were taken.

The whole sexy atmosphere of the period led me to reflect on the absence of any real work on sex *as it manifests itself in schools*. Even good, recent feminist work (e.g. Deem, 1980; Spender and Sarah, 1980) has not really covered this significant gap. I mean, particularly, how sexuality manifests itself in school as an axis of power relations and as a locus of social orderings.[1] I do not know, again, whether it is a male-biased absurdity but, as a commonsense recollection, large areas of school life seemed to have been suffused with sexual meaning and sexual longing beneath (or because of) the boredom. If this is even a quarter true for *most* people then it makes the omission even stranger.

The groping sessions were, as it turned out, the last manifestation of the sexy period, for after that time the protagonists were dispersed for various reasons. The girls who were most involved either went back to the main school or became defined as 'too old' for the centre and went on to another centre. The boys (who, so typically, had misunderstood the girls' intentions in the 'bundles' as we shall see) were left without any girls to 'practise' their sexist attitudes on.

In the next section I want to consider some of the attitudes and practices of the boys (and in less detail, the girls) that I argue are characteristic of their general class culture as well as of their age and location.

Some features of sexist sexual practice

The most common simple kind of sexist practice was a sort of feeding off the sight of the girls and of adult women teachers or visitors to the centre. Any slight revelation of flesh (a T-shirt, a skirt) focused the boy's attention on parts of the girl's bodies. In fact many hours must have been spent day-dreaming about the girls' bodies because at times a boy would come out with an unprompted sexist utterance to the air such as 'tits'! At other times the boys would giggle and grin and nudge each other about a particular posture of one of the girls. At this point it is very important to note what elements of redress were available to the girls. They were obviously not as weak as they were depicted by the boys, in fact they were often stronger. Not only did they have a strong group sense, at times some of them were stronger physcially than the boys. If sexism was one of the dominant modes of the centre it was *resisted by the girls*. The boys had to be careful that their sexist remarks were not seen to be personally insulting a stronger girl face to face. Here Tim, a leading centre joker, is talking to the air, extolling the virtues of parts of women's bodies. He is misconstrued by Lorraine (she thinks he is talking about her) who, being larger and stronger, can give him a sharp rebuke.

Tim:　　　. . . I like them with great big tits with great big nipples!

Lorraine　[*aggressively*]: What?

Tim:　　　I, er . . .

>   *Lorraine:*   Just shut up, O.K. Tim?
>   *Tim:*   Alright humpy.

I think the utterance is received as offensive by Lorraine really
because she thinks it is about her rather than as part of any
general attempt to correct Tim's sexism. (In fact there was no
evidence that any of the kids *at that time* had an articulated concept
of sexism as such.) However, the remark is only quashed by the
implicit threat of violence to Tim. As partriarchy so often finally
rests on male violence there is a certain piquancy to this reversal.

One of the specific features of men's sexism is the dissecting
approach that is taken to women's objectified bodies.[2] This came
out in the centre boys in numerous ways, for example, Tim's
selection of parts of the body, and was a crucial element in their
assessments of girls. It was externalised most frequently in sexist
slang; the part of the language capable of holding the most sexist
male meanings. This use of slang is common to the broader class
culture to which the boys belonged; it involves a detailed cataloguing of the female body in alternative terms, a literal naming of parts
whose use when 'skilfully' applied did seem to hold a certain power.
Perhaps part of its appeal was that it seemed to impart to the user a
tenuous sense of control. But, if this fierce objectification in slang is
a displaced attempt to control (and re-control each time?) the
object that it was labelling, then it also showed tell-tale signs of that
fixation which is part of an alientated view of the female body. Of
course one must be careful not to lose all precision, the use of slang
words for the bodies of *both* genders *by* both genders is a very old
business (as even a cursory reading of Chaucer will show). It is
doubtful whether the existence of such terms *per se* can be too
simply linked to a patriarchial system, however old that system may
be. Rather it is the tone, context, and use to which they are
attemptedly put, that makes sexual slang part of sexist talk. In terms
of the developing sexism of the centre boys it is the use of terms for
parts of the body *combined with* the intent to assess the girls in crude
and superficial ways that constitutes the element of attempted
domination. As we shall see, many conversations between boys
about women's bodies are premised on the idea that one can
reasonably assess a person solely in terms of the male opinion (for it
is men who presume to set the standards) of parts of their bodies.
Further, these parts – 'arse', 'legs', 'tits', 'boat' [i.e. 'boatrace' =

face] – seem to be almost interchangeable as 'good points' or at least one can be offset against another. Overhearing such an assessment discussion one might have got the impression that what was being discussed was some kind of grotesque snap-together doll. Once the parts have been divorced from the real bodies of real people they can be tacked on to any sentence and used as transferred derogatory labels, even adjectively: ('he's a cunt teacher he is'). It could be argued that facility with sexual and other slang is a sort of cultural 'skill' which can not only be used against those in authority but which will stand the boys in good stead generally in the world of working-class jobs. As Paul Willis (1979) argues, the 'culture of the shopfloor' is still one with a heavily macho orientation in many cases. I think he may also be right when he suggests that the workplace operates as a kind of pool of meanings (of a sexist type of masculinity) that spreads out into working-class culture as a whole (p. 190).

'Dogs', 'horny birds' and 'right whores'

Let us return to the topic of assessing women, especially according to their 'component parts'. The following extracts were taken from a conversation between two boys about which girls they fancied. This was also, incidentally, at the time at which the boys were trying in the most heavy-handed fashion to obtain sexual contact with the girls.

> *Jake:* I reckon Helen's got a nice face, she's good looking but her body, man! If she was slim . . . like her sister . . . she used to be really ugly didn't she, really fat? But now she's really slim, 'aint half nice now, she's got a nice body now . . . Lorraine, though, she's big. She ain't got a nice personality, too much mouth. She thinks she can rule everybody just because she's big.

The conversation passes on to assessing the younger sister of one of the girls in the centre. Jake urges Don to consider fancying her:

> *Don:* What's the sister like?
> *Jake:* Lovely! Ginger hair, ginger minge [minge = pubic hair]

Don demurs, indicating he is not attracted.

Jake: Oh my good God! Don't worry, you don't fuck the face!
She's got a nice body.

Obviously this discussion, very typical of the sort the boys would
have together to pass the time, is laden with sexist assumptions.
However, I do not think one can fully understand it only in those
terms without knowledge of the specific relationships involved.
Helen is being dismissed in as kindly a way as the boys are capable
of, because she is liked. Her friendly physicality and lack of
resistance to the boys' dominating ways secure her the lable of a
'nice personality'. Perhaps if she slimmed down they would do her
the big favour of fancying her! Lorraine on the other hand is not
going to suffer the boys' put-downs to secure some dubious
camaraderie (as her reprimand to Tim showed) and she has the
physical strength to take an independent line. Therefore, perhaps
what is most unfair about the boys' assessment of 'personality' is the
way it is not only traded off against looks but is considered 'not nice'
if it indicates a more-than-usual independence from male standards.

Early in the same conversation the boys had referred to Lorraine
as 'a dog'. This judgemental term (specifically on a girl's *looks*) is a
very common term within the sexist mode. Sometimes it seems that
all women who are not dogs ('dog rough' in the full phrase) are
automatically 'tasty' or fanciable. Of course it is absurd even by
sexist standards that 'dog' and 'tasty' should be a sort of binary
opposition. However, in that absurdity may lie the secret of the
power of the category. It relies for its power on the simplicity with
which it attempts to sort out the whole female gender and, perhaps,
the emotions of the speaker. How characteristic that is in fact of so
much of the lack of subtlety of male sexism. If vacillation is imputed
to women, then unwavering over-sureness may perhaps be, by
negative implication, very male. Besides which, the *pose* of sureness
is doubly 'functional' in that it obviates the need to find out if one
really does know one's own mind. Even if the boys want to
introduce the subtlety of considering a girl as 'a *bit* of a dog' the
clear, end position (dog) stands implicit and absolute behind the
indecisive judgement.

One could ask why males feel the need of this false security? I
follow Tolson's (1977) main drift that masculinity has at its heart
not unproblematic strength but often weakness, self-doubt and
confusion. In the light of this anti-'commonsense' view of masculin-

ity it is perhaps easier to understand why the boys make these superficial, dismissive judgements. Partly they are saying, 'we are the gender superior enough to judge women'. Looking down on the girls in the centre gave them an illusion of confidence. To put it another way, while the outward face of the sexist mode was characterised by confidence, brashness, fluency and 'presence' (the promise of power as Tolson puts it) the inward face was often the complete reverse. I think also the boys felt, obscurely, the need to by-pass the competitive relations between the sexes that their own behaviour perpetuated, but they were largely unable to do this. Thoughout I have put a question mark beside the idea of a sexist mode being 'functional' for the boys, and yet I have half-retained the notion.[3] There is always a danger of fixing an imbalance and of defeating opposition, or desire for change, by making structures seem *too* 'functional' and therefore impossible to alter. I do not want this analysis to be functional*ist* in that sense, but I do think it is vital not to flip over into complete voluntarism; we must look for structural (social and psychological) features of historically realised masculinity that are *not of individual men's choosing*, if we are to address the persistence of sexism and therefore stand a real chance of eradicating it.

As I have noted, the various abstracted parts of a girl are traded off against each other by the boys. A 'good body' beneath an ugly 'boat' may rescue the lucky subject! In this mode all girls are 'worth one' (i.e. worth having sex with) but this brings with it certain internal contradictions. Not least, the speaker must try to be a tireless Tarzan with the ability and looks to 'pull' any girl. Of course (and this is a *relief* to the boys) actual inter-gender encounters are much more *negotiated* and *real*, however one-sided. This must be allowed for too; any attempt to actualise attraction or act out fantasy may be rebutted which is why we have the classic sour grapes ploy. It is amazing how little discouragement from the girl is required to turn a 'tasty bird' into 'a bit of a dog anyway'.

'Unfeminine' girls – the case of Eve

The arrival of Eve during the time that the boys were trying more successfully to occupy a sexist masculine space, prompted some very interesting aspects of their ideology to come to light. Particularly, she brought a practical questioning of the vital, insecurity-producing area of the division between the sexes. Eve was fifteen at the time, she was short and physically very strong. She also had, as she put it, 'a bad temper on me'. Within ideological definitions she was plain-looking rather than the received idea of 'sexy'. The boys labelled her 'a dog' but also, making fantasies out of what was currently happening, imputed to her an instinctive craving for sex. Perhaps at the back of this labelling was the pervasive projection from the boys that *all* girls want sex (see earlier), without necessarily knowing it themselves. More than that, there was the unspoken notion that 'bad looks' or a shy personality prevent some girls from getting their fair share. Thus 'dogs' are constructed as being especially 'horny' because they cannot find any boy to have sex with them. (Gay sex was merely disgusting to the boys within their sexist mode.)

This of course also constructs the girl as passive, for she has to wait for a boy to condescend to seek her out. There was another belief, apparently deeply embedded in the boys at the time, that 'sexy' girls are 'right whores', but what exactly that last phrase signifies seems to be flexible. By a strange process of ideological addition Eve seemed to be lumbered with both labels. As I hope will be clear, this article is especially concerned with the complexities of the process of the imposition of sexist labels. Not least of the questions that Eve's case raises is that of the relationship of her 'plain' looks to the violence of the boys' stereotyping.[4]

Within a month of coming to the centre Eve had demonstrated her actual physical strength (and willingness to use it) by having a fight with one of the more peripheral male members of the centre. She inflicted a cut eye before the fight was broken up. The boys were especially disgusted with the boy participant for the weakness his poor showing implied for the rest of them. Whether they could have done any better against Eve at full strength was a question they were all, secretly, glad not to have had put to the test. An interesting reaction to female strength came up soon after in a less fraught situation. While the kids were playing Chinese arm-wrestling Eve beat all but the two strongest boys. As she strained and pulled one boy exclaimed: 'look at those fucking muscles, man! It's not human, she's a fucking caveman not a human!'

I have chosen only the most crystallised example of what I take to be a generalised ideological notion about the proper division between the sexes.[5] I take it to be a popular belief (in this country at least) that there are particular male attributes – of which muscular strength is only the most 'natural' – and that women who exhibit too much of these qualities can be said to be going against their natural state or damaging their femininity in some way; they are considered 'butch'. Of course this is nonsense even in its own terms because women exhibit prodigious strength in their work inside and outside the home. However, the question here, as with all ideologies, is one of the effectivity of ideas inserted into practice. This leads me to an admittedly speculative observation on power and living within ideological definitions. In order to operate with their ideas the boys must try to eliminate, by will and action, the discrepancy between their internal world (containing their 'desires' and 'biological promptings') and the external world (containing the necessary but puzzling opposite sex). In short, by acting in ways consonant with their men-over-women-views they attempt to force others to accept and validate these power-based views. Although (Barrett, 1980) ideology cannot be itself 'material' in any obvious sense the actions within it (prompted by it?) are so intimately linked with prevailing definitions as to be, at times, effectively indistinguishable. Similarly, resistance to ideologically-inspired action may consist of forcing apart, by one's actions, what has been elided by the actions of others. In the case of the boys groping (see below) their actions assume that there is only one definition of the situation. The girls are 'victims' of this in so far as it is up to them to prove that other definitions (theirs) exist.

Male constructions of women and sexist fantasising

I want to investigate further the mechanisms by which the boys effected their views with reference to actual practices: the centre craze for having 'bundles'. It was quite clear that these bundles were only thinly divided *in the boys' eyes at least* from crude groping sessions. At the time I asked two of the leading boys how it was that this sexiness was suddenly present now. Even allowing for the way my question is precisely geared to generate the boys' responses (research 'findings') the answer is alarmingly predictable.

J.W.:   Why is it suddenly happening now then, when it never used to?

Jake: Because we're getting all the horny ones, all the whores in here. They've heard of Don and Jake and Co., [we could] make a living; 'come to us, we fuck you, two pound a time, or we pay you'. Just the ticket. . .

Tomorrow. That's the next move. When he said, 'right, ready Dave?' . . . he goes, 'lights off!' She goes, 'now don't pull my trousers down.' [Jake implies that her tone of voice was a signal for them to do just that].

Don: What about what Ewan said? He said he pulled her trousers down and seen her bum – all black – and he goes, 'not washed that have you?'

The 'explanation' of the sexiness contained in the first part of the extract is unequivocal and appears at one level to be actually believed by the boys. Their lust is imagined to be naturally strong and constant so that action is simply facilitated by 'horny birds' apparently volunteering themselves for touching up sessions. In this context it is quite possible that girls do not know their own mind and that they can be easily embarrassed, which explains Eve's 'mock' physical resistance. As we shall see the staff, too, were sucked into this ideological definition at its more plausible point. However, I think it would be a mistake to formulate too simply the relationship between beliefs, this utterance, and actual reality. The boys believe that Eve is 'horny' (with all the background myths surrounding that) but there is a peculiar quality to this sexist sex *talk* which needs to be specifically addressed. Note for example the shading off into ridiculousness (the centre boys as paid studs!) directly after answering the question. Then there is the momentary complete reversal of meaning – 'or we pay you' – which contradicts the notion of being paid even though it does not countervail the sexist drift of the whole conversation. This lack of formal coherence is typical of the boys' sex talk, half the time they are fantasising.

I am aware that, in retaining a notion of fantasy without fully defining it, I am in danger of appearing to be simply defending this sex talk. I am *not* saying that what Jake and Don are up to is harmless. I do not deny, for one second, that male fantasy and action *can* be (and often are) related, and can have pernicious effects in our society. However, I retain the notion that there is a space, or function, partaken of differentially by *both* genders which I call fantasy. The immediate connection to the real world is attenuated in this space, in fact its relation to real life is largely characterised as one of distance and unreality.

For these boys, with their attempts to live out an internally-strained masculine position, sex is an area where they can attempt to construct themselves as masterful. Also, because sexual relations are rather scary in the real world, they are an ideal topic for wild talk and for 'having a laugh'. If some fantasising is harmless, the imminent possibility of a translation into practice is not, for that brings in the crucial factor of force, which is the lynchpin of actual domination.

Nor are all ideas to be excused just because they may remain as ideas. That would be to invite the untenable position that all ideas are equal as ideas. The actual unpleasantness of sexist modes as they manifest themselves in the second part of the extract is there to remind us if we start to be too soft on sexism in our desire to understand the kids. Nor I think should this kind of attitude be censored from our accounts simply because of its awkwardness for those who feel they should vicariously champion 'the working class'. Ducking, for the moment, the vexed question of whether this mode of expression *is* more or less specific to working-class males we must acknowledge that a disparagement of women's bodies is a feature of *male* practice in many societies and epochs. Extrapolating from this attitude I think it is not too fanciful to say that women as a whole are sometimes regarded by men as dirty, alien, even evil.

To return to the boys, the *tone* here is certainly what one could call, loosely, 'working-class sexism'. It is the same tone exhibited by 'the lads' in Paul Willis's (1977) *Learning to Labour* with their fascination for 'jam rags' (sanitary towels) and so on. Nor was I short of examples in my research: the reproductive and excremental aspects of the female body were constantly referred to by the boys in a fixated-disgusted tone edged with nervousness and surrounded by giggling. Arguably, this is a power-confirming form of speech, a 'discourse' if you like, for which there may not have been a real equivalent amongst the girls.

In a way it is surprising that the boys did not put more of the feeling behind this kind of 'smutty' sex talk into traditional dirty jokes (*the* way, according to classical psychoanalysis at least, of dissipating such fears). In fact the centre boys were very feeble joke-tellers and very few had built up a stock repertoire of such jokes.

The sequence of invasion

In this section I want to discuss what I call the sequence. I think the tendency to act out this sequence did reproduce itself, especially in the boys. This idea is itself located within the empirically-based assumption that men still do make most of the sexual advances in the early stages of heterosexual sexual encounters. Some readers may feel irritated by such an assumption and argue that this is no longer (or never was) the case. Again, as with many other forms of behaviour discussed here, we need further, theoretically-informed, research. (Incidentally, it is precisely in measuring kids against this unlocated sequence as an index of sexual maturity that Schofield's (1968) approach shows its unwitting empiricism.) I have tried to address the actual utterances and practices of the kids whilst, at the same time, not just celebrating these as 'authentic'. With this sequence, for example, we must hold against it first, the real elements of female activity in interpersonal situations; and secondly, we must stress that these forms are natura*lised* and never natural.

This invasion of female bodies, on male terms, cuts across class and is finally grounded in the male dominant aspects of the social order. Power and ideology are the indispensable 'supports' of the lived relations described. Things like the sequence act as an unspoken common ground beneath the level of immediate consciousness, but not removed from, or completely controlling, that consciousness.

It seems that, in initiating sexual contact, the boys operate a sequence from the least 'serious' regions of the body to the most 'serious'. That is, in petting, they would usually start by trying to get to a girl's breast before 'going below'. There is a sequence for forms of behaviour as well: that is to say, kissing is less serious than petting and petting is less serious than heavy petting. Of course, specific conditions may override this, such as the time available or the visibility of participants. I am assuming that most serious sexual activity still takes place in private (e.g. a room) or in semi-private (e.g. a party or a darkened public place). Of course, the breaking of certain of these codes or the attempt to refuse them altogether may form part of a strategy of resistance to normative order, especially in the subcultural groupings of the young.

The following short extract points towards the ideological uses of the sequence. The boys try to use it to grade and label girls. There is another way in which this labelling can be secured. If the girl does take some power and initiative away from the boy (especially in relation to the sequence) then she may be fixed in male views – by means of smirking and gossip – as congenitally licentious.

Whilst walking along with two of the centre boys I asked about a particular girl who had just left the centre. Alan, the eldest boy (he was sixteen), volunteered this:

J.W.:   Do you remember Tina?
Alan: Yeah! She's a right whore!
Rob: What did you get?
Alan: On the [school trip] man, I got fucking tits, a wank, everything!

A good deal about certain sexist assumptions can be told from this throw-away remark. Most obviously it attempts to signal to other males how competent this male is by getting so far down the sequence. Also, importantly, it indexes the girl's putative promiscuity as a shaping aspect of her whole personality. It is one of the oldest and commonest variants of the double standard, in which the girl is blamed for what she has done and for what is a 'virtue' in men. Looked at logically it is all very strange. If Tina is a 'right whore' what does that make Alan – a right client? But, of course, we are not dealing with logic or equitable views of the world, but with power-based distortions. Tina is, like Eve, forever the possessor of a hard-to-control un-feminine lust. Moreover, in the tone of voice there is real contempt, as if to say that this girl is really stupid for allowing herself to be had. Patriarchy always wants its dues paid twice. If she had been sensible she would have realised that male lust is supposed to be 'naturally' potent and rapacious and that boys 'only want one thing'. However, if she realised this *and* acted defensively against it she would be no fun! If Tina is to be written off as a 'right whore' what is it that she is not? A nice girl? There was some slight indication that the boys thought they would make their long-term choices (some years hence) from a category called 'ordinary girls' (but this, as we shall see, is not free from stereotypical views of women). It is a commonplace enough observation that these would be less threatening to the boys than the idea of a sexually experienced 'right whore'.

Sexist fantasising revisited – plans for a rape

Partly because of the tradition within which I was working, I went, time and time again, for the male and the spectacular in my ethnography. Perhaps I imagined it to actually equal youth culture (I take McRobbie's (1980) point here about male accounts of youth culture often being displaced autobiography and/or wish fulfilment.) The aspect of this that I have had to be most critical of, in this attempt to represent my material, is my effective identification with the boys. This becomes crucial in sections like the following. Having, semi-consciously, engineered conversations about sex, I withdrew from active participation in them. I did not attempt to explain my ideas about sexism. I made only a limited attempt to redress the balance by getting close to the recipients of the boy's sexism, and this only because the following conversation, and the whole period that spawned it, were so extraordinary to me (not to the kids) that I was *forced* to find out at least something about the girls. First let us return to the period in which the conversation took place – the period when Eve was first referred to the centre. What is being discussed by Don and Jake below, is a plan to get Eve back to Jake's flat so that they can force her to have sex with them both. Had it occurred it would have been a gang rape. However, the hallmark of this conversation (*as a conversation*) is its utter unreality. As much as anything, this demonstrates how the two genders (as presently constructed) can not only start from different premises but seem to be in different worlds. I do *not* say this to excuse the intent of Don and Jake in the rest of their dealings with Eve but to convey a quality which may have been lost in transcription.

> *Jake:*   . . . we get out at quarter past two and go to collect my
> sister at three. Forty-five minutes, that'll do. Get her on
> the bed, tie her up, say 'sit down you prat! you can scream
> as much as you like but you aint getting out of here till

we've fucked you' . . . have you got the bottle [courage] to fuck her?

Don: I've got the bottle anytime.

Jake: . . . 'not going to tell her that we're going to fuck her, I'm just going to say, 'do you want to come up the house after?' . . . I'll say, 'come up the house listen to some records'. I ain't going to say, 'I'm going to fuck you'. If she says, 'yeah', I'll say, 'alright then, just come up on your own', I'll say, 'have you got any money?' She'll say, 'yeah'. We'll get on a bus, get to my house, go in the pub, get the key from mum.

Don: Be quick in the pub.

Jake: . . . No, wait, this is dodgy . . . if me dad comes home . . . so if he comes in while you're there don't worry, just get off her, don't fucking be fucking away while he's there. Whoever's not doing it, right, at the same time keep watch, and anything you hear just jump off of her and pull her knickers up.

The whole of this transcript may (rightly) shock radical sensibilities, but, in terms of insight into the boys, it is important to understand how they relate to this sort of conversation. For them, though it is 'daring', nothing untoward has been broached and they pass on to discussing particular boys in the main school, leaving this 'fiction' hanging in the air. They did not try to pursue this idea in real life (leaving aside the bundles). The 'function' of this talk for the boys is titillative. Conversation being less constrained than practice, they can play with Eve's body here in a way which they cannot in real life. Of course some might argue that the unreality of the conversation is not a credit to the boys, who are still culpable in intent, but is a function of the constraint of the real world, as I have noted. Certainly, it is an open and challenging question as to what type of self-delusions and distortions of the social world are likely from carrying around this sort of ideological baggage in one's head. As I have also said before, sexist ideas are not neutral just because they are sometimes likely to remain as ideas (language has an effectivity and power of its own). In the next section we will look at when sexist ideas move into sexist practice. This part-fantasy, as I shall continue to call it, *is* extremely violent in its own terms. Perhaps it illustrates what a very fine line there is between 'normal' and 'abnormal' in presently constructed males and their desires. As regards Jake and Don it was because they had so misunderstood the nature of their contact with Eve (see below) that they stood no chance of developing *any* kind of relationship with her, sexist or not. These kids were fourteen and their material experience lagged behind their ideas. Despite 'advanced' *notions* about sex neither of them had had any heterosexual sex to speak of. Eve was altogether more realistic and had had relationships outside the centre. I asked her if she knew that Don and Jake had wanted her to go back with them after school to have sex. Of course she knew! 'I wouldn't have gone with them' she commented tersely.

The bundles – from sex talk to sex practice

The bundles were a particular craze that swept the centre for about two months. For the boys they were a chance to practise sexist sexual practices. Attempts at flirting had always been around in more or less submerged ways (e.g. Alan and Tina) but the bundles were definitely something extra which crystallised certain aspects of the boys' sexism. They started when new girls came into the centre and changed the balance of numbers between the sexes. The actual bundles would start when there were about four boys and girls sitting in the small back room. The staff were overstretched at this time and had to break their rule of continuous cover when they were called to the main school for ten minutes or so. At these unguarded moments certain kids who were not liked would be told to stay out of the back room by those who were going to have the bundles. This could be very humiliating if you were eligible by the criterion of age. Sometimes the lights would be turned out before the bundles began, and the room, which had painted-in windows, would be thrown into half-darkness. Amid whoops and giggles the kids would pile on top of each other and have bundles. They would never last very long (luckily for the girls) and could be stopped either when they all 'packed up' laughing, or became exhausted, or were disturbed by the sound of approaching staff or pupils. The other more usual way for the bundles to end was for a girl to apply the only veto the situation allowed and to protest vigorously that the boys were being too heavy-handed or too rough.

The bundles were used by the boys to find out how the girls

reacted to their pressure – they were games of invasion; though feminists might reasonably object that invasion cannot, other than very euphemistically, be described as a game. Even if they started on a nominally equal basis – a fair swap – they soon became more and more, by the boys' actions, just crude attempts at touching up. The boys simply could not draw the line, but always wanted to push it further and further. Every physical closeness afforded by the bundles became a chance for attempted sexiness which further encouraged them in their notions of female complicity, and, out of that, came the rape fantasy, and so on. If the girls thought the bundles were a bit of a laugh it was an absolute hallmark of the boys' developing sexism that they completely lost sight of the girls' feelings in the matter and, once on a runaway train of their own exclusively male meanings, pushed for more and more. If they had succeeded in touching a girl's breast, they would go for her crotch.

It was as if they wanted the girls to loan them their bodies on *male terms*. There was no question in this context of any relation to sharing time or pleasures outside the situation (unlike courting, where personalities are more properly on the agenda). Interestingly one of the boys had been out with one of the girls for a week but in the bundles that might as well have never happened. In going out together relations are a little more contractual, if not mutual, but here people of different genders who like each other, or have some things in common, are just in competing camps. The bundles did not seem to be about the production of actual physical pleasure, as in petting for example. For the boys (and for the observer) the other part of the pleasure is in the electric atmosphere generated. Again, the licence for this pleasure was simply the presence of the girls themselves, all other considerations being collapsed into what could physically be got away with. The boys were very rough. Partly to cover themselves from a straight rebuff and partly through ineptitude, the boys transferred the bundles into their own problematic – the problematic of roughness. The girls knew that it was this that represented the most immediate danger. The girls too wanted 'kicks', physical closeness, excitement, some exertion, with perhaps a few careless touchings, but they did not want to be suffocated or crushed!

Once again Eve is the key figure. In an informal interview with her I tried to draw her on the fact that the boys seemed to be more active in defining the situation. Not surprisingly she was extremely suspicious. She blocked me for most of the interview. She blocked me not just as an older person and as a man but specifically as myself. After all I had been silent observer at many of the bundles and I had not lifted a finger to help her. She denied that the bundles were a sexual thing for her, and insisted that they were just 'messing about'.

> *J.W.:*   So that is how it looked to you . . . It always seems to me, that it is the boys that want to touch the girls. Why didn't you or Mary touch them, or did you?
>
> *Eve:*   No. We was messing about, right? I said, 'Mary, come on let's jump them, right, for a laugh'. She said, 'Don't! They'll turn round and rape you, if I was you I'd forget it.' So she turns round to him [Ewan]. We jumped him, right? And they got hold of Mary – not me right, *Mary* – and I got out the room.

In setting the record straight, Eve's account, though mildly contradictory, outlines a justified fear of the boys' physicality; not so much their lust (elsewhere she said they were too young to rape) as their heavy-handed us of main force. However, we should not forget that the girls kept on lining themselves up with those same boys in that same specific situation. At no time did the girls say they were going if for anything other than a 'laugh' but that phrase can cover a multitude of meanings in their class culture. I am not trying to say the girls were two-faced, or that they were in any significant detail as the boys constructed them, but I do want to raise the issue of their continued re-entry into that room, albeit against their better judgement. The girls presumably hoped each time that they could maximise their 'laughs' and minimise or neutralise the worst aspects. So far so good, but *both* sexes seem partly constrained to repeat a sequence shot through with elements of distortion, rip off and oppression.

The other important factor in the bundles was the attitude of the centre staff. They knew about the craze, though not in detail (that is to say how far the boys were trying to push it) but they considered the whole thing in terms of the *individuals* involved in it. This common-sensical approach seemed to be based on the idea of free sellers at the sexual marketplace. My own analogy of invasion was countered by the empiricist argument that the girls had entered the room of their own volition (another vital reason for addressing the problem of the girls' 'collusion' and limits to their choice of types of sexuality. There were many other ideological distortions that intersected the staff's assessment. First, there was the idea that sex and sex-related activities are private (even though the boys were not hindered by such considerations). Secondly, and more specifically, they had no special liking for Eve because she was 'uncouth' and, perhaps by association, potentially promiscuous.[6] Lastly, they seemed to operate with the very common notion of adolescence as a problem period when sex is bound to raise its head. This is what I called the ideology of emergence, an empiricist construction on the apparent greater sexiness of lads when they reach their teens. Within this I think there is the idea that a person's sexuality is an innately formed miniature primed by nature to explode in the hot climate of adolescence. What exactly sexuality is, is here left to essentialism (i.e. that the essence of masculinity or femininity is biologically pre-given) without a consideration of how what emerges is due to culture rather than biology. There is also the idea here that boys and girls (especially boys) are prey to their own sexuality[7] but if you do not interfere the phase will be self-correcting. In terms of the centre bundles, the only way the staff felt they could intervene was under the rubric of procedures to prevent 'disruption' or the contravening of public propriety. It is perhaps an obvious point that ideological social relations 'justify' themselves. It *is* 'normal' for young males to try to dominate young females in a patriarchal society, and if it is normal, it seems, you leave well alone. Out of this power differential spring all the justifications of (as well as our reading of biological 'imperatives' into) social situations. How different would the staff's attitude have been if it was two stronger boys trying to touch up a weaker boy?

Michèle Barrett (1980, p. 63) argues that we have not adequately explored 'the parameters of erotic behaviour'. In particular I would like to say that, as far as the sociology of education goes, it has failed to tackle how sex is constructed and acted upon in school or school-like situations and how this is linked to power. Beatrix Campbell (1980) reports, most interestingly, almost exactly the same blindspots in youth work. (For an interesting exploration of gender relations and radical youth work, especially in relation to lesbianism see Nava, 1982.) Campbell says 'boys being boys, becoming men, at their leisure' comes out once again in actuality as the boys being crude, over-physical and contemptuous of the girls. The girls in the centre were beginning to be mistrustful of *boys as a whole*. In a place where even mildly sociable girls could be written off as 'right whores' it is perhaps not surprising to overhear conversations like this one: 'I wouldn't let a boy. [i.e. make advances] They fuck you and leave you, they do.' To return to Lorraine, the centre girl who was too strong for the boys to cheek, she regarded the immature boys as the main disadvantage of the centre. She cast her mind back nostalgically to the boys in the main school with whom she had been able to have a platonic laugh. This gave her a model of good inter-gender relations that was, even if too frequently disappointed, a living critique of the centre boys' practice.

> *J.W.:*   So you didn't find that the boys either tried to chat you up or ignored you? I mean, er, did you find that they could be friends with you without trying to do either of those?
>
> *Lorraine:* Yeah, they can be friends with you without doing either of them, because right, because I mean you get some of them [that are] really big-headed – they think they can just go over and chat you up. It's a load of rubbish that is, I mean you want the boys to sort of . . . policemate [a centre neologism for participate]. [laughs] You know, I mean not talk to the girls because they're boys, you know, I mean as friends . . . as *people*.

The middle class and sexism? – an autobiographical aside

I do not want to clutter this contribution with middle-class confessionalism, but I feel this is one case where the bringing to light of the researcher's own past behaviour can very usefully offset the discussion. It is consonant with the aim of the article to bring into question the un-class differentiated use of the word 'sexism' in order to sharpen the analysis of sexual practice. For one thing I would question the idea of a smooth, linear progression to a fixed state of sexism in the boys (as if they took a bus ride to emerge at the other end 'a sexist'). Instead, in the analysis of how sexist sexual practice becomes, on average, the norm for the boys, we must be sensitive to the lags and discontinuities present in all social situations. Nor will sexism, once generally established, do, even as a descriptive term on its own. We need to look at what *form* their sexism takes and how it is inscribed in other practices. The overlaying of the class struggle on the patriarchical order makes the relationship between class and gender relations the most complex and difficult of areas. The kids in the centre were all solidly in the working class, but that should not tempt one into too simple an equation between their type of behaviour and their class background. First, the question of whether each class has a distinct sexism is itself clouded by the problem of to what extent different classes have distinct sites and practices. (A question that Tolson's (1977) pioneer book fudges, as I have said.) Secondly, different aspects of sexisms adhere to specific institutions and practices, for example: the family, the street or neighbourhood, the school and so on. Thirdly, it is people like myself (in class origin terms) who still formalise most of the analyses into social science. Describing the boys' sexist sexual practice is itself a power-based operation. Not surprisingly, (but very significantly nonetheless) we do not really have a proper sociology (or ethnography) of the middle and upper classes. It is not to atone for this, but in the light of this absence, that I offer the following.[8] To the charge that this is nothing other than personal anecdote I can only say that I was present at both occasions (i.e. the bundles and the incident I describe below) and that the time difference is only proof, to me, of the persistence of some phenomenal forms.

When I was about thirteen (in a totally middle-class, private, day school) we had a school, gang hideout. It was a mixed gang but the girls were relegated to the subordinate role of 'gangsters' molls'. Around this age (and in the swinging sixties) we were developing the normal attitude to girls: a mixture of pursuit, disinterest, patronisation, fear and fixation! One day the moronic leader ordered his 'moll' to expose her breasts. When she of course refused he pinned her against a tree and ripped her blouse open. We all revelled in his power over her and laughed as she ran crying from the camp. Later, presumably after suffering imposed agonies of conscience, she went to the headmistress. The camp was closed in a hush-hush kind of way. As I recall, far from actual guilt (leading to group or individual self-criticism) all the boys involved were affronted and uncomprehending. First, we were self-righteous about the 'weakness' she showed in grassing; and secondly, we were angry that she had let the side down. *Whose* side, I am afraid, did not occur to us. All too soon we, like the boys in the centre, reached for the justificatory ideology that girls are fickle and that they do not know their own minds. We really thought that she must have wanted to be exposed but (being a girl) she was too silly or weak to face up to her own desires.

From practice to pick ups? – skating on thin ice

Some people may object that the 'sexiness' of the kids is quite abnormal or is solely because of the centre. I will try to show why I think this misses the point. It is conceivable that the fact that there were actual groping sessions was due to the local material conditions of the centre's regime: its isolated rooms, its occasional lack of supervision. But, surely such 'games' of invasion would have occurred elsewhere, such as at parties or in the kids' houses, at some time? This is not biological destiny pushing its way through at adolescence but an empirically informed guess. If they (the boys) are to adopt a mode, or modes, of sexual practice it *will* tend to be at adolescence and *will* tend to be like what occurred, given the world as it presently stands. From a standpoint of feminist intervention – in trying to *change* the pre-conditions for this 'emergence' – the real question that tantalises is, what is to be taken on and in what way? We should not be overly defeatist but we should be realists; empirical reality does not change at a stroke. The pattern is deep-rooted: the boys mainly chased and harrassed; the girls mainly fled, resisted or acquiesced.

Of course centre kids are not a separate species, and even in school time they had contact with other schools, at venues like the municipal sports centre. At the time of the bundles there was a craze for going to the ice rink at this sports centre. The boys would usually go around as boys together. They would crash around the rink at high speed, being as physical as possible with each other and laughing and whooping. (All this mateyness is not without its own buried homosexual meanings of course.) The girls used to skate round in pairs, as much for protection as companionship. When two of the boys spotted a pair of 'tasty' girls, the rituals of pursuit would be inaugurated. At first they would skate round them for a bit in a kind of ungainly dance to make sure the girls knew (they always did) that it was them that they were interested in. Then, rather than skating parallel and trying to 'chat them up', the boys would skate straight into them and send them flying. The girls rarely seemed to react especially aggressively to this – in fact they laughed and tumbled too – but that does *not* mean they would not have preferred a subtler approach. As with the bundles the boys seemed happier about the attempt to make contact if they translated it into their own problematic of roughness.[9] Of course, it may be that these boys were uniquely inept. They may become, in time, smooth chat-up artists (although this would leave untouched, or gloss over, the predatory nature of the encounters and the power relations involved). However, I suspect that this is allied to a general bluntness frequently found in males as presently constructed. In sexual relations it comes out as an attempt to define the transaction on a male terrain, to define the negotiations on a too-rigid basis (invasion or repulsion, yes or no). It is also an attempt to by-pass the subtler shades of meaning that would come more into play if relations were allowed to become more mutual. It is as I have noted, the terrain which forms, *de facto*, part of the girls' experience.

Mixed sex talk – some differences of tone

I have looked at boys' sex talk when there are just males together and I have tried to emphasise the dominating and disrespectful attitudes to women that develop in such exchanges. I have also tried to show that such talk is often very near to taking off into what I have called, *in a qualified way*, fantasy or part-fantasy. I have also tried to make a number of distinctions in what might otherwise be the monolithic concept of sexism. Most obviously I have argued that different aspects of sexism (imputing lust and inconsistency to women, feeling of the sight of 'alien' bodies and so on) are empirically observable as related to specific, actual situations. Last, but not least, I have tried to emphasise that while sexism comes out on aggregate as the general domination of men over women (grounded in patriarchy) it is individually discontinuous and, on the male side seen here, experientially insecure. I want to end with two very brief examples of slightly differently-worked forms of sex talk. The first is sex talk in a mixed crowd, and the second is solitary sex talk (sex thought?). The conversation below was taped during the centre's sexy period, in fact straight after a bundle had ended. The kids were sitting up, breathing heavily and adjusting clothing; two previously excluded boys drifted back into the room. It was not surprising that the conversation should turn to sex for it was almost as if it were hanging in the air, the whole feeling of the room was still tense, yet elated. Eve, who had been involved in the sex play (recipient of an invasion) broke the silence with a challenge to one of the newcomers.

Eve: No, don't lie, have you ever fucked a girl?

Ken: Don't you worry! I could take your trousers down, girl, right now and give you a right good fucking!

Tim: Ewan, he was about to get his out!

Mary: He wouldn't dare. Probably got none.

Ewan: If I showed you mine you wouldn't forget it!

Eve: [to the boys in general] No really, have you? It's nothing to be ashamed of you know.
          [General mumblings]

Tim: This mate, he was fucking this bird and he couldn't hold it, he come right up her.

Ken: That's something I'd never do. I'd never do that – spunk up a girl. If you do, you could easily get her into trouble. It's not worth it.

All: Yeah.

As I have said, the atmosphere is still rather strained, the participants are speaking with a decided hesitancy, as no one is quite sure what others' positions are or where the conversation might go. The crude phrases and exaggerated boasts are still there, but they are tainted with nervousness, if not humility. If it is partly correct that the sexes are in competitive relation to one another, this might help to explain the edge to such sexual banter; it is the charged meeting of parallel worlds, a swapping of confidences with the 'other side'.

When the cut and thrust gives way to tentative mutual enquiry the boys are relatively tongue-tied. It is Eve's challenging question that sets the scene. Notice that Ken does not answer the actual question, but everyone surmises his true position from the distinctly hollow ring to his boast. Words, no matter how assertive, cannot make Ken into the person he wants to be in issuing that statement. So, once again, we find that while the outward face of sexist sex talk is bravado, the inward face is another story. Furthermore, such talk and ideas weaken the ability to come to terms with the insecurities beneath them. The boast isolates the speaker from sympathy as well as from hurt. The fact of not being able to show 'softer' aspects of self to one's mates may push the boys towards a heterosexual relationship with an 'ordinary girl' who can listen to them and allow them to relax certain constraints of macho. Although the boys never showed any contrition about their dominating attitude to women (nor even looked like developing a forum where they could discuss this) they did seem to feel the need to develop other qualities in themselves. It could be argued of course that in getting the 'ordinary girl' to listen to them and sort out their problems they are not only heading towards one, power-imbalanced form of traditional relationship, but are making women suffer all over again for difficulties that men create for themselves.

This last extract comes from a kid talking into a tape recorder at home for a sort of autobiography and is different in tone from either the traditional boys' sex talk or mixed sex talk.

Jake: I like girls who are good looking, nice personality and not too mouthy – don't two-time you. Most do anyway. And a bit horny. That's the sort of girl. The ones that stand out in a crowd really. I don't like the tart ones, they think they are really beautiful and they just dress up as tarts, don't like them at all. I like just the normal little girls, normal girls . . . who just walk around the streets, they don't think they're lovely but other people do and they don't know it . . .

What attracts me about girls? I think it is their eyes and their hair. It's not the tits or their arse or whatever, it's their eyes and their hair. What puts me off a girl is being mouthy to people or something like that, acting really flash . . . got stupid habits, something I don't like it's that. And I don't like girls saying, 'I'll pack you up because you got the hump', sort of stupid things like that. I'll get married though one day I hope . . . until then I'll never

know . . . I like going out with girls. My mates wind me up.
They say I'm gay but I'm not. I get more birds than all that
lot.

Given all that has been said previously about the position and ideas
of the boys, it is not surprising that this extract shares many features
with the more violently dominating passages. It is certainly not a
self-critique of Jake's attitude to women, but it does constitute,
effectively, a distancing from the most one-dimensional view of
women that he perhaps feels is *de rigueur* in the company of his
mates: that is, a view that *completely* reduces women to their bodies.
Of course, objectification, which I have identified as a hallmark of
sexist attitudes, is still there. The parts that are swapped for the
cruder foci('eyes' and 'hair' for 'tits' and 'arse') are still component
parts with no real regard for what the owner of these features thinks
and feels. There is a question here that points well beyond the scope
of this article. Is this extract to be unproblematically condemned *in
the same way* as the rape fantasy before (just sexism with a human
face)? Or does this represent a kind of blocked, inflected sensitivity
and self-awareness? Of course, this is not a line of speculation that
will interest those who are still burning with anger about the
practices described. They might argue that these boys do not
deserve a kindly, liberal peroration. They might also point out that
Jake appears to be saying that girls should not really express
themselves *at all*, and that this is ultra sexist. (Jake may not want
girls to express themselves but, also, this 'not too mouthy' incident
refers to a specific girl that has just 'packed him in'.) My concern in
opening up these issues is not to make the boys seem nicer than they
were, but to think about weak points for intervention. It is true that
males will have to give up their privilege when there is an
equalisation between the sexes. However this will not come about
by a ten day sexual 'revolution', but by a combination of engagement from people committed to change, and through other
processes that will change at differing rates. It is in this light that I
ask to what extent can this reflexive impulse, if it exists in the boys,
be facilitated, drawn out and made to illuminate the contradictions
in their more sexist positions? If there is some validity in the analogy
of a scale of sexist positions (albeit complicated by different
referents) then what is it that lies beyond the worst the boys
produced or beyond this half-realised self-criticism?

Conclusion: notes for a continuation

It would be improper in some ways to have a conclusion for an article as inchoate and exploratory as this. Broadly, I maintain that we have to continue to pay very close attention to the dimension of gender as it is lived in relation to others and to ideologies. I started by pointing out that sexuality is still an extremely unclear field of study. It is perhaps because of this that highly complex theories can be spun with only obscure connection to lived experience and social relations. Michel Foucault (1979) is a case in point. His is a complex argument, but he seems to be saying that sexuality has progressively become identified with the whole truth about a person and that, therefore, it occupies a strategic site for the regulation of populations. Sexuality is 'deployed' – that is used – by operations of power that survey citizens via their bodies: its sensations, functions and pleasures. Even in the somewhat cryptic form here this is a provocative thesis. However, it is difficult to find a way through from this to the sorts of features of everyday life that I have described. Admittedly, this way of writing about sexuality is only just beginning to be elaborated but, I think, the objection to its overly-abstract nature is not inconsiderable. We are jumping the gun, and perhaps distracting ourselves, if we are looking for *one* water-tight theory of sexuality, or one (abstract) connection between sexuality, power and the modern social order.

This does not mean the collapse of the theoretical project, there are parameters to be explored: crucially, for me, the area of masculinity. Due credit should be given to attempts to open this up as an area. I have already cited Andrew Tolson's (1977) short, thoughtful book. I have objected to the notion that one can tie a mode of masculinity too simply to one class (*the* sexism of *the* working class etc.) but I applaud the direction. As a general idea I think it is quite right to examine the weakness within masculinity not just in the context of the uptight, fringe middle class but in the majority of males who may live out this weakness-within-strength[10] in different ways. This contradiction in masculinity must be rooted in deeper sources but it is built into the inherently contradictory, predominant, ideological relation to women. Obviously, it is at the meeting of the boys with the girls that sexism most actively takes its hue and sustains its preconditions in cultural terms. It is for this reason that Juliet Mitchell (1980) is quite right to emphasise that

sex differences are *differences* and only take on their full significance in opposition. As Cockburn (1981 p. 42) says the 'genders
presuppose each other'.

I am not even sure that the trust in theory, and the implicit
attachment to the idea of purely theoretical progress, is not too
mentalist in itself. I still believe we should take our *ideas* as far as we
can, but only so long as we have proper regard for the vast social and
material complexity that lies beyond, as well as within, our dim
circle of light.

NOTES

1. A very interesting contribution by Valerie Walkerdine (1981), does
    deal with the issues of sex and power in an actual classroom. The
    article tries to work with a notion of split subjectivities inspired by
    discourse theory. What is particularly notable (and alarming) is that
    the process of 'dismembering' women's bodies should so closely
    correspond with the sex talk of the boys in this present article.

2. Advertising, one of the most pervasive forms of representation in our
    culture, constantly dissects women and uses 'significant' parts of them
    in its attempts to 'glamorise' products and manipulate consumption.
    The extent to which this prompts, or reinforces, the boys' sexism is
    still undecided. That question certainly begs others about ideology
    and cultural production that are beyond the scope of this article.
    However, at the very least, such representations have a background
    saturation effect. Certainly, advertising usually heavily emphasises
    and celebrates sterotypical views of gender roles. For an interesting
    further discussion of stereotypes see T. E. Perkins (1979).

3. I am grateful to Phil Cohen for the suggestion that sex talk may have
    several different 'functions'. For example it may be confessional,
    seductive, therapeutic and educative (contributing to competence). It
    is also important to note that, depending on circumstance, one mode
    may stand for or promote another. Confessional sex talk may be
    seductive in some contexts, for instance.

4. It was most commonly at this point in the article that, I think, feminist
    friends who read it regretted the absence of a properly political anger.
    I accept that the case of Eve *is* upsetting. Some people felt that she was
    being made powerless in the situation solely on the basis of her face,
    and that the boys imagined that they could do what they liked with her
    without even having to pretend to be friendly. I accept also that I have
    found it difficult to raise these sorts of issues clearly enough. I still
    believe, however, that it would be tactically and analytically incorrect

to assume that the boys *could* totally 'scrap' Eve (in the sense of refuse to relate to). Though the boys' attitudes are seriously warped in relation to Eve, there is a subtle interplay of repulsion *and* attraction. That attraction is 'sexist' too and is not held up here as the opposite of rejecting stereotypes. However, if one does not also recognise that the boys wanted to contact Eve, then an important element of contradiction has been lost.

5. I take Loftus's (1974) point that school, especially by effectively emphasising the current divide between the genders, must play a fairly important part in reinforcing and 'teaching' sexist ideology in general. I think it is also generally correct that the domination of women by men depends partly on having 'feminine' women and 'masculine' men, and that too much crossing of this divide represents a problem for the system. With reference to the centre, there was a very interesting comment by one of the boys about 'feminine' behaviour from other boys. It was very much in keeping with the centre boys' homophobia and intuitive (repressed?) knowledge of the peripheralness and internal weakness of presently constructed masculinity. They were recounting to me a story of a boy who had been supplicating to a friend after losing a fight with him. Recalling his general demeanour they could find no more damning way of describing it than: 'he acted really feminine man, really bad'.

6. For interesting work on the ideological associating of active and 'delinquent' girls with promiscuity by the courts see Shacklady-Smith's article in Smart and Smart (eds) *Women, Sexuality and Social Control* (1978).

7. Foucault, paradoxically always best on ideologies, has written very well on the 'speaking sex' and the biologistic notion of sex drive as implied by theories of repression. See Foucault (1978 edn) especially pp. 3–35.

8. I dithered for a long time about this section and was in the end persuaded by the good sense and support of my friend Trevor Blackwell. What held me back was precisely that the story showed me in a bad light *but at such a safe distance*. I precisely did not want a pat on the back for its inclusion: the worst kind of left double think! What about the 'courage' of the centre kids who are fifty times more exposed?

9. There is some interesting work in America on men's liberation and the problem of men's relation to their emotions (e.g. Farrell (1974)). The main argument is that the macho shell that most men hide behind prevents them from acknowledging and using their softer 'more feminine' aspects and that this finally makes them insecure and 'uptight'. One aspect of ideology about men is that they are lusty and liable to want sex anywhere. However they may be confused by the

fusion of sex and affection(!) and by the question of what sort of behaviour is required when the two are linked. On male awkwardness I offer, anecdotally, the observation that if you see a heterosexual couple in public and the woman wants to be erotic *and* affectionate, to kiss and cuddle, it is *very often the man* who is perturbed and starts looking around to see if he is being watched.

10. It is sometimes suggested that masculinity is in need of the strongest of cultural supports because of the remote or peripheral part played by men in actual production of life. Thus, the argument runs, it is only by subjugating women and appropriating all political power, that men can counter their own uselessness. (See for example Christina Larner's 1981 review article.) I think this is a suggestive notion containing more than a grain of truth. My problem with it is that there is a danger of reducing patriarchy to a merely *compensatory ideology* (for weak men) while obscuring the actual power base of the system and the actual oppression of women that continues from these 'weak' men.

4

Drawing the Line: A Feminist Response to Adult–Child Sexual Relations

Mica Nava

The contemporary feminist movement in the United States and Britain and feminist ideas about sexuality developed in large part both out of, and in reaction to, the libertarian and liberation politics of the 1960s. Within the libertarian theoretical frame work, sexuality was understood as an energy and source of pleasure which needed to be freed from societal constraints.[1] Sexual repression was perceived as intimately linked to political authoritarianism: it was both a consequence of it and contributed to its persistence. Thus one of the tasks of socialists was to undermine the prevailing sexual codes, to explore hedonism both for its own sake and for what were considered to be its inevitably progressive political ramifications. Important among the targets of these libertarian critiques were monogamous marriage, the age of consent, legislation relating to homosexuality and abortion, and almost any other sexual taboo which placed limits upon the 'free' sexual expression to which every individual was entitled.[2]

Rooted as it was in this tradition, the women's liberation movement in the early days insisted upon the sexual liberation of women, and mounted a critique of the double sexual standard – of the way in which the constraints of the puritan ethic and monogamy operated most particularly for women. The campaign for free abortion on demand was (in part) an aspect of this general struggle to centrestage women's sexual freedom and pleasure, as was the focus upon the clitoris as the source of female orgasm. This in turn suggested, at least theoretically, the potential dispensability of men

85

and contributed to a gradual assertion of the radical nature of lesbianism. At the same time the early women's liberation movement formed alliances with the emerging gay movement because it was considered that homosexuals, both female *and* male, were also constrained by the existing rigid 'gender system' and its ideology (located somewhere 'out there').[3] However, alongside these liberationist-feminist celebrations and explorations of sexual possibility in which women were cast as active, initiating and powerful, there developed during the course of the seventies a new sensitivity among feminists to the ways in which sex and sexual relations could be as oppressive as the more conventional targets of feminist attack. In this more sceptical analysis, sex ceased to be perceived as a fundamental drive which needed to be liberated. Instead the nature of sexuality was increasingly understood as socially constructed, as shaped by a range of historical factors among which the differential in social power between men and women was quite central.

This shift away from libertarianism can be seen with hindsight to be associated with a diversity of theoretical and political developments. On the one hand it signalled a (minority) theoretical interest in what, for instance, Freud and Foucault could contribute to a feminist understanding of the production of sexuality. On the other hand, and this was both the dominant and the more directly political response, it ushered in a revival of emphasis upon *differences* in sexuality between men and women, and upon women as the *victims* of male power and sexual desire. This kind of perspective underlies the notion of sexual harassment, and draws attention to the way in which unwanted sexual attention from men towards women in, for example, the context of work, constitutes an exercise of power and a form of exploitation. The idea of women as victims of male lust has contributed to the focus of some feminists upon pornography as one of the key supports of male supremacy.[4] It is also evident in the withdrawal of some women into political celibacy and political lesbianism,[5] and in the division of the gay movement along gender lines. There are of course important differences both between and within these more recent concerns of feminism, but what they have in common is the underlying idea of women as often powerless (despite the fact that feminist organisation over these issues amounts to a counterattack), and sexuality, particularly heterosexuality, as often menacing and exploitative. The predominantly liberationist view, with which these more recent analyses are in conflict, cannot however be simply relegated to the past; here too the debate has continued and developed. Thus over sexual matters in general feminist positions are best understood as distributed along a continuum which (to extrapolate from Gordon and Dubois (1983)[6]) has at one pole the notion of sexuality as danger and women as victims of male power, and at the other, sexuality as pleasure and women as increasingly self-actualising and powerful in relation to men.

This is of course not the only polarisation to occur within the women's movement in recent years. There are a number of cross-cutting continua along which feminist theory and politics have been ranged,[7] and it is interesting to note that in these divisions individuals have not always found themselves aligned in any predictable fashion with others. However, this lack of consistency does not necessarily detract from the usefulness of the specific concepts, and in order to make sense of the issue under scrutiny in this article, that of sexual relations between adults and children, it is the sex-as-danger/sex-as-pleasure continuum which has seemed the most fruitful and apposite. Cross-generational sex pushes to the fore the contradictions between the libertarian and protectionist feminist perspectives. It also introduces interesting theoretical questions about gender and generational difference. In this article the discussion of these issues will use as a point of departure a specific instance; it will be based upon a case study of a sexual relationship between Phil, a boy of fourteen, and Mr Smith, a forty-year-old teacher at his school.[8] Although perhaps not immediately obvious, this peripheral and stigmatised sexual encounter between two males *is* a matter for feminists and feminist theory in that it has at its centre the question of sexual power.[9] It also challenges the idea of men and women as unambiguous social categories which stand in immutable opposition to each other, because in sexual relation to adult men, gender divisions within the category of youth are attenuated. In the context of cross-generational relations, boys may be as powerless as girls. Another purpose in examining such relationships is that they can cast some light upon the multifaceted nature of masculinity, a problematic often neglected by feminists, who have in some instances been guilty of retaining notions of essential (and disagreeable) masculinity while simultaneously refusing any notion of essential or natural femininity. Finally, and of particular importance in this instance, the question of sexual relations between adults and children is a relevant one for feminists in that it is most often women who have responsibility for the care and protection of young people.

This last point is crucial, because this article is not only about the struggle to achieve a coherent theoretical evaluation of sexual relations between adults and children in spite of the apparently irreconcilable positions taken up by feminists. It is also about the dilemmas posed for feminists by the moral principles which reside within these theoretical critiques. Feminist contributions to social analysis have always been characterised, either explicitly or implicitly, by the formulation of a range of moral-political prescriptions about ways of being in our every-day lives.[10] The essence of these feminist moral imperatives is that they require more than a merely abstract response to the terms of reference of any particular argument; in addition they frequently demand assessments of real-life episodes (which in all probability cannot be compressed into any specific theoretical framework) and also a material response – a course of action. This article then concerns itself as well with the response (the course of action) of Mary, an individual feminist whose responsibility it was to care for Phil.

Although this is a particular narrative, it raises a number of general points about cross-generational sex and about the often incompatible nature of the moral precepts which emerge from the sex-as-danger/sex-as-pleasure discourse. In addition it raises questions about the viability of individual feminist interventions in contexts which are already overdetermined by legal and bureaucratic factors and which therefore permit only the most limited of initiatives. It thus draws attention to the inadequacy of existing methods of dealing with such issues, yet at the same time this specific case is able to indicate to us what a more satisfactory procedure could look like. There is another point which must be stressed: it must not be assumed that the presentation in this article of a particular narrative amounts to evidence of the uniqueness of such an occurrence. Sexual encounters between teachers and pupils in secondary schools are commonplace. Since Mary communicated to me the details of the incident in which she and Phil were involved, numerous other such relationships all over the country have come to my attention.[11] The majority of these have occurred between male teachers and girl pupils, but as I shall argue in this article, this fact does not radically alter the way in which such events are to be understood. In describing Phil's case I have occasionally in-corporated aspects of these other incidents. What I recount here then, consists of a composite of a number of stories. I have chosen to present my arguments in this format, that is to say to use as a central feature a single constructed instance, since this is most effectively able to illustrate the complex and contradictory nature of real experiences which of course almost invariably defy easy categorisation. Finally, a case history – a particular rather than a general account – is able to prompt readers into considering what their own responses might be in such a situation; if it is able to accomplish this, then the use of a particular story amounts also to the construction of a practical political exercise.

The story

At the time of the incident Phil was homeless. He was an intelligent and independent boy who got on badly with his parents, and over the previous few years had a number of times been told by them to leave the house and find somewhere else to live. When this happened he would spend several months away from home; on this occasion he had already spent about ten weeks circulating between the houses of three or four of his school friends, his girlfriend Polly, and Mr Smith, a teacher at his school who had a daughter of about Phil's age. On the whole Phil seemed to like this itinerant existence, though sometimes he was obviously upset and would talk to his friends about the difficulties with his parents and the problem of having nowhere permanent to live. Then at one point, for one reason or another, most of his temporary accommodation options collapsed. Eventually he ended up living on a long-term basis with his school friends Mike and Anna Green and their mother Mary. After he moved into the Green household he told Mary about his friendship with Mr Smith. Mary had known that Phil and Mr Smith, who was an interesting and agreeable man, had always got on well together, that they enjoyed spending time together discussing ideas, and that Phil valued the way he had been singled out by Mr Smith for his special attention. However it became clear that Phil now wanted to talk in greater depth about the friendship. Thus it emerged that Mr Smith had also declared his romantic and sexual feelings for Phil, and that Phil had found these unwelcome. Phil told

Mary that Mr Smith had nevertheless persuaded him to have sex on two occasions. Although Phil cared for Mr Smith and was grateful to him for his support and interest, especially when he was having problems with his parents, he insisted that he had not wanted to have sex. However, he had agreed to it finally because he had not wanted to jeopardise the friendship, which he valued very much. But the sex had disgusted him, Phil said, and his strategy for coping with it was to pretend it was not happening. After the first time, which had taken place one weekend when Mr Smith's wife and daughter had been away and Mr Smith and Phil had got quite drunk together, Mr Smith had declared his remorse and concern and vowed it would not happen again. Phil had felt reassured by Mr Smith's promises and had continued to visit his house to show he still trusted him. Then one night a few weeks later Phil was feeling very depressed: he and Polly had had a row and split up; he had phoned his parents' house in an attempt to contact his older brother whom he had not seen for several months; when he left the message his mother had apparently not recognised his voice; his brother failed to return the call. So in the end, in despair he went to see Mr Smith, who took him out to a restaurant for a meal.

In the restaurant they chatted about different things, drank quite a lot of wine, and gradually Phil started to cheer up. Then Mr Smith apparently told Phil that he had recently had sex with Jeremy, another boy in Phil's year at school. Mr Smith told Phil that Jeremy had vomited after the incident, and that Jeremy's parents had told Mr Smith that they were worried about their son because he was looking unwell and behaving strangely. The story outraged Phil, who felt both that Jeremy had been exploited and, at the same time, that Mr Smith's protestations of love to himself could not have meant very much. He felt that his own position as the object of Mr Smith's affection and attention was being threatened, and he got quite drunk. After the meal he asked Mr Smith to drive him to Polly's house, but when he got there he felt unable to ring the bell because of his recent row with her. He said he felt too drunk and depressed to go to anybody else's place, and finally agreed to spend the night at Mr Smith's house. When they got there, Phil and Mr Smith went straight upstairs to Mr Smith's study. They had sex. Phil said he knew it was going to happen yet felt too miserable to say no. He said he felt that in some way Mr Smith was urging him to pay back all the kindness he had shown him, and that he owed it to Mr

Smith to respond. But he said that the experience was a nightmare, and the memory of it continued to be a nightmare. Afterwards he felt sick and ran out of the house in tears; he sat sobbing on the pavement for about fifteen minutes, not knowing where to go. Finally Mr Smith came out looking for him and took him back to the house. Phil fell asleep almost immediately on the sofa and left the next morning without seeing anyone.

As she listened to Phil's story Mary was struck by the way in which he held himself responsible for what had happened; he stressed that he had allowed the sex with Mr Smith to take place. At the same time she was aware that in spite of the irony with which he recounted the events, Phil was upset and confused. This combination did not have the seamless quality of fantasy; indeed because of its contradictory nature, Mary was from the beginning convinced of the truth of Phil's story (as were most people who subsequently heard it and knew both characters in it). She told me that it was clear to her that Phil wanted help in making sense of what had happened. He had apparently already told the mothers of two of his friends: one had assumed that Phil had wanted the relationship and was mature enough to make up his own mind; the other was shocked because she considered that all sexual activity for fourteen-year-olds was wrong. Neither approach had seemed satisfactory to him. Mary sensed that Phil wanted a different interpretation from her; he knew she was liberal over sexual matters, he also knew she was a feminist, and in addition, an advisory teacher for the education authority. What kind of help was he asking for?

Mary told me she reflected for some time before telling Phil that in her opinion Mr Smith seemed to have been insensitive to Phil's feelings and taken advantage of his trust and need for friendship during a particularly insecure period in his life. She pointed out that young people might sometimes appear quite seductive to adults, they might want physical affection, but that did not give adults the right to impose sexual contact. Adults, and particularly teachers, had a responsibility not to abuse their positions of power. The consent offered by Phil in the situation which he had described seemed pretty meaningless, since not to consent could well have threatened the friendship. Besides, in a legal sense consent was not at issue; even if a young boy or girl desired and enjoyed sex with an adult, which was apparently not so in this case, it remained that such relations constituted a criminal offence. Mary made it clear that she considered sex between fourteen-year-olds a different matter, even though that was illegal too, because two fourteen-year-olds were much more likely to be equal. She also made it clear that her reservations about what had happened had nothing to do with the fact that this was a homosexual encounter. Phil said it was a great relief to talk about everything, and that although he felt betrayed and used, he could probably cope with what had happened. But he still felt very angry on Jeremy's behalf; Phil had noticed how miserable and solitary Jeremy often seemed and thought that Jeremy had probably not been able to talk to anybody about what had happened.

Over the following days Mary struggled with the contradictory thoughts and feelings which Phil's story had provoked in her. At stake was whether the matter could be left or whether she had a moral obligation to do something about it beyond helping Phil to make sense of it and deal with it. How many other children had Mr Smith seduced? She needed to sort out in her mind the difference between this event and a relationship she knew of between a sixteen-year-old boy and his twenty-two-year-old woman teacher, to which she could find no serious objection. Did she find that more acceptable because there was less discrepancy in age, and the relationship therefore created fewer incestuous echoes? Or because the woman's power as a teacher was balanced by her pupil's maleness?[12] Or because the pupil had shown no ambivalence about his desire, and no emotional pressure seemed to have been involved? Or because that particular boy at sixteen was definitely no longer a child? Probably all of those things. What difference did the heterosexual nature of that relationship make to her response to it? Mary said the questions presented themselves ceaselessly. Her own biography was rooted in the libertarianism of the sixties, yet feminism in the seventies had made her far more aware of the exploitative nature of many sexual relationships, of how aggressive, indulgent and damaging they could be. Then again, was what Mr Smith had done more damaging than the punitive and undermining behaviour which was legal and quite routine among sections of the teaching profession? Perhaps not. In evaluating the issue it was important to distinguish between the moral-political and the legal. Legally this was an offence, yet so were certain other things that Mary condoned. So that was not decisive. Nevertheless it was an issue which would undoubtedly be significant if the matter were to be taken further. Should she take it further? What would happen to Mr Smith, to his wife and child? What did Phil want? By presenting her with the problem so soon after his arrival, was he in some unconscious way testing out the strength of her commitment to him as his new surrogate parent – playing the new mother off against the old father? To what extent was she responding to that test rather than to the issue itself?

Mary felt that if she decided to take it further, Phil must be consulted, but at the same time it was imperative that he should not feel responsible for the consequences of any action taken by her. In what manner should she take it further? Phil had obviously cared for Mr Smith; how much had he wanted the sexual encounter to take place (in spite of what he had said) and was that in any sense relevant? Legally it was irrelevant. Professionally it was irrelevant. As a teacher Mr Smith had a responsibility not to take advantage of children in his care, however infatuated they might be. And Phil had insisted all along that he valued the friendship, the attention, the caring that Mr Smith had offered but that he had not wanted sex. He had not welcomed the metamorphosis of father figure into lover. Morally, in terms of the moral principles constructed by feminism and socialism, it seemed untenable for a man of forty to take advantage of a child who was excruciatingly vulnerable by virtue of his homelessness and the rejection he had experienced from his parents. Besides Mr Smith was a teacher of the subject at which Phil most excelled and would undoubtedly wish to pursue through to 'A' level. What impact would the relationship have upon Phil's academic work if nothing were done? And then there was always Jeremy to consider, and any other children in the past and future.

Mary pondered upon the matter and discussed it at length with friends over a period of days. She considered the implications for Phil, for Mr Smith and his wife and daughter, and for the other children at the school. She concluded finally that there seemed to be three options open to her: to do nothing; to approach Mr Smith; to approach the headteacher. To do nothing, she eventually decided, would constitute a form of collusion; it would also be a denial of Phil's request for help. She reminded herself that whatever the consequences of some form of action, the ultimate responsibility would not lie with her, but with Mr Smith who had failed to consider the personal and professional implications of his own actions. *The issue had been initiated by him.* To approach Mr Smith directly would be to offer him the opportunity of presenting his version of the events. But Mary felt that the likelihood in such an instance was that Mr Smith would simply deny everything and the matter would thus turn into a personal confrontation between the two of them in which she would have insufficient authority to achieve a satisfactory outcome. Alternatively, Mr Smith might admit to the relationship and Mary might be able to exact a declaration of intent about the future, but what value could such apologies and avowals have? By that time the most appropriate resolution seemed to Mary to be that Mr Smith should leave the school quietly with a reference which would indicate that he was not a suitable candidate for teaching in primary or secondary schools. The option of approaching Mr Smith directly would not accomplish this. Mary also felt that if at a later date Mr Smith repeated this kind of behaviour – perhaps with serious repercussions for the child – and it emerged that she had been in a position to prevent it, she would not be able to justify her course of action to the school – or indeed to herself. During the period of these reflections Phil was becoming as indignant on his own behalf as he had been on behalf of Jeremy. He was also angered by the fact that Mr Smith had ignored him totally since the second incident; it confirmed his growing sense that Mr Smith's attention and concern were evidence of a sexual interest only. He was absolutely willing for the matter to be taken to the headteacher and uncharacteristically asserted that he did not mind if in consequence he was seen as a child in need of protection. To approach the headteacher directly was the course most often advocated by the many friends Mary had consulted, so finally this was what she decided she would do.

The Head was sympathetic, sensitive and, predictably, disturbed about the matter. She too saw such incidents in terms of an unacceptable abuse of power, and stated categorically that the homosexual nature of the event did not enter into it. As Mary had expected, the Head agreed that if Phil's story were true, then Mr Smith should not be allowed to remain in the school. However what Mary had not anticipated was that the matter could not be dealt with at the Head's discretion. The local education authority had devised a set procedure for such questions and it was incumbent upon the Head to report the incident to her superiors. The procedure was thus set in motion and the matter was suddenly out of Mary's control. Phil was instructed to write down in detail what had happened to him – not an easy task. The following day the Head presented Mr Smith with a copy of this statement and suspended him pending an investigation of the issue. Mr Smith apparently made no comment and was understood to have left his home immediately. The procedure also demanded that Phil's mother report the matter to the police. The Head, Mary, Phil and Phil's mother (whom Phil had not seen at all for almost three months and who knew nothing about the incident) were all extremely unwilling to involve the police, but the education authority insisted that as this was a criminal offence it was obligatory to do so. They said that their own internal inquiry could not proceed if the police were not informed and pointed out that no other method existed for dealing with the issue. Phil's mother therefore reluctantly took Phil to the police station to make a statement, and he accompanied her reluctantly. Phil spent three harrowing hours there, arguing with his mother and with the police, who acted in the style for which they are notorious in cases of rape by subjecting him to an aggressive and humiliating investigation that included probing for intimate details about the sexual encounter. The police also insisted on raising the issue of consent by referring to a recent case of an eleven-year-old girl who had had sexual intercourse with an adult man and who had, according to the police, 'acted provocatively'. At this Phil quite properly told them that consent was not at issue and walked out of the police station in tears, abandoning the uncompleted statement and determined, both for his own sake and for the sake of Mr Smith, not to return.

However, the education authority procedure was apparently too inflexible to allow for this. Once Mary had reported the matter to the Head, it seemed that Phil was obliged to pursue it according to the rules regardless of the personal cost to all concerned. Thus it was suddenly revealed by the authority that if Phil failed to continue with his statement to the police, this would amount to an admission that he had made 'a malicious allegation'. The consequences could well be that Mr Smith would return to the school, and that Phil would have to leave it, would leave his friends, and would have upon his record a statement to the effect that he had made a serious and untrue accusation against a teacher. Yet to pursue the matter with the police seemed as bad if not worse. It entailed the continuation of the traumatic and degrading interrogation at the police station, as well as a court case in which Phil would undoubtedly undergo a rigorous cross-examination in order to establish in minute and sordid detail the precise nature of the physical contact he had had with Mr Smith, for which in any case there was no substantiating evidence. Furthermore, in such a context Phil's unstable background would in all likelihood be exposed and held against him by Mr Smith's legal representatives. There was certainly no guarantee that the veracity of Phil's statement would be accepted in a court of law. Though if it were, the consequences would also be appalling. In that case there was a real possibility that Mr Smith would receive a gaol sentence (probably in isolation since that is the lot of sexual offenders) a punishment which neither Mary nor Phil felt was at all commensurate with the initial 'crime'. The matter was out of their hands and in the hands of a government bureaucracy and legal system with which, over this question, they could not agree.

The dilemma was acute, indeed overwhelming. Mary had never before experienced such moral turmoil. Phil insisted that the prospect of the court case as well as the responsibility for Mr Smith's possible conviction and sentence, and the effects of these upon his family, were all much worse than the original experience. He could not go through with it. Yet the education authority had warned that the consequences of withdrawing his allegation at this point would be extremely severe. Why should Phil have to suffer twice over for Mr Smith's indulgence and lack of responsibility? There no longer appeared to be an acceptable way out of the situation. Mary regretted that she had not researched the likely repercussions of her intervention more thoroughly; all she had ever intended was for Mr Smith to leave school-teaching. She felt no more able to tolerate responsibility for a gaol sentence than Phil could. But then neither could she stand by and tolerate Phil's exclusion from the school for being unwilling to go through with an allegation which had in the first instance been presented to the authorities by *her*. No alternative options seemed available.

In despair, Mary sought legal advice. The lawyer whom she consulted made it clear that a refusal by Phil to testify against Mr Smith in court did not legally amount to a withdrawal of his allegations. Phil and Mary felt enormously relieved. However, a few days later the Head phoned Mary to tell her that Mr Smith had returned home. He had contacted his union solicitors and was categorically denying the whole episode. Apparently the education authority had decided that as the police felt they had no case (since

Phil refused to testify) then they could not proceed with their own internal inquiry. According to the Head, the consequences of this would definitely be that Mr Smith would be free to return to the school and that Phil must leave it. Because Phil was unwilling to pursue the matter with the police, the assumption continued to be that his allegations must therefore be malicious. It appeared that there were two standards of justice in operation here: Mr Smith could not be made to leave the school because there was insufficient evidence that the accusations were true, yet Phil could be thrown out in spite of the fact that there was no evidence that his statement was false. The implications were both paradoxical and extremely disturbing: it looked as though the result of Mary's attempt to protect the child was that he was going to be more damaged and victimised than ever. This would be the ultimate irony.

Since the education authority appeared to have no power either to proceed with an internal inquiry or to prevent the return of Mr Smith to the school unless there was a criminal conviction, Mary felt the most that she could salvage from the imbroglio at that point was an agreement that Phil would not be expelled. Phil himself agreed that under the circumstances to stay at the school and co-exist with Mr Smith was the remaining option most worth fighting for. So Mary phoned the authority again; stated unequivocally that Phil's refusal to testify was not the legal equivalent of a withdrawal of his allegation; reiterated her support for Phil's decision not to proceed, since that seemed the least traumatic course of action for him personally; made it clear that she would vigorously oppose any attempt to exclude Phil from the school; and demanded to know on what grounds this was being proposed. It was then that she discovered that the 'set procedure', to which the authority had often referred, was not nearly as immutable as had been implied. At that point it emerged that in spite of the threats, there was no statutory obligation to exclude Phil from the school in such a case. His continuing attendance at the school would only be in question if Mr Smith insisted upon his expulsion from it, and was in addition able to convince his fellow trade unionists to support such a demand with industrial action – an extremely improbable event given the particularities of the context.

Thus it came to pass that Mr Smith also opted for co-existence, and although he neither demanded Phil's expulsion nor minded being seen chatting to him in the corridor, most of the time he continued (when asked) to deny the accusation which had been levelled against him. By then a number of people attached to the school in various ways (staff, students, parents) knew about the incident, and as far as Mary could tell, found the substance of Phil's story quite credible. However, on the whole the return of Mr Smith to the school appeared to receive an extremely low-key response. To all intents and purposes then, the closing scenario of the drama looked remarkably like the opening one.

What can be concluded?

One of the things that this case history does is to draw attention to some of the complexities of those occurrences in real life which demand from feminists both a form of moral political assessment and also a decision about a course of action. Mary, in her attempt to evaluate the events recounted in this story, referred to a number of principles deriving from feminist theory and politics, yet these proved insufficient to enable her to develop a consistent and unambivalent response. At the crux of her dilemma lay a number of contradictions. The first of these was rooted in the diversity of feminist theory and its inability to offer a coherent analysis or set of principles which could act as guidelines for instances of this kind. The second was rooted in the dissonant and frayed nature of the circumstances themselves; the particularities of this case were not easily categorised. Finally the whole matter of Mary's response was made more complex by the inadequacy of existing official methods for dealing with such issues. What would a more satisfactory procedure look like? These are some of the questions and contradictions which will be addressed in greater detail in this final section.

I shall start by examining some of the arguments which have been put forward both for and against sexual relations between adults and children. But before doing so I shall focus briefly upon a terminological point. In this article the phrase 'sexual relations between adults and children' has on the whole been used in preference to 'paedophilia' because the very expression paedophilia appears to foreclose certain debates. Its use serves to reaffirm the category of 'the paedophile',[14] who is thus cast as an aberrant personality – a total identity – defined by the fact of sexual attraction to pre-adolescent and early adolescent children. To refer instead to 'sexual relations between adults and children', though more unwieldy, may help to avoid the pitfalls of definitions which pre-empt certain readings, and may perhaps offer the possibility of a less partisan interpretation of the issues.

The defence of such sexual relations has been most forcefully put by a certain (very small) section of the gay libertarian Left (predominantly by men, but also by a few women who identify themselves as part of the feminist movement and who tend to cluster at the extreme end of the sex-as-pleasure continuum).[15] Although in principle the debate has included heterosexual relations, it has focused primarily on what has been termed by its advocates as 'man-boy love' (statistically a tiny minority – estimated at 10 per cent (E. Wilson, 1983a, p. 121) – of cross-generational sexual relations). This has partly been because among libertarians, men lovers of girls have been less outspoken in their own defence. It has also been a consequence of the inordinately heavy gaol sentences meted out to men found guilty of homosexual relations with children in the United States during the seventies compared with those guilty of heterosexual (including incestuous) relations with girls under the age of consent. Quite properly it has been pointed out that this is evidence of the massive prejudice which exists against gay relationships rather than of the concern to protect underage children. This is also borne out by the status in popular (male?) mythology of sexual relations between adult women and boys, which although a largely undocumented and unverified phenomenon, retains a romantic and quite distinct image from that of the archetypal man-in-raincoat-molestor-of-boys. Sex between women and girls also remains relatively undocumented and uncommented upon, though Pat Califia (1981) in her discussion of man-boy sexual relations, argues in its defence.

Although differences exist between those who defend cross-generational sexual relations, on the whole the most interesting arguments have tended to make the following points. Childhood must be understood historically as a relatively recent social construction, children in advanced capitalist and patriarchal societies are oppressed within the family; they are financially dependent and have no right of political or sexual expression. The relations of domination and subordination between adults and children are not dissimilar to those between men and women. 'The language of "protection" and "innocence" is precisely that used to subordinate women in the nineteenth century' (Presland, 1981, p. 76). In fact, the argument goes, children are no more sexually 'innocent' than women have been presumed to be. Children experience sexual desire and pleasure from a very early age, as psychoanalysis has revealed, and sometimes the objects of their desire are adults. Children must have the right, as adults do, to initiate, consent to and derive pleasure from sexual encounters, 'to define their own sensual relationships with adults' (Moody, 1981, p. 153). Califia has stressed the importance of distinguishing between a 'consensual sex act which takes place between two people of different social status and a sexual assault (which can easily take place between people of equal social status)' (1981, p. 138). A child's consent must not be taken less seriously than that of an adult; children are capable of and regularly do both consent and refuse to do many things requested of them by adults. It must not be assumed that such sexual relationships are imposed upon children or that they are necessarily distressful for them.[16] Proponents of man-boy love have pointed out that their critics – who have drawn attention to the power disparities between adults and children – have focused upon sexuality (and primarily upon gay sexuality) to the exclusion of other spheres in which power disparities exist, such as the family, education and the economy. Gayle Rubin (1981) has emphasised the need to avoid playing into the hands of the Moral Right who deny the very existence of childhood and early adolescent sexual feelings, both gay and straight. However, although defending the 'diversity of human sexuality' and the rights of 'stigmatised sexual minorities', she does concede that young people can be abused and exploited in such relationships. Finally Moody (1980) draws attention to the frequently aggressive and bigoted police interrogations of the victims of sexual assault which he argues are very likely to be more traumatic for the child than the initial sexual encounter. On the whole the literature about sexual relationships between men and boys by those who are advocates of it, tends to concern itself with the task of justifying such relationships, with attempting to dispel prejudice, emphasising the sexual desires of children, claiming for cross-generational sex an innocence and purity,[17] and re-addressing the issue of consent. Although drawing attention to the social construction of childhood, that is to say to the way in which definitions of childhood and modes of protecting children have varied historically, the category of paedophile itself

appears rarely to be problematised. I have come across no attempts
to deconstruct sexual relationships between adults and children.
The paedophile is, he exists.[18] The why and how his desire is
constructed remains unexamined.[19]

The principal arguments against cross-generational sexual relations which also emanate from within the feminist and gay
movements, probably represent the overwhelming majority of
individuals and occupy an enormously wide range of positions along
the sex-as-danger/sex-as-pleasure continuum. Divisions between
positions (and most certainly between the poles) are particularly
acute and acrimonious in the United States. But in Britain also there
are significant differences between those who take up a kind of
latter-day 'social purity' position of extreme protectionism (more
often in relation to girls than to boys), and those who locate
themselves somewhere between the midway point and the libertarian sex-as-pleasure extreme, but who nevertheless oppose sexual
relations between adults and children.[20] The arguments outlined
here do not represent a specific position in this spectrum, they are
intended to convey the main points made by most of the feminist
critics of cross-generational sex. These start by questioning the
nature of childhood sexuality advanced by the defenders of
man-boy love. Although agreeing that children have sexual feelings
and desires, the opponents of cross-generational sex argue that it
should not therefore be supposed that what children want is to
engage in sexual *acts* (that is to say in mutual masturbation, fellatio,
penetration); theirs might be a far more diffuse desire for physical
contact and affection. As Elizabeth Wilson has said in relation to
incest between adults and children:

> Because we believe that children do have sexual desires, it does
> not follow that adults should engage in sexual relations with
> them; nor does it follow that, because a child may have
> *unconscious* incestuous impulses of a vague nature towards a
> parent, it consciously desires the adult expression of them.
> (1983a, p. 123)

Thus the recognition of childhood sexual feeling does not mean that
children's sexuality can be unproblematically equated with adult
sexuality. There are likely to be disparities not only in the nature
and object of desire, but also in 'experience . . . physical poten-

tialities, emotional resources, sense of responsibility, awareness of the consequences of one's actions, and above all, power between adults and children' (Gay Left Collective, 1981, p. 60). It is this issue of disparities of power which has been most focused upon by feminist and gay opponents of cross-generational sex. In a social context in which inequalities of power between adults and children are the norm, 'consent' cannot maintain the meanings that it might have between adults with similar social positions and perceptions, or between adults and children in some utopian world. As Angela Hamblin and Romi Bowen have argued:

> To consent a person must know what it is she is consenting to and she must be free to say yes or no. We argue that a child does not have the power to say yes or no. Children do not have the knowledge or independence to make a decision about sex with an adult. They have been brought up to obey adults. They depend upon adults for the resources to live. (Hamblin and Bowen, 1981, p. 8)

In a social context in which adult men can give or withhold gifts, money, affection, approval, even a home, the notion of consent merges imperceptibly into coercion. Robin Morgan, one of the more vehement feminist opponents of cross-generational sex, has stated that she thinks that 'boy-love is a euphemism for rape, regardless of whether the victim seems to invite it ... When somebody powerless is getting fucked, literally and figuratively, by somebody who is powerful, that is a rape situation' (quoted in Califia, 1981, p. 137).

If consent and coercion cannot be properly separated out in cases of cross-generational sexual relations, then it is irrelevant to point to the greater social power of boys compared with girls. What is at stake is boys' relationship to adult men, in which they are relatively powerless, not to girls. (Indeed boys as victims may experience an added anxiety and shame because of the particular taboos associated with gay sexuality; however they may also possess an added strength in that they can use those taboos against their assailants by threatening to expose them.) Since such sexual relations so frequently occur between children and the adults who are responsible for their care and with whom they have an emotional relationship (like relatives and teachers), the issue is not merely one of a confusing and possibly unpleasant sexual experience which can afterwards be easily forgotten. Although such events are not invariably traumatic, they very often are and many victims of such relationships have only in adulthood been able to reveal how they continued to experience a sense of horror, betrayal and self-blame for very many years. As children the possibility of refusing to consent had not seemed available to them. Of course most proponents of paedophilia insist that consent is essential and they argue that it can easily be distinguished from coercion in that sexual relations are often initiated by the child and enjoyed by him or her. One critical response to this assertion has been to draw attention to the fact that, ironically, the principal spokespeople on behalf of cross-generational sex have been adult men, not boys or girls (e.g. Millett and Blasins, 1981, p. 81), and that until recently the argument was posed in terms of the rights of men to have sex with children rather than the rights of children to have sex with adults. It is important to stress that many feminists and gays who oppose adult-child sexual relations because of disparities of power and the likelihood of exploitation, support the right of boys and girls to have sexual relations, gay or straight, with each other, and oppose recourse to consent legislation in order to inhibit these. Where some feminists have argued to maintain the legal age of consent this has been primarily in order to protect abused young people (mainly girls) from the ordeal of having to prove, as happens in the case of rape, that they did *not* consent to sex with adults. It has also been to provide young girls with a legal prohibition to refer to if they feel under pressure to have sex, whether from adults or their peers. However this protectionist feminist position has by no means been uniformly accepted by young people themselves on the grounds that it can reinforce the sexual double standard, limit sexual activity and be used to justify the non-dissemination of contraceptive advice to those most in need.[21]

This discussion has only marginally addressed the more common manifestation of child-adult sexuality in schools, that is to say the covert (sometimes overt) sexualising of certain teacher-pupil relations in the pedagogic context, in spite of the fact that Phil and Mr Smith's relationship represents an extreme expression of this process. The subject demands an article to itself. I would like to point out however that as an issue it is encumbered by similar sorts of sex-as-positive/sex-as-negative contradictions to those encountered in an examination of cross-generational sex. For example, does the sexualising of teacher-pupil relations in the classroom amount to a form of sexual harassment, and disadvantage those who are singled out in this way? Or alternatively, could the essence of successful learning precisely lie in the investiture of certain subjects and pedagogic relationships with a covert form of sexual desire? Perhaps a bit of both, but all this represents a divergence from the principal topic under scrutiny in this article – the seduction of Phil by Mr Smith – that is to say *the actualisation* of the fantasy and innuendo (both conscious and unconscious) which permeate the social context of schooling, yet usually remain unrecognised.

Mary's reaction to this 'actualisation' of what most often remains fixed at the level of fantasy, indicated that she had referred to aspects of both sets of arguments – to those opposing and those defending sexual relations between adults and children – in order to make sense of the event.[22] Part of the difficulty in arriving at a coherent evaluation stemmed from the contradictory nature of the circumstances themselves. Phil at fourteen could not easily be categorised as a child. He was street-wise, well informed, and astute both about his own feelings and the complexities of family life. Yet he was *also* sensitive, innocent and vulnerable. Physically not out of puberty he could not, either, be categorised as an adult. What ultimately seemed to define him as a boy rather than a man in this particular context was his immaturity *in relation* to Mr Smith. If Mr Smith had been twenty instead of forty, the power disparity and incest symbolism could not have had the same significance. If Mr Smith had been a woman of twenty, the power disparity would have been even less. Thus both masculinity and youth as social constructs possess meaning in as far as they are counterposed to and interrelated with on the one hand, femininity and on the other, age. Phil in relation to his fourteen-year-old girlfriend was situated in a different discourse. But in terms of his power relations to Mr Smith (though obviously not in terms of his sexual desirability) his masculinity made very little difference.

The issue of consent in Phil's story seems to present fewer problems. Although he formally consented, the nature of his consent was hardly free from those features, like indebtedness and the fear of withdrawal of affection, which suggest that consent cannot be easily distinguished from coercion in very many instances. Yet the fact that the sexual act itself was not pleasurable for Phil should not on its own be used as evidence to convince us that the consent was in fact coerced. For of course many sexual encounters to which adults consent, which they desire, turn out to be disappointingly unpleasurable. On the other hand, the fact that the experience of sex with Mr Smith was such a 'nightmare' for Phil might precisely be evidence of the specific and distinct nature of pubescent sexuality. One could speculate that what Phil found exciting was the discovery of his own power as the object of Mr Smith's desire. But being aroused by the power to arouse is not at all the same as enjoying the sweaty and focused urgency that the real-life adult thing too often is – as many women are well aware.

Then there was the question of Jeremy who had apparently vomited, and all the other children for whom Mr Smith was responsible in his capacity as teacher – with whom he went on schooltrips, to whom he gave extra lessons after school, and whom he might invite to his home in the future in order to become better friends with his own daughter. There was also the unpalatable fact that Mr Smith might well have referred deliberately to his encounter with Jeremy as part of a strategy to seduce Phil again. Phil was, after all, homeless and drunk, he had recently broken up with his girlfriend and not been recognised by his mother; he was therefore particularly likely to feel displaced and open to persuasion. There is no doubt that Phil had felt deeply betrayed and disturbed by the transformation of Mr Smith from attentive and attractive father figure into sexual assailant.

Thus on balance, having considered the full range of the debates and having taken into account the details of the particular instance, Mary continued to feel that Mr Smith's behaviour had been indulgent, exploitative and indefensible. He should not have done what he did and should not be in a position, such as teaching in secondary schools, where he could do it again. Nevertheless, in spite of this, she was not sure that her course of action in going to the Head was something she would repeat were the same circumstances to recur. What had been clearly revealed to her by the incident was the inadequacy of the existing procedure for dealing with such matters. For a start, the 'set procedure' devised by the disciplinary department was opaque in the extreme. No information was given to Mary about the scenario which was likely to unfold, about the possible nature of the police and court interrogations, about the likelihood of a criminal conviction for indecent assault and the range of possible prison sentences. No formal statement was provided about the authority's policy and past practices in such instances, nor about the principles which determined the establishment of an internal inquiry. No explanation was given for the fact that an internal inquiry could be conducted only if the police considered that there was sufficient evidence to proceed with a criminal prosecution. Why, if an obligation of the education authority was to act in *loco parentis*, was it insisted upon that Phil undergo a harrowing police investigation and cross-examination in court in which the most intimate of details would be publicly inspected. The demand seemed particularly misplaced since, given Phil's 'unstable background' and the fact that there was no substantiating evidence for his allegation, whether Mr Smith would be found guilty remained in question. The determination of the authority to involve the police at all costs as part of the set procedure was of course a consequence of the criminal nature of the occurrence. Yet it seemed remarkably unconducive to the promotion of trust and good relations as well as unlikely to encourage the co-operation of young people in similar instances in the future, since for many of them the experience of the police and courts might well be more painful than the original sexual encounter.

But not only was the education authority procedure opaque, and open to criticism on the grounds that both its refusal to conduct an internal investigation and its insistence upon the introduction of criminal proceedings could be counterproductive – as in this instance they were – it also appeared to Mary that its representatives had acted in a calculatedly dishonest manner in suggesting that Phil would have to leave the school if he did not go through with the police inquiry. Since it had been hinted to Mary that Phil's story was considered extremely plausible, it seemed that the threats to expel him could only be understood (with hindsight) as part of a strategy designed to persuade and pressure him to continue with the police statement and to testify in court. This was the only chance of obtaining the legal conviction required in order for the education authority to prevent the return of Mr Smith to teaching. Yet, to put it bluntly, this would be to sacrifice Phil for the sake of the school and other children who might be at risk in the future. It was this contradiction which most starkly exposed the weaknesses of the institutional procedure. Theoretically designed to protect the child, in practice it appeared to offer two options only: Phil should either have said nothing, or be prepared to endure the whole mortifying business from the beginning to the very end – *on his own*. Forced into being the isolated representative of all other victims in the past and future, Phil himself would have been victimised several times over.

It was precisely the crude nature of the procedure which rendered it ineffectual, or at least at first glance appeared to do so. Because it so thoroughly bludgeoned the fine gradations of Phil and Mary's judgement, they withdrew from it. Yet paradoxically the very limitations of the procedure were ultimately to contribute to a more subtle and satisfactory solution than anyone could have anticipated. The fact that a complaint was embarked upon but not pursued, that Mr Smith finally went back to the school, did not simply return the matter to square one. On the contrary, a considerable amount was accomplished through this aborted attempt to do something about the matter. For a start, when it was finally all over, Phil felt pretty good. He had demonstrated unequivocally to Mr Smith that he would not be taken advantage of. At the same time he had gained from Mary substantial evidence of her commitment to protect and care for him. In addition Phil had largely managed to avoid the traumas of the police and court. His friends had been extremely supportive and loyal. Although he felt not entirely approved of by the headteacher of the school because he had not seen the matter through, this was compensated for by Mr Smith's understandable appreciation. Under these circumstances therefore, the prospect of co-existing in the school with Mr Smith was not unpalatable.

The procedure embarked upon but not completed had other positive effects as well. Mr Smith had received a warning. It was not unreasonable to assume that he was a great deal less likely to repeat such incidents than if nothing had been done, in which case children in the future would be less at risk than Phil himself had been. One other consequence of having taken the matter a little way along the route of the set procedure and then abandoning it, was that it allowed the subject to emerge from its traditional regime of silence. Since the issue was raised, but not judged, it provoked Mr Smith's friends and colleagues to make assessments for themselves. And interestingly, the response of the other teachers suggests that they too believed the gist of Phil's story in that none demanded his exclusion from the school, *yet* neither did they instantly demand the dismissal of Mr Smith (though they would henceforth be alert to a possible repetition of such conduct). Thus it appears that, haphazardly, by dint of the failure of the set procedure, an opportunity arose for the members of the community of the school – those most familiar with and sensitive to the personal circumstances of both Phil and Mr Smith – to begin to address the matter. Through attempting to avoid the harshest consequences of legal intervention, a way was fortuitously found which provided local surveillance and some measure of protection, which in principle (and in this instance) was more appropriate to the particular than the institutionalised procedures of the law and education authorities are capable of being.

One could argue then, that the option arrived at by Phil and Mary, that of going half-way and then stopping, could be recommended as an example of how to deal with such issues under present circumstances. As a method it could undoubtedly be refined. An imaginative and detailed strategy lies beyond the scope of this article, but, for example, ways could be devised within schools of convening committees (of which students would also be members) in order to alert the whole school community to the problem of sexual harassment and to insist that it receive the attention it deserves. The focus in this article upon the relatively uncommon phenomenon of a sexual relationship between a male teacher and a male pupil must not be allowed to obscure the fact that it is overwhelmingly *girls* in schools who, on a daily basis, are the victims of unwelcome attention from both male teachers and male pupils. It must also be stressed that a proposal for an alternative procedure of this kind is not an argument for abolishing the age of consent, since this legislation continues to provide a form of protection for young people and continues to define the issue as one which is serious.[23] What the proposal does represent is the possibility of recourse to additional and distinctive forms of regulation. This itself is indicative of the more general contemporary shift in the location of illicit and taboo sexual practices away from the realm of law and penalty (Foucault, 1979). However, this shift must not be interpreted simply as a more subtle and sophisticated form of surveillance. Nor should it be interpreted merely as a relaxation of regulation, part of the more general liberalisation of attitudes and law towards sexual behaviour. The proposal constitutes a distinct but continuing and emphatic form of vigilance which is fuelled by the feminist insistence upon the centrality of the exercise of power in many sexual relations, whether between men and women or between men and boys. The focus upon power may ultimately be able to transform our understanding of the substance of these relationships. Instead of locating and analysing them within a paradigm of sexual behaviour – in terms of sexual freedom or sexual variation – they must be decoded and read as practices which are above all manifestations of *domination*, and are profoundly intertwined with the social and historical contexts in which children and adults, male and female, are positioned.

Notes

1. See for example the work of Wilhelm Reich and Herbert Marcuse. Lynne Segal (1983) discusses this background in '"Smash the Family?" Recalling the 1960s'.
2. For example David Cooper said in *Death of the Family* (1971): 'Making love is good in itself and the more it happens in any way possible or conceivable between as many people as possible more and more of the time, so much the better' (quoted in Segal (1983) p. 53). See also *The Little Red Schoolbook* (Hansen and Jensen, 1971).
3. The argument is elaborated by Fernbach (1980).
4. Much has been written about this issue. See for example: 'What is Pornography? Two Opposing Feminist Viewpoints' in *Spare Rib*, 119 (1982); Rosalind Coward and WAVAW (1982); Paula Webster (1981); Andrea Dworkin (1981); for a very useful overview see Chapter 7 in Elizabeth Wilson (1983a).
5. See discussion by Hilary Allen (1982).
6. Linda Gordon and Ellen Dubois (1983) in their article 'Seeking Ecstasy on the Battlefield: Danger and Pleasure in Nineteenth-Century Feminist Sexual Thought' examine theoretical and political differences between nineteenth-century 'social purity' feminists and early twentieth-century women sexual radicals. They suggest that aspects of these different traditions are echoed in today's divisions between feminists. Elizabeth Wilson (1983b), in her introduction to the Gordon and Dubois article in *Feminist Review*, no. 13, situates these observations in the context of the American debate, though they are clearly relevant to discussion in Britain as well.
7. The capitalism-patriarchy debate has provided another. For a discussion of these differences see Anne Phillips (1981).

8. These are of course pseudonyms.
9. It is of course vital to keep in mind that the overwhelming proportion of adult-child sexual encounters take place between men and girls.
10. This argument is developed in Nava (1983).
11. I know of no systematic research in this area. Information is difficult to obtain since incidents of this kind are often only known about locally; details of them tend to be hushed up and frequently do not even reach the administrative levels of the education authority.
12. Valerie Walkerdine (1981) has drawn attention to a remarkable instance of this process.
13. An astonishing 90 per cent of education authorities in this country have not banned corporal punishment; a high proportion of schools continue to use it on a regular basis.
14. A historically specific category constructed in relation to legal and psychiatric discourses of the nineteenth and twentieth centuries, though details of this process are hard to come by.
15. For example Pat Califia and Gayle Rubin (both contributors to Daniel Tsang (ed.) (1981) *The Age Taboo*, a collection of articles which examines the issue of sexual relations between men and boys) are known among feminists in the United States for their libertarian defence of sado-masochism.
16. PIE (Paedophile Information Exchange) in their pamphlet *Paedophilia* (1978) quote a study by Lauretta Bender and Abraham Blau: 'The Reaction of Children to Sexual Relations With Adults' *American Journal of Orthopsychiatry* (1937), in which it is claimed that: 'The emotional placidity of most of the children would seem to indicate that they derived some fundamental satisfaction from the relationship. The children rarely acted as injured parties and often did not show any evidence of guilt, anxiety or shame. Any emotional disturbance they presented could be attributed to external restraint rather than internal guilt.'
17. In fact of course there are (at least) a few known cases where individuals associated with those groups which defend, theorise and attempt to cleanse paedophilia, have deceived and taken advantage of boys in council care and other difficult personal circumstances.
18. The paedophile is almost never a she.
19. Elizabeth Wilson (1983b, p. 38) has made this point in relation to sado-masochism and Gayle Rubin's libertarian defence of it.
20. Of course virulent criticism has also been articulated by right-wing moral crusaders, such as Mary Whitehouse, who oppose all forms of sexual behaviour unsanctioned by marriage, most particularly those which are homosexual. These views are not considered in this article since they did not enter into Mary's deliberations when evaluating the issues.

21. Under-age sex has also frequently been used as a pretext for taking young girls into council care, see for example Deirdre Wilson (1978). A number of astute and persuasive criticisms of the age of consent legislation are made by young women in 'Sex Under Sixteen' in *Spare Rib* 108 (1981).

22. How individuals end up 'selecting' a particular set of views is of course a very complex business and cannot be understood without also taking into account unconscious mental processes.

23. The age of consent is a very complex issue which is only superficially addressed in this article. An argument could be made for abolishing it and putting in its place a professional code of practice in which sexual relationships between teachers and pupils, although not illegal, would be grounds for dismissal (as they are between client and practitioner in the medical profession). This would be likely to improve the rate at which such offences get reported, since the police and courts would not be involved, and might therefore be more effective than existing procedure. However a reform of this kind would fail to protect those children assaulted outside educational institutions – a very high proportion of child abusers are family friends and relatives who are not covered by incest legislation either.

I would like to thank all those people with whom the ideas and events in this article have been discussed and who have helped me organise my thoughts about the issues. Most particular thanks are due to Phil and Mary both for their constructive comments and for trusting me with their story.

5

Family Fortunes: A Practical Photography Project

Adrian Chappell

The following account describes a practical photography project recently undertaken by Tina, an eighteen-year-old working-class girl, and myself, a male tutor, working in the ILEA's Cockpit Cultural Studies Department. The project spanned six months, half a day a week, culminating in a photographic exhibition.

The project was intended to help Tina explore the relationships within her family. To do this she drew upon her experiences of three families: her own (with whom she no longer lived), her boyfriend's and her boyfriend's aunt's family. Recently Tina had left home to move in with her boyfriend's family. It was the experience within this family that provided the main focus for her photographic work. The project enabled Tina to recognise the expectations members of the family held about her own future role as wife, daughter-in-law and mother. However, our work together did not begin by looking directly at these expectations or the pressures they gave rise to. These were to surface slowly through our collaboration, eventually forming the basis for Tina's photographic exhibition.

The exhibition is reproduced here in a scaled-down version. It is shown in chronological order. The first panels depict the families, represented as 'family trees'. The second section develops themes embodied in Tina's relationship to different members of the families, ending with some observations about her relationship with Mark, her boyfriend, and their future together.

Cultural studies: photography as a popular practice

Since 1978 one of the teaching and research projects undertaken in

112

the Cockpit Cultural Studies Department has been to explore cultural issues with young people through the practical use of photography. Originally this had been established through the Department's 'Schools Photography Project' which formulated approaches to using photography within the secondary school curriculum. The Department has also always been concerned to relate the experiences of school to the wider context. Latterly our interests have widened to working beyond school with school-leavers, connecting themes of transition to both employment and unemployment through focusing on peer-groups, family, community and class-cultural identity.

Before going any further with a discussion of Tina's work I should clarify the basis of our approach to using photography as a cultural and educational practice. In our view photographs are about the expression and conveyance of meanings, of ideas, values and information. Photography is a social practice through which representations of the world are constructed. Two governing principles, or guides to practice, help shape this definition. The first concerns our choice of photographic convention with which we invariably begin our photographic work with young people. This is embodied in the 'snapshot', the sphere of popular amateur photography. Most families own a camera. In all probability this will be the instamatic type, the basic 'point and press'. The logic of this commodity form dictates continuous technological innovation in both styles of cameras and machine colour-processing techniques. And if most families take photographs then most will have some means of displaying them, the special ones being framed and the rest stored safely in family albums. Usually the camera is only brought out for special occasions, for weddings, holidays or at Christmas time. In assuming this it would be difficult to deny the substantial popular base this form of photography has in our culture, structured into private domestic consumption.

The second point follows. As a popular convention the 'snapshot' is increasingly recognised by historians and cultural analysts as a form which represents detailed aspects of family life, family traditions and pastimes − as visual records of specific family occasions, recorded by the participants themselves. Through the family album, the 'snapshot' is a form for representing every-day life, albeit selectively. In this sense the evidence of the photographer's selection process (the choice of what to take pictures of) will pose problems for the cultural interpreter. There will inevitably be gaps between what is portrayed and what is not. This is because as a convention it is never understood as a systematic process; if it were it would fall within social documentary. But the distinction we draw, as photography tutors, between these two conventions – and the limits of both – is overcome by building a photographic practice with young people in which their interest in taking pictures is based first of all upon a taken-for-granted aquaintance with 'snapshot' photography. Working within this frame is always a starting point because it is situated within the familiar, and operable through a known convention. Often then, young people's choices about what to take pictures of will be organised around establishing their own family album, this time organised around their own interests and priorities. But *contexting* these interests and experiences, however, is a far harder stage to attain; the underlying objective in our project work with young people is to help transform the 'taken-for-granted' into a reflexive, self-critical practice. Tina's photography began with the 'snapshot', then moved on when she realised that what she wanted to show in her photographs necessitated a search for other conventions.

Working with Tina: setting up the relationship

Tina was born and brought up with her two sisters and brother in Kentish Town, North London. Though she is still close to her parents, she recently left home to live with her boyfriend Mark in his family's flat down the road. Tina's family already had close connections with Mark's; Maria, Tina's elder sister, had married Georgie, Mark's cousin. All three families had lived close to one another for many years, moving locally when additional larger council accommodation became available. Within these strongly defined working-class families Tina's future was already prescribed, expectations set, destinies marked out. In one powerful sense this community pattern was based unequivocally on survival, of 'looking after our own'. This was brought into even sharper relief when set against a background of economic and ideological restructuring bent on breaking the relative autonomy of working-class communities. Tina had figured out a version of this for herself but it became especially pertinent as she and Mark surveyed their future prospects

together. Mark was twenty-one and since leaving school had spent
long periods on the dole.

It would be tempting to continue this description of Tina's
present situation, but to a degree that is beside the point, for the
central purpose of the work with Tina was to develop *her*
perceptions of what was happening in her domestic life, not mine.
The project was to help Tina explore the issues in her own terms: in
her own words 'to see what I don't want to see'. I am aware through
many conversations I have had with other tutors that the role I
adopted in my relationship with Tina did raise some important
pedagogic questions, in particular the question of intervention. For
instance, it became apparent to me through early informal discussion with Tina that her life was being marked out along very explicit
patriarchal lines. It was a male expectation that was shaping her
future for her. Mark's mother Pam and her sister Enid had long
since been installed to service the needs of their respective menfolk
through their roles as wives and mothers. Their next logical step it
seemed was to prepare Tina for her place within the family. That, at
any rate, was the reading I made. But whether it was relevant to
Tina was another matter, for I was far less concerned with making
my own readings on the reproduction of female subordination than
I was to help find appropriate methods for Tina to consider her
position, and to make practical interventions for herself, on *her*
terms.

Establishing the photography project

I should like to develop some of the educational issues by referring
now to Tina's photographic work. The panels accompanying this
article appear in the order in which they were produced and visually
represent the different stages of the project.

Tina was one of four unemployed students who made contact
with the Department through a local social services and Manpower
Services Commission (MSC) clearing house. We had already
established several projects along similar lines with this age group.
All were designed to focus on the concerns of the young unemployed, to help them formulate and express their own priorities
through practical photographic work. Tina's enthusiasm was
immediately apparent. Though she had never taken photographs

before, they were an important part of her social life. This was evident when, having gauged that doing photography with me could be about her own family and life style, she produced a stack of family photographs brought from home for us to look at. Many of these had been lifted from family albums at home. It next seemed appropriate to suggest that she should have her own album and take photographs of her family to supplement those she had brought in. So, over the next few weeks, Tina borrowed a camera and flash to take pictures at home, in her own time.

A routine quickly established itself – films back each week for processing and printing, two prints from each negative. One print was stored in the department and the other taken home in the album for the families to see. Throughout this period I observed that Tina's attention was concentrated less upon her own family than on the other two – her boyfriend's, and her boyfriend's cousin's. I did not push her to explain this because her main objective appeared to be a 'mapping' of each of the three families. Perhaps, I imagined, we could take that up later. In the meantime the 'mapping' was beginning to present some problems of organisation; how could the photos be arranged and classified? At one level this was a question I was asking for myself because Tina herself obviously knew who was related to whom. Each of the three families could be shown in separate albums but even then their actual relationships would still be difficult to show. In the event, through working together, Tina and I began to assemble her prints in generational groups, on the lines of a pictorial 'family tree'. This idea appealed to Tina and she soon saw the potential in re-photographing (copying) original album prints, scaling them up to required size in order to make a unified presentation. In the process of organising her prints Tina's next move was to change format by presenting her work on display panels instead of through albums.

The panels provided a covenient way for her to cross-reference and detail the relationships within the families. They were designed to read from top to bottom, from 1950 (her chosen starting point) through to the present (1983) (see panels 1 and 2). The bottom line represented the present family groupings with the key figures printed up larger than the rest. Tina was surprised at the unity of her pictorial assemblages, particularly with the copying of older prints in which the same members of the family appeared more than once. (See for example Tina's parents' wedding portrait, then further

1950

1960

1970

1980

1983

TINA'S FAMILY

Tina:
I've been working on this exhibition for 6 months, half a day a week. I like coming to the Cockpit; it's different from anywhere else. When I first came I had the idea of doing a family tree, one that's made up of three families — mine, my boyfriend's and my boyfriend's mother's sister. But the work has gone further than a family tree, further than I had planned at the beginning. The exhibition (part of which is printed here) starts with my family tree and my boyfriend Mark's. The rest of the exhibition is about the way we live in our families and some of the things we do and the places we go.

Panel 1

1950

1960

1970

1980

1983

PAM'S FAMILY

I live with my boyfriend Mark. We all live in his mother Pam's house. I've been doing a YOPs course for 3 days a week at Readers and Writers. I'll have to go down to careers again though in a couple of weeks. Judy, my MSC supervisor, suggested now I've turned 18 I should go on a TOPs course at college. But I don't want to go from course to course . . . know what I mean?

I think the exhibition is accurate in the things it shows. But it hides a lot of things: I'm working on the pictures . . . I see what I don't want to see.

Panel 2

down, Tina's photograph of them 23 years on – panel 1.) The pyramidal structure of each 'tree' was not unlike a cast list, or television credit, a metaphor Tina became increasingly fond of. There was a powerful sense, often hinted at by Tina, in which she felt as though she was orchestrating (directing) the images of those three families, a sense in which she had seized temporary control over them, albeit through black and white photographs. Was there, however, a danger that her photographs would become representational substitutes for real relations? At this stage (six weeks into the project) Tina's photographs did arguably provide a concrete fixing point through which she and I could talk about her families and her relationship to them. The question begged in this process seemed to be this: could Tina take her photographic work beyond the initial process of mapping to explore social relations?

Transitions: 'private album, public exhibition?'

The transition of form from album to panel marked a critical stage in Tina's project. On the one hand Tina had always had her 'private' album: from the beginning she had assumed its function. But the new format of the 'family trees' suggested developments not possible within the album form. Could Tina push beyond 'closed' relations embodied in her album, to 'open' representations through which her own position could be addressed. Her original aim had now begun to shift, and she found herself increasingly as both representer and represented. And potentially the new format of panel display suggested a very different use-value when compared with the album. With the inclusion of text both to complicate and elucidate the photographs, the panel version offered an extended 'open' mode of address. The transition then, was attempting to make explicit all that was implicit in her album work. At the same time, making the work 'open' meant making it accessible to a wider audience, something Tina was still unsure about at this stage.

Over the next three or four sessions Tina considered whether or not such a development actually helped *her* to understand the relations she was representing. Her deliberations led her to conclude that if she felt she was benefiting, then she had no principled objection to other people looking at and commenting on her work.

Representing family relationships

In Tina's own words the project became an exhibition 'about the way we live in our families and some of the things we do, and the places we go'. We still needed a structure, however, which, through specific examples, would demonstrate the tensions between surface experience ('this is *what* happens') and deep structure ('this might be *how* and *why* these things happen'). Tina's certain priority was to make sure there was positive space for herself in the eventual display. She made clear that she required a section within the panels in which her needs could be represented; these were not idealised but were based upon what she felt could be realistically achieved in the context of her present domestic relationships.

We decided we needed a way of organising the images so that the different social activities within the families could be addressed. By this stage Tina had something like 200 photographs of the families, showing them in their homes, in the local pub and the laundry. Spreading these on a table it quickly became apparent that in some of the venues one sex was more heavily represented than the other. For instance, most of the photographs taken in the pub showed Tina's boyfriend and his father; contrastingly the kitchen interiors always showed women either cooking or washing-up. A lot of comparisons were quickly drawn by Tina. The material was eventually divided into two gender specific categories: areas of 'social exclusion', and areas of 'social interaction': the heart of this new 'mapping' exercise became an exposition of sexual power relations within and across each of the families.

The sharpest examples are shown in Tina's contrasting panels on the pub (panels 3 and 4) and the laundry (panel 5). Tina made repeated visits to both, something she had done anyway for sometime. However the photographs she was now taking began to demonstrate clear differences in how each of the social spaces was used, and how each was perceived. The laundry for example, although a workplace paying appalling wages, was, more importantly, a very significant female meeting place in the neighbourhood. It was a space relatively free from male interference in which women – as wives, mothers, girlfriends and daughters – could share and enjoy each other's company. It was particularly the warmth and humour that was noticeable for me when I began looking through Tina's photographs. For the security the laundry offered was based

The Mitre:
My dad and Martin (Mark's dad) go down the pub. Mark'll go when
he's got some money, or when he's bored. Pam will go in the pub at
weekends for last drinks at about 10.30. But they'll be in there till 2.00
in the morning. I only go sometimes . . . don't like it really. I've just
turned 18 and I thought, well, may as well . . . but I've done it before.
Often when I go to the pub it's to get Martin to give us some money to
go shopping. He goes straight down the pub when he gets back from
work. We know he's in there if his van's parked outside. He'll stay
there till Pam comes over to tell him his dinner's ready. If Pam hasn't
any money she has to go over there and ask him . . . she has a moan
. . . then he gives it to her. Sometimes. She has to give him a nudge,
then he shouts at her.

Panel 3

This is the way men are. Martin being pissed and Georgie acting stupid. The one of Mark in bed . . . ? Well that *is* Mark. Mark's always in bed. He loves his bed. He hasn't got a job and there's nothing for him. Well he wakes up when I do and then either goes back to sleep or has a fag. He smokes like a trooper. That is normal for Mark. Really he should be looking for a job I think.

Mark gets spoilt. Mark is Pam . . . she loves him. He's his mother's son. She gives Mark whatever he wants. but Martin knows Mark is old enough to get things for himself. Me and his mum spoil Mark. He gets his way so much. Even though I might have an argument with Mark, Pam says you always give up in the end. Pam will always tell me not to give in . . . but she always does. **Panel 4**

Pam and her sister Enid work in the laundry. They get 30p for a service wash and split it between them. They work seven or eight hours a day, in shifts. This includes Saturday morning and Saturday and Sunday night. They get £27 a week. The bloke who does the cleaning at weekends get £7 for two hours; if Pam and Enid do it they only get £5 between them.

Enid always makes friends with anyone who comes in, like Pauline in the photos, well Enid hardly knew her before she started playing around with her. That's the way Enid is. Pam likes the laundry too, she can have a laugh. But Enid's got the front to go up to people. Different families are always dropping in. I come here on Mondays and Thursdays to pick up the washing on the way home.

There's more of a laugh in the laundry than in the pub. This is because everyone knows everyone else here, and no one gets embarrassed when we have a laugh. It's not like that in the pub. **Panel 5** on a taken-for-granted reproduction of traditional domestic roles – now transposed to the workplace – in which the menfolk had no particular claim or interest. The laundry posed no challenge to male hegemony. Compare this for a moment with the pub. 'Time off' rules OK here for the men, freed from work and domestic responsibilities. Male leisure time is characterised defiantly (panel 3), the women always playing a secondary supporting role (panel 4). Insofar as the male ego needed constant replenishment the pub was one environment which fulfilled this task. What did Tina make of this, and how would she organise her photographs around her own feelings about these two venues?

The organising framework we were working from ('social exclusion' areas) had presented Tina with the two venues. At this point the organisation of Tina's photography took another significant leap forward, the juxtaposition of photographs veering towards photo-montage. Each photograph she took was potentially another facet in her photo-construction of family life. We next began thinking about how text, taken from tape interviews we had been doing together, could contribute an additional element to the existing photos. Once typed and photocopied the texts could be manipulated and juxtaposed as readily as the photographs themselves. And like the photographs, new permutations of text could produce new meanings. As a practical experience this process served as the clearest example of how Tina began to *construct* representations of her family through photos and text.

So far, in her photographic work Tina had not yet been involved in looking closely at her relationship with Mark, her boyfriend. He was, after all, the main reason she lived where she did, and he was the person with whom she still had every intention of sharing her life. It was the work Tina had done on the laundry that gave her a way into understanding something more about Mark and her own relationship with him. The confidence she had gained in examining why the laundry was such an important venue gave Tina the impetus to look more closely at the domestic lives of the women who worked there. The domestic worlds of Mark's mother, Pam (panel 6) and her sister Enid were to provide Tina with powerful insights into how her relationship with Mark was being shaped by family pressures. In particular she was to notice the extent to which male-dominated assumptions shaped her boyfriend's attitudes and at the same time determined how she herself was expected to respond. She began to

Me and Pam do all the house-work. But sometimes, when Martin comes in and the house is in a mess he'll help clear up. But the kids won't. Martin will come in sometimes and grab hold of me or Pam and say 'you're the woman here . . . do my shirts'. Martin thinks that women should do this. And the rest of the men think the same as he does.
So what do I think about it? I don't. There's not much I can do about it. But when me and Mark are in the house on our own Mark will do things for me. Sometimes, that is. Like when I was ill. He made me a cup of tea and some soup. But the one thing he won't do is make the bed . . . I have to help him with that. He has his moments . . . but if he thinks I can do it he'll leave it to me.

Panel 6

see her relationship with Pam, Mark's mother, as a kind of apprenticeship in which she was to acquire the domestic skills of wifehood. Yet Pam's own relationship with her husband exhibited all the characteristics of deference and servitude that Tina was quite aware she wanted to avoid in her relationship with Mark.

Towards the completion of her work Tina began to demonstrate an increasing anxiety about living where she did. In particular she began to feel the hopeless trap of subordinate female role into which she felt she was being pushed. One panel expresses Tina's mood very clearly (panel 7). But it also suggests a different and more independent future. Here Tina has attempted to represent the relationship between Mark, Pam (his mother) and herself. The panel is dominated by Mark in the middle foreground. Behind him are Pam and Tina, Mark's pet dog Jody, and four bordered prints. Jody sits at his master's side, epitomising man's best friend. Behind Jody, and standing between Mark and Tina, is Pam; she is looking across towards Tina who is reclining on a bed, fingering her engagement ring. Between Tina and Pam, and stretching into the background are three material possessions that Mark would most like to own – a motor-cycle, a Porsche and a Jaguar. In the foreground another bordered print depicts Tina and Mark together. This print nestles within Mark's physical embrace. But the angle and the print's fall out of frame suggests that the embrace is not certain. The text then offers a more realistic view. It recognises the tensions between the three people. It hopes there will be a mutual willingness for Tina and Mark to make a go of things, but it retains the option for Tina's material independence – the eventual flat will be in her name, if and when she gets one from the council. This panel represents a critique of the present and a cautious eye to the future; but the whole is rendered from past and present experience.

Tina's final exhibition comprised eleven panels (of which eight are reproduced here). It represents an impressive attempt to look into her own domestic life through the use of photographs and words. In the process she has managed to look critically, though sympathetically, at the important relationships in her life. Tina has her own copy of the exhibition which she took home to show the rest of the family. Their responses, predictably enough, were mixed – though not hostile. The men found their portrayal humorous and true to life. The women, particularly Pam and Enid, also thought Tina had portrayed them in an accurate and honest way. Neither

This is the way I look at it: I know I mean a lot to Mark, and I know Pam does too. If anything happened to Mark, Pam'd go mad. And he's got something about his mum. He'd kill anyone who touched her . . . he'd kill anyone who touched me, but there's something about his mum. I think I'd get on better with Mark on my own. Not married to him mind. Mark and me want our own flat. He knows it'll be hard when we've got our own place. But he wants to be away from the family too. The flat will be in my name though. For the simple reason that if we split up he's got his mum to got to. But I've got no one. I can't go back to my mum. The flat will give me my own ground too, to argue back to Mark. At the moment I can't argue back.

Panel 7

My panel is important to me. I've got lots of people and lots of things in mine that mean a lot to me. Cassie, the little girl, for instance: I looked after her when she was a baby till she was about 4 years old. I looked after 3 kids but Cassie was my favourite. Then I met Mark, and stopped going out.

If I had one more panel, and this was about the future? Well, a flat, a baby, Mark, and a dog . . . and that's all. But I'd be working, and if I had a kid I'd still be working. See Mark's got nothing behind him. I've hardly got anything behind me, but I'd probably get a better job. Then my mum would look after the baby – but I'd pay her for it.

Panel 8

Tina nor I had ever imagined that producing a set of photo-texts would change attitudes in her family. The work was presented as an expression of *Tina*'s views and aspirations, and demonstrated a change in *her* ideas.

Postscript: four months on

Four months after completing her work Tina returned to the Cockpit's photography project. During the intervening period she had found a part-time job, but more significantly she is expecting a baby and appears pleased to be pregnant. Her top priority now is to secure a flat – in her name of course – which she will share with Mark and the baby; she is entitled to council accommodation and the process should be a formality, though, as she said, she will believe it when she sees it. But being pregnant has also speeded up her next role, certainly so far as Mark's family is concerned. Preparations are well in hand, with presents for the new baby stacked high to the ceiling in her bedroom. The new baby will affect everyone in Tina's and Mark's families. Their parents will become grandparents, their brothers and sisters, uncles and aunts. Tina has now acquired a camera of her own – a Nikon EM – and she is taking many pictures of herself and her environment. These will form an autobiographical piece: a photo-diary of events and reflections on becoming a mother. Taking pictures has become a firmly established part of her everyday world. The photographic documentation of her pregnancy is helping her to express and to make sense of the rapid changes which are occurring in her life.

6

Dance and Social Fantasy

Angela McRobbie

Deciphering dance

One of the first books I remember reading, I mean really reading, still lies within quotable reach on a bookshelf upstairs. It would hardly qualify as unusual taste for a seven-year-old girl, then or now. For some reason I prefer not to look at *Dancing Star*, (a children's biography of the life of Anna Pavlova written by a woman called Gladys Malvern) again. I would rather leave it lying there and rely instead on memory for what struck me about it then and how that relates to my concern in this paper..

But perhaps I should begin by explaining what my intentions are here. By drawing on research material I have been collecting sporadically over the past two or three years, and by adding to that a more recent analysis of the TV series *Fame* and the feature film *Flashdance*, I will be presenting a number of arguments which focus around the various meanings dance has for women and girls. I should add that my mode of presentation here is unashamedly unconventional. What I offer resembles more a series of snapshot profiles than a thorough academic thesis. I will be trying to hold onto what are, for me, the three most important instances in the circulation of dance as a social experience. These are, first, dance as image second, dance as fantasy and third, dance as social activity. In fact rarely are each of these absolutely separate from the others. But, for the sake of facilitating what is undoubtedly a preliminary account, my intention is to use this classification as a working schema.

In fact I do not have much choice in this respect. There is very little substantial written material to guide my interest in dance. Of

Camden Palace 1984

Photographed by Zadoc Nava

all the areas of popular culture, it remains the least theorised, the least subject to the scrutiny of the social critic. Even the most illuminating comments, particularly those found in the field of social history, rarely add up to more than two or three pages (Burke, 1978, pp. 116–18). And when dance has found its way into accounts of working-class culture, it has tended to be either derided as trivial or else taken as a sign of moral degeneration. In his well-known study of Salford in the 1920s, *The Classic Slum*, Robert Roberts (Roberts, 1971; pp. 222–5) combines both of these attitudes, linking the popularity of the mass dancehalls with the inherently unserious attitudes of young women. Richard Hoggart also thought that girls were 'silly' in this way (Hoggart, 1957, pp. 50–1). In *Uses of Literacy* he accused them of having an almost unhealthy interest in all the paraphernalia of femininity and described them as 'surely . . . flighty, careless and inane?'

It is unfortunate too that recent interest in the subject of dance by sociologists like Mungham and Pearson (1976) and Simon Frith (1978), has not been followed up by closer study. Dance is, after all, a vital feature of leisure culture, entertainment and sexuality, and its neglect marks an important absence in both sociology and cultural studies. Feminism has also been slow to consider its social role, despite the fact that women's discos have become a solidly entrenched part of feminist culture today.

This leaves us with a number of other points of entry into the subject. Christopher Lasch in *The Culture of Narcissism* offers one such possibility (Lasch, 1981). Much of what he says could be applied to the disco boom of the past eight years and particularly the dance-exercise craze which has drawn women and girls of different social background to the dance studio or exercise class Lasch sees this recent obsession with 'work-outs', dance, aerobics, and other forms of strenuous exercise, as a sign of a culture which has lost touch with its past and which possesses no positive focus for thinking about the future. It is, he suggests, indicative of desperation and despair. My view however is that Lasch's analysis, though interesting in its focus on how uses of the body have taken on new cultural meanings, cannot provide us with the source of the attraction of dance for women and the social possibilities and fantasies it provides. My own interests here are not so specifically in these health-oriented activities, but I would still nonetheless dispute Lasch's pessimistic account. For women and girls, dance has always offered a channel, albeit a limited one, for bodily self-expression and control; it has also been a source of pleasure and sensuality. Even though it has often been directed towards men, the spectacle of women dancing has been linked unambiguously with female pleasure . . . more of which later.

There are other possibilities. Subcultural analysis has fleetingly considered the part dance has played in youth culture. And Dick Hebdige's examination of punk dancing (pogoing) stands out for the close attention it pays to the individual movements which make up the dance (Hebdige, 1979, pp. 108–9). Apart from this there have been several lengthy accounts of various dance cultures reported in the music press: Northern Soul, Heavy Metal dancing, New Romantics and New York 'break-dancing'. But these are all quite far removed from the more standard disco scenes inhabited by the majority of young working-class and middle-class girls. Despite this gap I want to try to hold both these strands, subcultural and mainsteam, together, the one offering a deviant leisure and lifestyle, the other fastening onto more traditional gender patterns.

If dance exists and has existed as a mass popular leisure activity, and if in turn it has gone largely unconsidered by sociologists and social historians, the same holds true for images of dance and for the way dance finds itself inscribed in other visual texts, particularly film. This latter is surprising given the great interest which semiologists and structuralists have afforded the popular media in recent years. It is also surprising when we consider just how much viewing time is devoted to images of (usually young) people dancing. Both dance and music are staple features of 'light entertainment' from *The Grace Kennedy Show* to *The Val Doonican Show*, from *Top of the Pops* to the recent non-stop dance series *Hot for Dogs*. In all of these, many of the movements and the conventions of dance have been so naturalised we hardly notice them, e.g. the inviting 'foxy' expressions on the dancers' faces, the up-the-thigh shot, followed by the smiling complicit wink to the camera.

Alternatively dance has also been conventionalised as it is performed within cinematic narratives. These take a number of forms. Either simply as 'numbers' punctuating the plot or else as a kind of symbolic climax, a piece of strongly visual erotics. This latter can be found variously in both Hollywood and high art cinema. In most of Bertolucci's films dance plays this highly sexual role, and it was his portrayal of Dominique Sanda as the ballet mistress in *The Conformist*, surrounded in her studio with all the paraphernalia of dance: the ballet shoes, the mirrors, the bar and the leotard; which first alerted me to the mysterious eroticism of the rehearsal room (so obsessionally pursued in the visual arts by Degas). This is also the scenario which forms the central backdrop for both *Fame* and *Flashdance*.

A final introductory point remains to be made. This refers to dance's status as a prime vehicle for sexual expression for women. This is by no means a simple function of dance. Rather it carries a range of often contradictory strands within it. There is, on the one hand, the social pressures which direct little girls towards dance as a suitably feminine form of leisure. And dancing here is linked with being pretty, graceful, controlled and an object of admiration. But this conformist role does not deny the way dance carries enormously pleasurable qualities for girls and women which frequently seem to suggest a displaced, shared and nebulous eroticism rather than a straightforwardly romantic, heavily heterosexual 'goal-oriented' drive. As a purveyor of fantasy, dance has also addressed areas of absolute privacy and personal intimacy, especially important for women and girls. And there is I think a case which can be made for forms of fantasy, daydreaming, and 'abandon' to be interpreted as part of a strategy of resistance or opposition; that is, as marking out one of those areas which cannot be totally colonised. Dance and music play an important role in these small daily *evasions*, partly because they are so strongly inscribed, in our culture, within the realms of feeling and emotion. They are associated with being temporarily out of control, or out of the reaches of controlling forces. Thus we have the experience of dance being linked, linguistically, with the onomatopeia of the letter F: *Saturday Night Fever*, *Fame*, *Flashdance* – as though, with a quick slip of the tongue, to move rapidly to fever, frenzy, feeling.

Work and leisure, pleasure and pain

The biography of Anna Pavlova was important for me in this respect. It introduced me to the idea of work as a commitment, even an obsession, and also as something which could be immensely satisfying and pleasurable. This was a way of articulating childhood play with work, and with making work compatible with play. I do not imagine that this feeling was expressed then in terms such as the ones I have just used. I would also suspect that my childish reading of the book bore some, perhaps distanced, relation to my own class and cultural upbringing. Still, these ideas did take a very tangible form. Pavlova's life certainly balanced pain with pleasure, hard work with rewards and recognition. And although dance was central, it allowed other experiences to emerge. There was for example the graphic description of Anna's first truly intense experience. Taken by her mother to see the ballet in St Petersburg for the first time, Anna was so moved that her fingernails dug into her hands and made them bleed. The hardship! The pain! The symbolic forerunner to a magnificent career! Who wouldn't have been won over by a narrative like this? Who would fail to be excited by the endless travel to exotic foreign places, or by the thrill and mystery of pre-revolutionary Russia?

And so this 'tale' stands as a classic narrative of childhood femininity. It asserts the absolute value and romance of art and of art being worthy of great sacrifice. Like so many other schoolgirl stories it suggests an escape from the trappings and boredom of a conventionally feminine existence.[1] In neither *Dancing Star*, nor in any of the texts which fall into the category of girls' fiction, is there anything very much to be found on domesticity, children, motherhood or sexuality. Instead there are images of girls and women operating quite outside society's normal expectations of what they should be interested in.

There is also a kind of utopian egalitarianism running through all these fictions which states quite clearly that you do not have to be rich, privileged, or special, to fulfil these fantasies of the self. All that is needed is hard work, talent, and determination. These are I think, powerful and significant messages. On the one hand they are so familiar, the myths upon which bourgeois capitalist society and its protestant ethic is founded. And, in this context, these stories, so classically worked out in *Fame* and *Flashdance*, are merely more feminised versions of the kind of rampant individualism which is synonomous with the so-called 'American Dream'. And yet it is not quite as simple as that.[2] For a start, these texts address a very special audience, it is not so often that girls get encouragement to put marriage and motherhood in second place and to put all their energies into achieving some much sought-after goal. Narratives like those found in *Fame* or in ballet-school stories find themselves in fierce competition with the much more narrowly feminine plots set out in *Jackie*, *My Guy* or in popular romantic fiction. And consequently it is this determination, zeal and energy which marks out texts like *Fame* and *Flashdance* as of special interest to the feminist critic.

Anyway, the American Dream was never without contradiction. Nor were those qualities invariably denounced by socialists as 'bourgeois' or 'individualist'. It would be possible to argue that the effort needed to make a better life possible, the kind of visionary dedication described in so many narratives, fact and fiction, has indeed been just as much a part of, for example, working-class life or black culture, as it has been an ideology hand-made to fit the needs of a capitalist economy and its striving middle classes. Part of what we know and often praise as working-class culture is precisely the outcome of these kinds of impulse. And certainly much of working-class youth culture is best understood in these terms. It is not surprising, given the nature of working-class labour, that these images and these desires have been most frequently articulated in leisure forms, in popular fantasy, in carnival, in music hall, in pop music, in dance, and in street night-life. For both the black and much of the white working-class populations (male and female), sport, art, leisure and entertainment have provided this utopian space, carved out between, against, and amidst stronger forces of domination and control. Such gestures do not then exist *outside* dominant cultural forms. They are rather continually locked into a slow-moving love-hate relationship with them. Presented back as packaged and polished cultural products, the impulse finds its keenest expression in Hollywood musicals, the generic category into which fit both *Fame* and *Flashdance*.

Women's success and the power of the gaze

One of the core strands underpinning my interest in dance, is the way in which in fiction and in visual texts, it presents women and girls with the notion of a vocation, or a career. Not simply a way up, or a way out, but something which is also immensely satisfying, a job which demands dedication, but promises rewards. Even if the power of this narrative remains purely at the level of fantasy it is still a fantasy which cannot be quickly dismissed.

In this next section I want to chart out in a little more detail some of the consequences of this. It could be suggested for instance that women have been allowed to achieve a higher degree of visibility or success as dancers, or for that matter as actresses or models, because all of these occupations entail positioning women as objects of the (male) gaze. In this context some feminists might see the profusion of female bodies in *Fame*, and the strong visual interest in Alex's body in *Flashdance*, as indicative of the familiar practices of sexism. They would point to the heavily sexual mode of performance, the pouting lips, the high kicks, and the almost soft porn sequences in *Flashdance*, as evidence of this. They would subsequently see little of significance in a critical analysis of dance under these conditions save to condemn it as not so far removed from prostitution. It is indeed a great irony of the female labour market that those fields which are held out as promising the greatest rewards socially and financially, have consistently depended on the exploitation of the most traditional sexual qualities. In each of them the body is sharply in focus and with it appropriate gestures and appropriate presentation. What is more, it is in these fields that girls are, quite unrealistically, given the most encouragement to succeed.

Other feminist critiques might conceivably take up a different tack. They would argue that the point is not to do away with the visual element in these practices *per se*, nor to write off dancing, modelling, acting, or even waitressing, as essentially sexist occupations. The emphasis would rather be placed on overturning the social relations which at present characterise these. This would lead into a discussion about how women watch other women performing in these contexts. In her important article, 'Visual Pleasure and Narrative Cinema', Laura Mulvey argues that it is as though women have been forced into looking, in instances like these, as if through the eyes of men (Mulvey, 1981, pp. 206–16). She suggests that frequently the structure of the shot, the implied positioning of the camera so that it conforms exactly with the gaze of the male hero, means that the mode of looking is therefore male. *Flashdance* offers a series of perfect examples of this. Much of the dancing is set in a Pittsburgh equivalent of a working men's club. The only women in it are either 'go-go' dancers or else waitresses, which is to say that the audience is wholly male, rowdy, and viewing the girls in a directly sexual way. Throughout almost all of these dancing sequences, the camera's look dissolves with that of the men and then locks into ours. Thus we watch the girls through the eyes of the customers in Mawby's Bar, and the film severs the space between the fictive audience shouting for more, and the cinema audience waiting, more politely, for more.

This has two immediate consequences. First as I have already stated, the women in the film are performing for men, and this makes the film audience implicitly male. But, since much of the text has more in common *narratively* with what we might call a woman's film, this problematises the way in which women in the audience are expected to look at the film. This second point raises more questions than it can answer. What is the effect on women of all this looking at images of other women's bodies? Do we look uncomfortably as voyeurs or jealously, as perhaps we are meant to? Or do we look narcissistically, as though to say 'Yes, that's me, I'm like that, just as thin and just as desirable'? Do we look subversively with desire, or do we simply, at this point in the film, turn off or else get angry?

What is certain is that when women's bodies are used in these contexts it is inevitably to help sell some product, in this case a film or TV programme. Selling and serving have always been women's work and young women have been at the forefront in the drive to sell, to advertise and to attract consumers. The female body is used here because in our society the act of consuming has to be pleasurable. That is to say, buying is based round, not direct physical need, but the more nebulous areas of choice, desire and want. And since sex is most intimately connected with pleasure, it is employed as a hook to encourage more and more consumption. Sex here however means the availability, or at least the fantasy of the availability, of the woman's body for men. Thus we have the familiar and much documented images in advertising in which sex and femininity are intricately combined, making new inflections of meaning within the traditional sex and gender equation. It is almost impossible to imagine a situation where this was not the case. But just as viewers are not all men, so equally consumers – of meals, clothes, food, cars, insurance, and cigarettes – are not invariably male. Indeed, it is women who do the bulk of consuming, and this can only mean that either women ignore the address made in these adverts to male sexual desire, or else they slide into somehow participating in the pleasure on offer. Either way it is a confusing situation. And it demonstrates just how difficult it is to ascertain what female sexuality is. It is everywhere but for whom? It is you but of course it is not! It rivals you, flatters you and degrades you. Still, to stress the degradation as though to deny the pleasure, is to miss the opportunity of exploring further vital features of women's culture. What I am suggesting then, is that the process of viewing or looking at women performing in some way, from the point of view of a woman, demands more theoretical and concrete analysis, part of which would have to entail an interrogation of the form and nature of both the pleasure and the pain which this involves.

Breathless and exuberant

The main point here is that the opportunities for this kind of looking are multiple. It would be difficult to spend more than a few hours without having some images of this type foisted on any viewer; on the tube, on the television, in magazines, on the street, and so on. The concentration of these forms and visual signs means that dance-as-image can only really be understood within a field of *related* social phenomenon. Dance has not only an integral relationship with music, but also with youth culture, fashion and style. It performs a function as both climax of the action and the necessary backdrop against which many of these other 'performances' can be carried out. It is therefore with the idea of going out dancing in mind that a range of other activities are carred out, like shopping, flicking through magazines, or dancing to records at home. Together these form a constellation of tightly inter-related instances in sexual expression, in the presentation of self in everyday life and in the articulation of modes of pleasure.

Top of the Pops, the weekly music programme on BBC1 plays a central role in bringing together these various strands. Its festive, fast moving, party-like format, helps secure the link between dance, leisure, and excitement, with fashion, sex, display of the body, and youthfulness. The studio dancers help to make it seem 'live' (and thus spontaneous, almost natural) by applauding, cheering and 'getting down' when the music starts. They are also part of the visual theatrics and the camera wanders among them when there is no video, or when the band or group in question do not appear live. The show also confirms and illustrates the convention of dance as sexual invitation. This is evident in the *Top of the Pops* resident team of dancers, previously 'Legs and Co', and more recently 'Zoo'.

But this 'come-on' dance style is combined with displays of the most recent shifts in fashion and style. So these spots function also as unofficial free advertising for fashion manufacturers. They are almost like moving fashion shots. In their presentation we see, televisually, similar 'looks' to those seen monthly in *Honey* or in *19*, and also in the more subcultural magazines like *ID* and *The Face*. What these representations do is construct a kind of 'regime of looking'. At the present moment (summer 1983) most of these styles are still a definite re-working of mid to late seventies punk. They each involve re-appropriating from the least expected sartorial cupboard and subjecting these items to rapid cultural upholstery. Thus the 'nappy' shorts barely held together round the thighs of young adult men and women, and there is also the wardrobe of soft and hard core porn. Black leather minis, studded belts, caps and braces reminiscent of *The Night Porter*, dark glasses, whips, and chains. Post-punk style has also put the tart or the call-girl back in the heart of fashion, combining this 'brassy' look with 'hard times chic' a combination of thirties and forties ragged clothing, echoing films like *The Grapes of Wrath* and *Angels with Dirty Faces*.

Dance provides an ideal display site for the rapidly changing face of current fashion (despite youth unemployment and widespread financial hardship). Together these two forms work across each other. Dancing necessitates energy, vitality and at least a show of natural spontaneity, and so fashion photography often uses *its* conventions to place the model as though caught dancing, suspended in mid-air momentarily, and so breathlessly, exuberant. A state supposedly brought about by the purchase of the objects or clothes on display. In this way the accessories of leisure and femininity – perfume, clothing, make-up, shoes, deodorant or shampoo, are injected with qualities which have the power to send the consumer dancing off into the future. Dance therefore signifies intertextually across a range of different discourses. What brings these spheres together is their emphasis on the body and the pleasure they promise, which will bear not only on the body but on the 'imagined other'. They also offer simultaneously an escape from work and an opportunity to make something of work.

Texts, readers and viewers

And so dance accumulates its sense as it combines with other forms and other discourses. But this still does not really address the question of how, as image up there on the cinema screen, or over there on the TV, it makes sense for its viewers. It is important here to dwell on this because one of the marked characteristics of most academic writing on youth has been its tendency to conceive of youth almost entirely in terms of action and of direct experience. Attention has been paid to young people in the school, on the dole, and on the street, all sites where they are immediately visible to the social observer. This has had the effect of reducing the entire spectrum of young people's experience implicitly to these moments, neglecting almost totally those many times where they become viewers, readers, part of an audience, or simply silent, caught up in their own daydreams. To ignore these is to miss an absolutely central strand in their social and personal experience. It means that in all these subcultural accounts we are left with little knowledge of any one of their reading or viewing experiences, and therefore with how they find themselves represented in these texts, and with how in turn they appropriate from some of these and discard others. This absence has also produced a real blindness to the debt much of those youth cultural expressions owe to literary texts, to the cinema, to art and to older musical forms.

The problem is that it is immensely difficult, if not impossible, to assess how meanings are drawn out from texts, from music and from images, and how in turn these affect the feelings, actions and behaviour of their audiences. In the field of popular culture it is often as though they simply feed into the currencies of everyday knowledge and become embedded in what we all know and take for granted. In this way the kids from *Fame* enter the same kind of field of popular knowledge as say the image, look and style of Princess Diana. These all flicker on in the background, images that things are done to, as if they were merely a domestic accessory. *Fame* is simply *on*, hair can be washed to it, the ironing done, meals eaten, and even the paper read to it. And there is a sense in which as a pre-dominantly feminine text, *Fame* slots easily into the culture of everyday femininity, like gossip, shopping or flicking through a magazine.

This deep imbrication between visual texts and lived experience illustrates exactly the point I have just made about youth culture. These viewing experiences are just as *lived* as kicking a ball around the football pitch or going out dancing. Similarly having watched, looked at or read some text is not the end of the story. That experience frequently floods into the more social sphere of the classroom or workshop. This is because it is these more private actions which form part of daily linguistic exchange, which in a social setting act as mediators in the building up of common or shared knowledge. This can mean things as simple as talking about who was on *Top of the Pops* the previous night, or about what has been going on between Deirdre and Ken in *Coronation Street*. How we look at TV one moment and then how we talk about it the next day can hardly be precisely categorised with any accuracy. Work-place discussions like those I've just described can mean as little as finding a way of passing the time. And this emphasis also raises the possibility of *Fame* or *Flashdance* requiring specifically feminine knowledge of the social sphere, acquired *prior to* experience of this film, or that TV programme. This knowledge would have a similar status as Barthes' symbolic code; that is, where he refers to those recurring narrative features requiring or referring to extra-narrative knowledge of, and familiarity with, particular aspects of the everyday world.

All of which leaves the social critic with few options other than to limit strictly the range of his or her analysis. It also means working with a consciously loose rather than tight relation in mind, one where an inter-discursive notion of meaning structures and textual experience leads to a different working practice or methodology. Instead of seeking direct causal links or chains, the emphasis is placed on establishing loose sets of relations, capillary actions and movements, spilling out among and between different fields: work and leisure, fact and fiction, fantasy and reality, individual and social experience. One reason why these relations are so difficult to tie down is that despite their concrete material existence, they are nonetheless formative influences in the construction of deeply and largely private internal processes, that is human psyches and human subjectivities.

Dance and fantasy

If thinking about dance as a set of images or as something which is represented in various written or visual texts presents difficulties when we try to be precise about its effect or its explicit meaning, then, when we shift to dance as simply an activity, a practice which most people indulge in with greater or less frequency, a different set of problems emerge. Dancing seems to retain at its centre a solid resistance to analysis. So deeply have we absorbed its rules and its rituals – the preparation, the mirror, the anticipation, and of course the dancing – that somehow we avoid subjecting all this to the scrutiny of analysis. Even the simplest of conventions have eluded sociological comment. One of the most obvious of these might be the way in which a girl or a woman going to a disco or dance *alone* is deviant. This does not hold true for men or boys. Where in general they may also go out dancing in groups, to go alone is in no way remarkable. But for girls it means a great deal more. It is a sign either of having no friends, or of being on the look-out and therefore morally out of line.

The second convention which marks out the different experience of dance for men and women lies in the strength of its attraction as a pleasurable activity. Up until very recently dance has been inextricably linked with femininity, which has made it either an ordeal or something faintly ridiculous for men to show more than a fleeting interest in. There are a whole string of literary, cinematic, and sociological accounts which offer ample evidence of this. These have shown how men have seen dance as an unfortunate pre-requisite to courtship. Mungham, amongst others, has described how men at the dancehall he studied, would stumble clumsily from the bar towards the end of the evening to strike an often ungainly pose on the floor and to survey the mass of dancing girls (Mungham, 1976).

Recently, as dance has become more popular among men, its connotations of cissiness, triviality or silliness are rapidly disappearing. Men can now demonstrate sophisticated dancing styles with expertise and pleasure without inviting criticism or disdain from their male peers. Black (Afro-Caribbean) culture has done much to bring about this change, with the massive increase in dance technology ('ghetto-blasters' and walkmen, hi-fi's and sound systems, 12″ singles and pop videos) and in dance music style (funk, rap, disco, soul, lovers rock, and pop), advertising its appeal and facilitating its spread. Most new dance styles have come out of black youth culture, with men tending to take up the most spectacular gymnastic and acrobatic variations. Leroy, one of the main characters in *Fame*, exemplifies this exactly. He started off as a rough street boy who loved to dance. Then, in true Hollywood style, he gradually became the school hero, a kind of hip head boy who will always see justice and goodness prevail. In his dancing, however, he displays a combination of sexy masculinity with controlled half-balletic, half-gymnastic movements.

There are a few other more general points which can be made about the conventions surrounding dance culture at the present moment. The most important of these is the way in which dance can no longer be reduced simply to the level of promising or providing sexual opportunity. For girls and women it has always been an absorbing and pleasurable activity in its own right. And often, despite the pressures of romance, girls have been content quite simply to dance. The most important shift has been that men are now beginning to participate in dance in a less sexually frantic way. They too have taken up its narcissistic, auto-erotic dimensions, and its features which are predicated more on patterns of friendship than on its possibilities for sex or romance.

But even if it does not have to lead to romance, dance still affords the opportunity for fantasy. Like the cinema, the dancehall or disco offers a darkened space where the dancer can retain some degree of anonymity or absorption. This in turn creates a temporary blotting-out of the self, a suspension of real, daylight consciousness, and an aura of dream-like self-reflection. Where the cinema offers a one-way fantasy which is directed solely through the gaze of the spectator towards the screen, the fantasy of dancing is more social, more reciprocated. This is because it allows simultaneously a dramatic display of the self and the body, with an equally dramatic negation of the self and the body. This latter works through the whole structure of the dance-floor. The crowded mass of bodies, the insistent often trance-like disco rhythms and the possibility of being at once *there* and *not there*.

Dance evokes fantasy because it sets in motion a dual relationship projecting both internally towards the self and externally towards the 'other'; which is to say that dance as a leisure activity connects desires for the self with those for somebody else. It articulates adolescence and girlhood with femininity and female sexuality and it does this by and through the body. This is especially important because it is the one pleasurable arena where women have some control and know what is going on in relation to physical sensuality and to their own bodies. Continually bombarded with images and with information about how they should be and how they should feel, dance offers an escape, a positive and vibrant sexual expressiveness and a point of connection with the other pleasures of femininity like getting dressed up or putting on make-up.[3] But how exactly does fantasy function amidst the semi-darkened space, the mirrors, corners, music and alcohol? And how, as a sociologist, to cull from so many multiple sources, from personal, general, feminist and 'normal' accounts? And also, of course, from the narrative representations so obsessively repeated in *Jackie*, in pop music (–'he walked up to me and he asked' . . .), in popular romances, on TV and on film? From all of these I offer the following. (I should also add that since my sources are predominantly heterosexual these fantasy scenarios make no claim to represent gay or lesbian experience.)

The first is possibly the most obvious and relates to the absence or presence of the object of desire. The presence is awaited, anticipated, and then acted upon through the use of mirrors, the positioning of the body within his gaze. This allows the dancer to have one partner in fact, and another in fantasy. His absence too can generate fantasy-structures based round loss, around what might have been, and of course around a possible future presence, and thus with what it might still be like. Equally, concrete loss of this object of desire can precipitate the fantasy around suffering and pain so familiar in the pages of *Jackie*. To see him disappear with somebody else! To catch him in an embrace with someone else! To be left alone, to dissolve in tears! And then slowly to plan – to get him back, to find somebody else, to play hard to get, or simply to wait!

It is in terms of these small theatrical tableaux that so much of women's culture can be made sense of. The last dance, the waltz, dance as memory, dance as sexual expression. Like all fantasies dance signifies in these contexts as something to be lingered on, referred back to repetitively and imagined as future pleasure. This means remembering precisely minute details of dress and appearance, another seemingly trivial, but nevertheless stubborn and

recurrent feature of women's experience. Dance and the excitement of going out dancing, retains a special place in the female
memory for the very reason of its dispersed, fluid and often
ambiguous pleasure.

This is particularly the case for working-class women for whom
getting married, settling down and having children marks such a
decisive break in their patterns of leisure. Many of the young
working-class mothers interviewed by Dorothy Hobson recalled
with nostalgia and more than just a hint of regret the days when they
were able to go out dancing whenever they felt like it (Hobson,
1978, pp. 79–96). What they said had a particular poignancy
because as married women their desire to go out occasionally to a
disco was inevitably destined to be misconstrued by their husbands
as a desire to go out on the town with the idea of picking someone
up. Neither did the husbands welcome the notion of their wives
being the object of other men's gaze.

From getting down to getting home

While the private aspects of dance, the self absorption and the
fantasy might have a special place in the rituals of dance culture, it
would be quite wrong to pay less than equal attention to its more
explicitly social dimensions. And the observations I offer here focus
on precisely those more material and concrete actions which
characterise dance. Generally I am restricting these comments so
that they refer, not to all kinds of discos, but rather to two fairly
typical 'scenes'. These are 'respectable' city discos frequented by
young single people usually under twenty-five-years-old and for
whom Saturday night dancing, though extremely pleasurable in its
own right, is still nevertheless a stop-gap between youth and settling
down. My other area of interest is what could be described as the
subcultural alternative. Here I argue that what this 'scene' offers is a
suspension of categories, there is not such a rigid demarcation along
age, class, ethnic terms. Gender is blurred and sexual preference
less homogenously heterosexual, but I'll expand on this later.

There are a number of features which recurred so frequently
during the time I was researching these mainstream discos that they
seem worthy of comment. The first of these hinged around the

problem of how to combine the enjoyment of dancing with the real prospect of romance, and two features here seemed to take on a special significance. These were the maintenance of some notion of 'respectability', and the minimising of the danger of sexual violence. Each of these were grounded in a real fear of assault by a stranger (i.e. a dance partner) on the way home from the disco and this fear resulted in a set of codes relating to 'getting home'. Basically this meant not accepting the offer of being 'seen home' by someone unknown, no matter how 'juicy' he was. In the discos I visited it was customary instead to suggest a mid-week date as though to prove his 'real' rather than fleeting interest. This was a practice adhered to by the majority of girls attending city discos regularly. To ignore this code or to break the rules not only put oneself at risk but also the other girl or best friend who would have to find her way home herself. This was seen as a kind of betrayal of trust and could result in the end of a friendship. Indeed, the city late at night, and the lonely suburban streets held great fears for these respectable girls and also for their parents who would frequently give them the taxi fare home rather than have them walk the streets. Even then the evening frequently ended with one girl 'stopping over' with her friends. In every way this meant that a Saturday night's dancing was more expensive and more perilous than it was for their male peers. And whilst in one sense their mothers' advice about taking care and not accepting a lift home in a strange young man's car is an excellent example of feminine good-sense, often its other side was offered implicitly as a solution and was actively advocated as such by the mother. This was simply to find a reliable steady boyfriend whose company would make unnecessary these costly and time-consuming practices. And such a partnership would also mark the end of dangerous jaunts into the city centre dancehalls. But these mothers too regretted the loss of their own dancing days, and so their advice was also tinged with sadness, and offered, if not reluctantly, with some cynicism.

Still, if in contrast to the fun and excitement of the earlier part of the evening, these difficulties seemed more like a headache, they certainly were not sufficient to keep anybody at home. Apart from the dancing itself, these straighter, more 'respectable' discos provided a forum for a number of other games and rituals. Many of these were played by the girls at the expense of the boys. First they would set out to chat up a couple of lads and get them to buy, or 'con' them into buying, a round of drinks, then disappear rapidly with the gin and tonics, into the ladies. Some minutes later they would slink off in the opposite direction. The next strategy was a little more demanding. Here two friends would pretend that they were French and working as au pairs in Birmingham to improve their English. This allowed them the pleasure of masquerade; their temporary identities as French or Spanish returned them to the narratives of schoolgirl fiction where the 'Mam'zelle' was allowed to be extravagent and extrovert in all kinds of ways.[4] These games also entertained a fantasy of travel and a desire for some*thing* else, some*where* else. And following this it is not surprising that the other favoured fantasy was to pretend to be either a model or an actress, or to be terribly 'posh', living in a large house in Sutton Coldfield with horses and a swimming pool.

In subcultural, or more specifically, punk discos, the rules were quite different. Ideas of being cool and of being seen 'posing' were internalised to the point of becoming automatic response. Yet strangely this was balanced out by the girls in fact being allowed to act much more extravagantly without being penalised. Thus where respectable girls fearful of losing their reputation or of losing their way home would restrict their alcohol to a couple of drinks early in the evening, punk girls would frequently go out with the objective of 'getting smashed'. In every way they were more fearless than their straighter peers. Less time would be spent here on traditionally 'chatting up' boys and more emphasis was placed on dancing, drinking or simply hanging around talking. Frequently there would be, in discos like these, large groups of people who all knew each other. This minimised the problem of getting home, and anyway having chosen to take up a subcultural identity implicitly meant also being deviant enough to gladly wander through the streets at all hours, drunk or sober, in groups or in pairs; as though to be punk was to refuse to be intimidated into submissive femininity. This did not make dancing unromantic or lacking in fantasy. It is more that the nature of fantasy was displaced into all those precious gestures of sub-cultural lifestyle: into style (wearing the right clothes at the right moment); into the pleasure of being illicit or deviant, or at least of entertaining this self-image; into dancing in the right way to the right kind of music.

Punk, new wave or 'alternative' clubs do not preclude the idea of romance. It could even be argued that the 'alternative' dance circuits are more romantic, certainly more utopian, than their more respectable equivalents. This stems from the core desire at the heart of the subcultural discourse, that it will not stop. It may get boring but nonetheless the choice has been made and the associated lifestyle has become rooted. It is not that subcultures seek to prolong adolescence or singleness but rather that they seek to overturn the relations marking out singleness as a short period of excitement before real life, hard work and settling down sets in. Which is to say that what a subculture like punk expresses is a breaking with such normative definitions and expectations altogether. This has a definite effect on the aura of the 'alternative' or punk disco. It takes out all the edge, the slightly desperate quality which Mungham (1976) describes in his study. Gender in his Mecca halls is tantamount, where in The Tincan, The Duma, the Hacienda, the Camden Palace, or wherever, it is either parodied through perversity, taking up the earlier shock effects of punk and parading them (as in leather-night at the Batcave or the Mudd Club), or else it is simply subordinated to the music.[5] One way or another it is nothing to get frantic about – class, race, and sexual preference are all at once *there* but not *there*. Punk might be risky, it might represent a stepping out of line, but on the dance floor and on the road home it inoculates the girls both against some danger by giving them a sense of confidence, and against the excesses of sexual discrimination by giving them a lifestyle which adamantly refuses the strictures of traditional femininity.

The dynamics of dance: Fame and Flashdance

Possibly the only thing that links *Fame* and *Flashdance* with this kind of standard, British punk disco scene I have just described, is that here too, in these texts, we find an *image* or *set of images* of girls untrammelled by their sex or by femininity. Neither *Fame* nor *Flashdance* devote the usual amount of time to romantic *dilemmas*, affairs of the heart, or other emotional activities so frequently linked with passive femininity. There is an undeniably romantic thread running through *Flashdance*. But it does not dominate the film; it provides instead a kind of constant tension, something which has to be held at bay so as not in any way to threaten the larger obsession which is the desire to win a place at dance school.

As a starting point for analysis we are presented in each instance with an image of girls as extremely strong minded and determined. Their work is their overriding passion and no mention is made whatsoever of those concerns so dominant in other teenage popular media. Marriage, motherhood and domesticity are, in other words, remarkable in their absence. This is not to proffer in any simple sense either *Fame* or *Flashdance* as exemplary or progressive feminist texts. Much of their interest lies instead in the complex way they both combine old and new elements, inflecting them first in this direction, and then in that. In fact they share this characteristic with a number of other contemporary cultural products especially those aimed at a youngish market. Lucy Fisher and Marcia Landy (1982, pp. 4–20) in their extremely interesting analysis of the film *The Eyes of Laura Mars*, show how the film skilfully concertinas into its time a range of interests which could be said to appeal to a market ranging from critical intellectuals (references and images of other films and well-known books litter the text); to feminists (it is a film which takes up the question of violence against women and pornography); to the 'trendy' youth market (in its use of pop music, its narrative location in the world of fashion photography, and in its representation of the hip world of New York) – and so on.

In their different ways both *Fame* and *Flashdance* do the same thing. They place together images and moments of overwhelming conformity with those which seem to indicate a break with Hollywood's usual treatment of women. This seems like becoming a distinctive trend in popular entertainment, and is evidence of some popularisation of feminist issues. *Tootsie* plays at being a woman, discovers what it is really like, gets a nasty shock and is pleased to return chastened to masculinity. In *Kramer v. Kramer*, a mother leaves her child to be looked after by her workaholic husband, he changes, but she is not sure if she wants to come back. It is almost as though films like these succeed at least partly in the extent to which they fulfil the very function I described when I raised the question of how we watch films and TV. That is, they give us all so much to talk about the next day. So much so, that *not* to have seen them is to find oneself out on a limb in terms of everyday conversation and discussion. In this way the polysemy (or multiple meanings) of the text rises to the surface provoking and pandering to *different* pleasures, *different* expectations and *different* interpretations.

Alex in *Flashdance* shows all the signs of the 'new' woman. She works as a welder, lives alone, rides a bicycle, and dances in a night-club in the evenings. She is dedicated to getting on as a dancer, she is tough and does not put up with the crude sexism of her workmates on site and in the bar. But then in the end she falls for her startlingly handsome boss. Alex may play it down by playing hard to get, but the romance is a vital theme in the narrative. Everything about the camerawork from start to finish alerts us to this possibility and then follows these deeply charged hints all the way through. In the most traditional terms both Alex and Michael positively radiate good looks and beauty which leap out at the viewer as being in stark contrast to the bleak industrial landscape and the seedy working-man's club where most of the action is set. If dance *dominates* the narrative its *subtext* is visually romantic, so that these elements end up in narratival tension only to be resolved in the final moment of the film where Alex wins a place in dance school and forgives Michael for interfering in her career.

Fame also produces a seemingly endless chain of similar ambiguous strategies. The girls here are spunky, cheerful, untroubled by overt displays of male chauvinism amongst their male peers, and, in any case not particularly interested in striking anything other than friendly relations with them. Julie, Doris and Coco care just as much for their female friends as they do for the boys and, along with the equally strong teacher figures, Lydia, and Sherwood, they hold the narratives together. Amongst none of these characters has any talk of marriage or motherhood appeared. And yet what surreptitiously replaces romantic interest and traditional femininity is an unrelenting respectability and an unending, almost gross, sentimentality about the family. Both boys and girls from *Fame* occupy an almost childlike position in the family and an excessive amount of narrative space is devoted to setting up family problems for each character and then working through to some resolution. At points *Fame* suggests an obsessive pre-sexuality rooted in family relations so strong as to discount the importance of finding a boyfriend or falling in love.

If the narratives trade in ambiguities and contradictions, how exactly do the musical and dance sequences articulate with these? How do these traditionally non-representational spheres find meaning? In fact these displays or performances take the form of narratival interludes and function so as at once to heighten and to illuminate the preceding stage in the plot. Thus when Alex is alone in her warehouse after a hard day's work, and when her dreams of making it to dance-school seem most unlikely, her dance, performed as though for herself but of course also and exclusively for the viewer, takes on a distinctively yearning quality. Both the music and the movement, (slow, elongated and introspective), at once suggest the difficulties which lie ahead and also, because of our expectations about a film of this type, look forward to some happy resolution.

This emotive code of music and dance follows a similar pattern in *Fame*. Doris is depressed about her forthcoming exam but, bursting into song, finds some way of overcoming her fear. A boy feels rejected by the glamorous Julie but gets over his misery by singing a duet with another girl, the lyrics of which extol the values of friendship above everything else. Lydia has had bad news about a forthcoming visit by a well-known impresario. Feeling let down by his cancellation she encourages her dancers into an even more 'grimly determined' routine. And Julie, in turmoil about her father's forthcoming re-marriage, clings even more desperately than usual to her 'cello and gives a performance of startling 'intensity'. These virtuoso performances suspend the action and highlight its critical features. But they also in themselves are made to possess, by their very practice, the ability to work towards a restoration of happiness.

This repetitive coding conforms absolutely with Richard Dyer's account of the conventions in the musical (Dyer, 1982). In *Fame* every single performance carries almost ritualistic qualities. Like religious singing, the song and dance routines in *Fame* are constructed so as to seem to bind people together, uniting young and old, teachers and taught, performers and audiences in an expression of celebration (American-ness). The style of the songs, if not sorrowful or directly sentimental, are most often hymnal, even anthemic, so as to bring the audience to their feet. And the camera endorses this by focusing in close-up on the glowing young faces which so clearly speak of sincerity, faith in youth and the new generation, and a continuity of young and old values. These moments function so as to flood the audience and therefore the viewer with emotions of this type – the naturalness of love and the importance of trust, friendship and hope. And then the lights go up and applause breaks the sanctity of the preceding moments.

Music and dance here raise the emotional temperature and become an act of faith not only in the self but also in the social values which these various characters in *Fame* represent. *Flashdance* is not quite so straightforward. The main focus of attention is on one figure, Alex, and on her struggle to get into an institution like the one in which *Fame* is set. Alex is only a dancer in this film, and music accompanies her instead of being performed by anyone in the narrative. It is however significant that the title song, '*Flashdance. What a Feeling*' which made no. 1 in the American Top Ten is performed by Irene Cara, who appeared in the original film version of *Fame*, and also performed its title track. The musical and lyrical qualities in each text have much in common. In both cases the woman's voice 'reaches out'. It starts off controlled and moves, rapidly rising, to an effusive chorus: 'Fame I'm Gonna Live Forever . . .', 'What a Feeling . . .': the conclusion in both texts invariably works towards joy and optimism rather than sorrow or failure. Often it is a case of them (Alex or the Kids) winning over us – the stuffy judges in *Flashdance*, the audience, or spectators in *Fame* – to what they represent, like a massive job of public relations on behalf of popular culture. (In *Flashdance* this is marked by the gradual smiles on the faces of the 'highbrow' judges and the tapping of their feet in time to modern pop music.)

Dancing in the streets

How to assess the popularity of *Fame* and more recently *Flashdance*? I don't want to spend too much time itemising the more obviously economic aspects of this success. Earlier in the article I drew attention to the way in which popular meanings taken up in one sphere work their way across a range of others. I suggested that these meanings were tightly bound up with the generation and proliferation of material signs like dress, style and music, as well as with active pursuits, like the explosion in dance following the success of films like *Saturday Night Fever* and *Fame*. That is to say that *Fame*'s popularity can be, at least partly, understood in terms of all its spin-offs: the taking up of leg-warmers, tracksuits, casual sport-style dress, *Fame* T shirts; in the return of the *Fame* film theme to No. 1 in the pop charts following audience interest in the

154

Photographed by Zadoc Nava

Camdem Palace 1984

TV series; and the high sales of the album of *Fame* music, released soon after the start of the TV series. I also described how *Fame* characters seeped into popular consciousness to be absorbed into the fluctuating stock of public knowledge, making guest appearances on *Top of the Pops*, on *Nationwide* or on its equivalent on the other channels.

The success of *Flashdance* is more difficult to assess. Certainly ticket sales have been proportionally much larger in the States than they have been in Britain. But then cinema is always more difficult to break audience resistance to than TV. Cinema audiences have to be positively lured away from their screens at home, which means that popularity in this field is something quite different from small screen success. Cinema has, as John Ellis (1982) points out, to rouse the curiosity of its desired audience. It has to provide them with a more intense visual experience than the one they will, with the flick of a button, get at home. One result of this is that cinema has to be, and is permitted to be, a much sexier medium. Both *Flashdance* and the original film version of *Fame* contain much more explicitly sexual material than their televisual counterpart. They also allow fairly free usage of the word 'fuck' and discuss issues not usually held compatible with 'family viewing'. The film *Fame* features one student trying to come to grips with his homosexuality. It also confronts the issue of unscrupulous porn merchants exploiting the youthful enthusiasm of students like Coco (here played by Irene Cara). In contrast with the sexual spectacle offered in *Flashdance*, *Fame* on TV has all the antiseptic charm and excitement of a schoolgirl's comic. Both *Fame* and *Flashdance* have been popular in a youth-oriented market, but what distinguishes them is the emphasis in *Flashdance* not simply on sex but on the kind of sexual looking appropriate to the cinema screen and dependent on that mode for its existence. This raises questions about how women and men view these texts differently, an area of debate I referred to earlier in this article. How do women and girls watch *Fame* and *Flashdance*? Are their interests catered for differently from an assumed male audience? Or is it the case that the special needs of the male viewer are *less* directly met in *Fame* because the assumed audience is solidly male *and* female, young *and* old, and all positioned within the family? Which is like saying that men and boys would tend not to make dirty jokes or pore over page three of the *Sun* or flick through *Playboy*, around the kitchen table. But in the cinema where men are sought more directly as consumers or ticket-buyers, then this *family* moral code can be dropped. Apart from anything else this guarantees greater financial return than would be the case if the films were promoted as just a matter of song and dance.

Indeed, this very point is significant in any attempt to understand the dispersal of pleasure in this film and in the large-screen version of *Fame*. For women, Alex is confident, pretty, interested enough in femininity to read *Vogue* during her tea break and keep her body in shape at night. She is loyal to her girlfriends and is dismayed when one of them decides to work in a much seedier topless bar after she loses a skating competition. Alex then takes it upon herself to save her friend from this scene of exploitation and degradation. But whilst she represents one thing, the camera focuses on something quite different and bestows more than a series of lingering looks around the aforesaid bar, just as it almost caresses the bodies of the dancing girls in the more respectable Mawby's Bar. This sets up a duality of perspective which actively constitutes the kind of polysemy I referred to earlier. Likewise, in the cinema version of *Fame*, Coco is lured to the flat of the porn dealer, made to strip and is set down in front of the video camera. Because Coco is a central and likeable character in the narrative, the audience is on one level being asked to sympathise with her plight as she sits sobbing with shame and fear. Yet still the audience is allowed to see her sitting there, *not* directly to the camera but through the video-screen and hence through the *eyes* of the porn merchant himself, as in a classic Peeping Tom situation.

There are other more general and less contentious pleasures which find expression in both *Fame* and *Flashdance* and which consequently add to their popularity. In each case youth is linked with drive, ambition, idealism, health and energy. Everyone in both texts is always in a hurry. In *Fame*, students and staff alike are invariably rushing and in *Flashdance* Alex flies on her bike from her daytime work to Mawby's Bar and then back home. The Kids from *Fame* leap from one class to the next and then they seem to leap across New York on their way home. This is an important point because once again in our society, to be in a hurry is to be somehow an important person or at least someone who is going to be important. There is no lazy lounging about in the New York School of the Performing Arts. We cannot help as spectators being impressed by the confidence and exuberance, and because women are equally if not predominantly represented, then this spectacle of women out there doing things, enjoying life and not getting bogged down by lack of confidence or by shyness is, I think, an extremely pleasurable vision. But, no sooner do I write this than the voice of realism begins to make itself heard. 'Is this not a very neat fantasy to offer young people', it says, 'especially in times of such high youth unemployment, to give them this absolutely unrealistic image of themselves, with no problems, with supportive parents, street kids as well, with loads of talent and appearing to get somewhere with it?' The voice goes on: 'Dressed up too in the language of American democratic values; the "kids" aren't rich, many of them are black or Puerto Rican or Jewish and they're not being held back, they have co-operated with the system and look where they are getting!'

Much of the power of this fantasy lies precisely in its mobilisation of the concept of youth – it offers images of intensity and of great effort without actually going on to assess the eventual outcome. Which means that what is covered in *Fame* and *Flashdance* is not the desired results but the hard road leading implicity, but not definitely, to success. At this stage in their careers both Alex and the Kids can afford disappointements and failures simply because with these come also scope for improvement or room for a change in direction. The young in this sense are not accountable. And if fame itself is not *achieved* or won within the narratives, then neither are the disadvantages that go with it. And what is standard for youth – to keep trying, to retain an innocence and an absence of cynicism, would be undignified in adults and hence not pleasurable when presented to an audience of viewers.

Finally there are other equally significant outlets for pleasure in both *Fame* and *Flashdance*. And in each instance they have a direct bearing on our focus on gender. First there is the backdrop of the city. What is interesting here is that both New York and Pittsburgh are presented as livable urban spaces for women. The Kids from *Fame* and Alex in *Flashdance* take this freedom of movement about the city they live in for granted. They are hampered neither by fear nor harassment. Alex presents a striking figure cycling to and from work, and then doing the same, after a night's dancing, through the deserted streets of the city in the early hours of the morning. Coco too is unfearing as she pursues a disillusioned Leroy throughout the streets of the Bronx. And Doris even goes so far as to play at being a prostitute by hanging out on Times Square so she can get the feel of the role for one of her character parts. In these fantasy representations, the city is a site of social pleasure and much of this derives from its multi-cultural atmosphere. Black kids are as much in focus in *Fame* as white students, and Alex in *Flashdance* is no WASP (White Anglo-Saxon Protestant) herself. In fact in both cases the students seem to benefit *positively* from being black, Puerto-Rican, Jewish, Italian or Greek, as though the richness, the warmth and the intensity (stereotypically constructed) of these family backgrounds, prepare them all the better for the dedication needed for their chosen careers, more so than their WASP friends. This is obvious in the case of Julie, the beautiful girl who specialises in classical music. Frequently she is presented as suffering directly from her cold, anxious, WASP background. She lives with her divorced and nervous mother and is the only girl in *Fame* who possesses little push, whose good looks almost handicap her and who seems already less than confident about her ability. In this sense she stands in sharp contrast with Doris around whom so many of the narratives focus. Doris is stereotypically Jewish, has problems with her weight and is attractive but not beautiful (the Barbra Streisand of the New York School of Performing Arts). Often she goes too far and overwhelms both her friends and fellow students with her loud personality, but it is she who comes across, throughout the series, as possessing the 'right stuff'. Devoted in the extreme to her extended Jewish family . . . Mum, Dad, brother who was a draft dodger, Grandmother who turns out to be just as spunky as her grand-daughter . . . and so on, Doris has the proverbial heart of gold.

Part of the pleasure here is that the struggle to make it from backgrounds which are not rich, white and culturally confident, produces characters with little time for angst or nervous introspection. Material necessity and the social demands made on the individual by a large noisy family do not leave much space for self-indulgent reflection. And because so much emphasis is placed on talking it over and working it out, a problem no sooner arises than it has been solved. Nobody tolerates racism and the Kids' confidence is such that they challenge rather than dwell on what seem like petty injustices. All of which adds to the Utopian qualities of the community which is represented in *Fame*: everybody needs a family, everybody benefits from warm and loving family relationships, to deny them is unnatural, ageist, or downright antisocial (a far cry indeed from the 1960s and 1970s images of youth in revolt against the family); a re-alignment as though both sides have learnt from the other, so that there is no longer any need for drawing up battle-lines around generations. In *Flashdance* this subject is re-worked subtly. Alex appears to have no close family and so, as a single girl living alone in a large empty warehouse guarded only by her dog, we are invited to admire her pluck and her independence, but also to worry about her isolation. In this way she is both problematised and exemplary. When her friend and mother-figure, another Jewish émigrée named Hanna, dies, Alex's resilience and determination multiply as does her attraction to Michael. The film closes with her falling into his arms and hugging him warmly.

In *Fame* too the hug punctuates the ebb and flow of friendship, family and sibling love, and even the occasional romance. It marks an intensely human moment, one whose emotional contours are at once strong and ambiguous. In popular imagery, hugging is frequently something in which women take the initiative: men are hugged, rarely do they rush up to a woman with childlike exuberance. Hugging is partly what links fantasies about the self with the need to prove oneself to another. It looks back to childhood and the desire to win parental approval: look what I've done! Aren't I clever!

Not surprisingly this latter dimension makes the pleasures of hugging problematic. Is it because it is based on the assumption that where boys *will* achieve, that they *have to* achieve, for women it is still something that has to be struggled for? The hug is both the recognition and the reassurance, the parental reward, the sign of absolute affection. No wonder it has such resonance in memory and in expressions of desire.

When I wrote, some years ago in an article on *Jackie* (McRobbie, 1981) about what was wrong with the picture stories, about how they make life revolve around romance and therefore be defined either in terms of joyful moments or else painful interludes, my complaint was grounded in the search for a realistic account of girls' lives. I wanted images and stories that were more down to earth, more real, and I commented sourly on how the picture stories ended with a kiss as though there was nothing else beyond. I consciously played down or ignored the role of fantasy in popular fiction and implicitly argued for more representations of *real* girls confronting *real* issues. As I have already indicated, this is a distinction which I no longer hold to be so helpful. Daydreaming during work, as an added and therefore positive input, or else just as a distraction, is still nevertheless as much an *experience*, a piece of reality, as is babysitting or staying in to do the washing. What is more, to ignore these more private aspects of everyday experience is to avoid considering their function and how they make sense in terms of politics and social change. Are they open to change or do they insistently remain the same? This is a question that is impossible to engage with here. Nevertheless, what is significant about the two texts I have been considering is that in each case the fantasies focus around hard work, its costs and its rewards. And as fantasy-type narratives, although ostensibly offering viewers an idealised future, they are in fact providing them with a set of pleasurable moments. Where in *Jackie* equivalent moments, because they are always heavily romanticised, signify *closure*, signify the *end* of the search, the relief, 'she need look no further . . .' and so on, in *Fame* and *Flashdance*, the narratives leave things a lot more open. In *Fame* the closing hug sequences suggest a kind of emotional recharging of batteries, and in *Flashdance*, the hug offers an image of pleasure and relief as a result of hard work having paid off. These are in marked contrast to *Jackie* and, especially, *My Guy*, where the final narrative sequence seem to celebrate only the possibility of long-term female inertia. *Fame* and *Flashdance* manage to retain therefore a dignity on behalf of their female characters by using these motifs and these moments to mark out mobilisation, movement, and the pleasures of social engagement, not alone but in conjunction with friendship and sexuality.

Notes

1. For a fascinating analysis of schoolgirl fiction see Gill Frith forthcoming (1985).
2. The fragment from Jacques Rancieres *Proletarian Nights* translated in *Radical Philosphy* no. 31, contains a dramatic challenge to those who have dismissed individual cultural expressions coming from working-class writers, musicians, poets or artists, as petty bourgeois or merely individualist. The problem for such radical critics, states Ranciere, is that too often these expressions are not all compatible with the political expectations or desires of the (frequently) middle-class intellectuals

anxious to ascertain a fit between ideas of class, party and their eventual unity.

3. It is interesting that sequences like these in films have recently been given over to men. First, I think, by Scorsese in *Mean Streets* who shows Michael (Harvey Keitel) in front of the mirror with a shirt, lovingly pressed by his mother, getting ready for the night's action. Then of course, in *Saturday Night Fever*, there is a much less subtle version of exactly the same scene where the camera lovingly shoots upwards from behind John Travolta's legs and thighs. Finally there is also in *American Gigolo*, an equally narcissistic moment showing Richard Gere surrounded by a multitude of silk shirts.

4. This is taken from the article by Gill Frith (1985).

5. Well-known clubs in London, Birmingham and Manchester frequently reported on in the music press.

7

Some Day my Prince Will Come: Young Girls and the Preparation for Adolescent Sexuality

Valerie Walkerdine

Introduction

My first inspiration for the title of this chapter came from a fragment of childhood memory told to me by a friend, now adult. It was of her grandmother, seated at the piano, surrounded by her family, playing her favourite song, 'Some day my prince will come . . .'. Judging from the rendering of the song, it acted as a catalyst for an outpouring of unfulfilled desire and it is clear that, old as she was, her prince had not yet arrived. That an old woman can still harbour desire for romantic fulfilment encapsulates the theme which I want to explore: the way in which girls are prepared for entry into heterosexual practices, and, in particular, for romantic love. Here I intend to explore this theme by examining some aspects of the ideological preparation for adolescent sexuality in children's fiction, particularly girls' comics. I shall use this examination as a vehicle for discussing the relation between the psychic production of feminine desire and cultural forms and practices.

It will be my argument that young girls of primary school age are presented with, and inserted into, ideological and discursive positions by practices which position them in meaning and in regimes of truth. In the insertion of young girls into positions which serve to produce and reproduce feminity, the organisation of psychic life embodied in the dynamics of the family is centrally and strategically important. In psychoanalytic studies of the preparation for feminine sexuality, the strategic dynamics relate to the shifting for the girl of desire from the mother to the father (or more particularly the symbolic form of the Phallus in Lacanian theory, as I will explore later). I want to show that cultural products for girls, by exploring those dynamics in symbolic form, may be of strategic importance in presenting psychic conflicts lived out in fantasy situations, and also in presenting resolutions and potential resolutions to these conflicts. They may also serve to prepare the ground for the insertion of the little girl into romantic heterosexuality. In his discussion of feminine sexuality, Freud said that 'The constitution [of the little girl] will not adapt itself to its function [heterosexual femininity] without a struggle' (Freud, 1933, p. 117).

I want to explore some of the cultural practices which locate the girl in that struggle. Contrary to some classic approaches to feminine role models, I shall not argue that young girls passively adopt a female role model, but rather that their adoption of femininity is at best shaky and partial: the result of a struggle in which heterosexuality is achieved as a solution to a set of conflicts and contradictions in familial and other social relations. That the girl appears willingly to accept the position to which she is classically fitted does not, I would argue, tell us something basic about the nature of the female body, nor the female mind, but rather, tells us of the power of those practices through which a particular resolution to the struggle is produced. Girls' comics, because they engage with the production of girls' conscious and unconscious desires, prepare for and proffer a 'happy ever after' situation in which the finding of the prince (the knight in shining armour, 'Mr Right') comes to seem like a solution to a set of overwhelming desires and problems.

Current approaches to sexism in literature

The issue of 'sexist bias' and stereotyping in literature for children has long been an important issue in feminist analyses of educational practices (see for example Glenys Lobban, 1975; Bob Dixon, 1977). While these approaches have been of critical importance in raising the issue of content, they have tended to minimise the importance of the text itself as productive of meanings. Such approaches rely on a view that sexist literature presents stereotyped images which offer a biased and distorted picture of reality. For example, by showing women always at the kitchen sink they do not reveal that many women engage in paid labour outside the home.

Gill Pinkerton (1982) in an article on producing non-sexist materials for the primary school classroom aimed to

> extend children's thinking beyond stereotyping, both through in-depth discussion and by providing a range of material – stories, pictures, films, people – which presents broader images of what girls and boys, men and women are really like.

The objective here then, is to get the children to see that other views and images are possible, and therefore to bring about a change in thinking and action.

Now, all this may seem fine, since indeed it forms the basis of the taken-for-granted approach to sexism in literature in school. However, I think that there are at least two difficulties with this position. First, it assumes that by presenting a 'wider range of experience', children's views of themselves and of possible courses of action will change; secondly, that unproblematic transformation will come about through the adoption of non-stereotyped activities. Such an approach assumes a passive learner, or rather a rationalist one, who will change as a result of receiving the correct information about how things *really* are. It assumes that when the little girl sees the veil of distortion lifted from her eyes, she too will want to engage in those activities from which she has been forbidden by virtue of her gender. There are two important points in response to this position. The first deals with the central importance of cultural practices in *producing* forms of thought and positions for women, the second deals with the inscription in those positions, of desire – that is, how we come to want what we want. Recent work in the field of cultural practices has stressed the importance of the way in which texts, such as books, films, advertisements and so forth, operate in terms of systems of signification. Thus the text has to be actively read in order to engage with the way in which images and other signs, verbal and non-verbal, are constructed.

In this sense then, we can say that texts do not simply distort or bias a reality that exists only outside the pages of books – in the 'real world' – but rather that those practices *are* real, and in their construction of meanings create places for identification, construct subject-positions in the text itself. So we need not point to some untainted reality outside the text, but to examine instead how those practices within the text itself have relational effects that define who and where we are. They are not just images which are distasteful, to be tossed away and replaced by more politically acceptable ones. I suggest that we have to engage with the production of ourselves as subjects in and through our insertion into such cultural practices, of which children's literature forms a part. The content of such literature is not just grafted onto a cognate and waiting subject, who can be so easily changed. Rather, the positions and relations created in the text both relate to existing social and psychic struggle and provide a fantasy vehicle which inserts the reader into the text.

Fantasy in children's literature: the case of girls' comics

Girls' comics are a very powerful form indeed. They implicitly offer guidance as to how young girls may prepare themselves to be good enough to 'win' the glittering prizes: the man, the home, the adventure and so forth. They do this, but they do it at a level which the alternative images or role models for girls simply cannot reach: they work on desire. In her analysis of the adolescent magazine, *Jackie*, Angela McRobbie (1982a) discusses the codes through which adolescent femininity is constructed and therefore may be read. The positions that magazine offers relate to heterosexual practices about 'getting and keeping a man', and while pre-teen comics do not do this in any overt sense, what happens is that they engage with the construction of femininity in such a way as to prepare young girls for the fate that awaits them. How then are young girls prepared? The textual devices turn around stories which are based on classic fairy tales in most cases. They end with happy-ever-after solutions, mostly around the insertion of the girl into an ideal family. Meanwhile, in getting there, the girls in these stories are apparently hapless victims of circumstance, scorned, despised and hard-done-by. The resolution in the family is, I will argue, the Oedipal resolution played out. The happy family is produced through the traumas associated with the loss and abandonment of the mother in favour of the Oedipal love of the father. And, as we know, the father simply precedes the prince. The heterosexual practices of *Jackie* then offer a solution, a way out of the misery of the femininity struggled over in the pages of these comics.

The comics that I have chosen are two of the most popular amongst junior school girls: *Bunty* and *Tracy*. For the most part, these stories develop themes of family relationships. To do so, they use particular kinds of narrative device. I shall not attempt a comprehensive examination of these devices, particularly the use of strip cartoons, the style of drawing and so on, but will concentrate particularly on those devices which allow certain very distressing issues to be the focus of the stories. Often these stories contain a catalogue of dreadful events which befall their heroines. How can comics full of frightful stories sell so well and be so gripping? Why are the heroines of the stories more often than not helpless victims? I shall attempt to answer these questions by outlining the themes of the stories, mentioning some remarks made by Freud which relate to similar content which emerged in his clinical work. There are eighteen strip stories in these two comics. They are nearly all about girls who are *victims*: of cruelty and circumstance. Eleven are about girls who do not have, or do not live with, their parents. Indeed, the circumstances are so fantastic that they would, on the surface, appear to bear very little relation to the lives of their young readers. I say *on the surface* because it is precisely the organisation of *fantasy* (rather than the realist approach of anti-sexist literature) which is so important in understanding the relation of such literature to the psychic organisation of desire. After all, fantasy is the tool *par excellence* of psychoanalysis.

Fantasy and fiction

Freud, in his early work (1906, pp. 237–41) discussed the importance of fantasy[1] in the production of the material which was the subject matter of the analysis itself. He posited various structures and mechanisms through which, in his terms, reality was 'mediated' by fantasy, such that the material of everyday life was not lived in any simple sense through mechanisms of perception. In particular he argued that it was quite common for children to fantasise about alternative parentage: 'Chance occurrences . . . arouse the child's envy, which finds expression in a phantasy in which both his parents are of better birth' (p. 239). Such fantasies have certain effects upon the lived relations of the family themselves, but are also devices which allow certain difficulties, to be dealt with. What is the effect of fantasy, and how does it operate? I want to explore this in two ways. First, I shall examine the content of the two girls' comics in question, then I shall go on to relate this to other cultural practices in which fantasies are produced, particularly in this case fantasies connected with romantic heterosexual love.

It is my contention that the very 'unreality' of the stories presented in these comics is one basis of their strength rather than weakness. That is, they engage precisely with the kinds of issues mentioned by Freud. They allow engagement with difficult emotions and less than perfect circumstances by devices which allow the young readers to identify with the heroine in the text. Thus they permit the working out and potential resolution of certain conflicts.

The market for these magazines is working-class pre-pubescent girls. The stories themselves therefore relate to fantasies about family, sexuality and class. In several ways the stories construct heroines who are the target of wrong-doing and whose fight against private injustice is private endurance, which always triumphs in the end. By contrast, boys' comics deal with public bravery and public fights against injustice which are rewarded openly. Now, as I have said above, it has classically been the position, in relation to issues of sex and class in children's literature, to regard such material as biased, bad and unreal and therefore to be countered with an appropriate realism. but the alternative realism is based on politics of rationalism, of rational transformation, change through the imposition of the 'right line', the undistorted picture of reality. 'Reality' is not in this simple sense hidden or distorted. What we have to examine is the materiality of the fantasies created in these comics, in terms of what is spoken, what is understood, and how it is resolved.

Readers are constructed in the text, readers construct readings of the text – a complex interplay which does not recognise a simple split between a pre-given psychological subject who reads and a text in which meaning is produced (Henriques *et al*, 1984). Realist approaches to reading, which prevail in the radical work on children's fiction, treat readers as pre-existing classed, gendered and racial subjects who are formed through certain material relations of production, who have a 'lived reality', a material base, which stories help or hinder. It is in this sense that we can understand the movement towards more 'real' texts which 'reflect the reality' of (predominantly) working-class life. What, then, are these children, faced with what is represented as their 'reality', to do with such realist texts? What if the readers do not 'recognise themselves' and their lives in the stories, or what if they do not *want* to recognise? And what about desires to have and to be something and somebody different? Classic fairy tales are quite fantastic: they do not bear any resemblance to the lives of ordinary children. Yet they act powerfully to engage with important themes about 'what might be'. In other words, I am arguing that they engage with the very themes, issues, problems, fantasies (of escape, of difference) which the realist, 'telling it like it is' stories do not engage with at all.

The comic stories do. Certainly they present miserable circumstances, difficult lives, but they do so in such a way as to provide solutions and escapes, ways out, in fantasy and in practice by the proffering of what and who one might be. The stories romanticise poverty and portray a way of dealing with it which is almost masochistic – it is desirable precisely because it can be suffered virtuously and moved beyond. Poverty is presented as the result of tragic circumstances; so too are families who are wicked, oppressive – the result of some dreadful accident of fate. The major narrative device which renders these difficult circumstances palatable is precisely that they *are* fantastic. That is, they are removed from the everyday in various ways: a different historical period or geographical location, and the overwhelming use of 'surrogate' parents and siblings. In the majority of stories, the children do not live with their biological parents or siblings, but are removed by various tragic circumstances to surrogate families who are cruel to them. It is my contention that it is these devices which help make possible the engagement with difficult material. That is, identification is possible at the level of fantasy – where an identification with a 'reality' presented as mirroring the life of the readers may well be rejected as 'not like me' or indeed 'too close for comfort'. The argument is then, that the distance, the difference, renders these stories *more*, not less effective, and such effectiveness is not to be easily countered by a simple realism.

The realist text and approach to change using stereotypes concentrates on *images*. Images can be good or bad, true or false. The concept of fantasy being put forward here is one which does not present a rational or passive appropriation of an *image*, but an active engagement with, and construction of, the imaginary fulfilment of a wish. It is in this sense that fiction is not a mere set of images, but an ensemble of textual devices for engaging the reader in the fantasy. Because the fantasies created in the text play upon wishes already present in the lives of young children, the resolutions offered will relate to their own wishes or desires. In this conception of change, there is no simple response to a positive image, but a complex psychic organisation. So the reader who engages in this fiction lives a 'real' life which is at the same time organised in relation to fantasy. To understand children's fiction in this way gives quite a different view of the presentation of fiction and its effect on, and relation to, the lives of young girls.

Let us now examine in greater detail the content of *Bunty* and *Tracy*, for their thematic organisation. Apart from the *eleven* stories about girls who do not have, or do not live with, their parents, the other *seven* are as follows:

1. A girl who is helpful and does good and kindly deeds for others except when she puts on a glove puppet, at which point her character completely changes and she becomes vicious, angry and evil. Of course, at the moment she takes off the glove-puppet, she has no recollection of her evil deeds.

2. A girl who is perfect at school: clever, beautiful, helpful, sensible, but whose cleverness and good deeds make her the object of envy, and therefore unpopular and unhappy.

3. A girl who lives with her mother, the latter having been made redundant. The girl is saved from having to sell a precious camera by her ingenuity in using it to make money by taking and selling photographs. These turn out to be related to good and kindly deeds for others.

4. A girl whose mother is a teacher, who has chosen to teach in a 'rough' comprehensive and is constantly trying to reform the children. Her daughter by her ingenuity and good deeds, helps her mother to manage the school (of course without her mother's knowledge).

5. A girl who was a Victorian serving girl but who has been frozen for one hundred years in a block of ice (!) and is found by a family with a daughter of the same age who passes her off as a cousin.

6. A girl gymnast from an Eastern bloc country who is helped to escape by a British girl gymnast.

7. A horse who develops the theme of jealousy: another horse is jealous of her but the heroine's horse helps the other unselfishly despite the other's jealousy.

Even where the girls are presented in an ordinary family setting, the stories tend to centre on the resolution of certain problems – often to do with internal family relations. For here, too, the girls are often in receipt of gross injustices. They are constantly misunderstood and misjudged, but the theme that is played out again and again is, that despite everything, the girls engage in selfless acts of helpfulness and courage in the service of others. These can be illustrated by the resumés of the 'story so far' given at the top of each picture-strip. In the story, 'Joni The Jinx', the caption reads as follows:

> When orphan Joni Jackson was adopted by Kate and Robert Stewart, she looked forward to the kind of happy family she had always dreamed of. But things didn't quite work out as planned.

In this story, the adoptive parents are keen to do their best, but they argue over how to present themselves properly to the social worker, and tensions between the husband and wife are brought to the fore. In each case, Joni, helpful and thoughtful as she is, takes this to be *her* fault in the sense that it is her presence which has caused these tensions to surface.

In another story, 'Cherry and the Chimps', an orphaned girl is found living with chimps in Africa by a wicked couple, who use her as a slave to serve them and to run their chimp circus act. She is constantly abused. The misery and unhappiness is only resolved by the reappearance of her real parents who were thought to have been killed in a plane crash.

In 'She'll Stay a Slave', the heroine, Jenny, is an orphan, a slave to her cruel cousin, but she is predictably very clever and helpful, despite the fact that her wicked cousin is always exploiting her, trying to spoil her success and so on. The caption is as follows:

> Jenny Moss lived with her Aunt Mary and Uncle John. Her cousin Paula treated her like a slave and Jenny put up with it as she mistakenly believed that Paula had saved her life after an accident. Jenny was one of three girls being considered for a scholarship to Redpark College – but Paula tried to spoil Jenny's chances of winning as she did not want to lose her 'slave'.

These tales of cruelty go on and on. They range from a girl who is made to act as a robot in a circus act by wicked relatives and who

Thanks to Sarah Webb

suffers pain and humiliation in silence because she believes her relatives are paying for hospital treatment for her sick brother, to a girl who is forced to act as a ventriloquists' dummy because the real ventriloquist, her grandfather, is ill. Then there is the tale of Victorian orphan sisters who go from disaster to cruel disaster: at the end of one episode one sister suddenly goes blind!

I want to examine certain themes which appear constantly throughout the comic stories. The first theme which I shall take is that of the production of girls as *victims*. I have already noted the large number of girls in the stories who are victims of circumstance and of cruelty. Let us examine how these aspects of the stories function in the circulation of meanings and the presentation of key signifiers at the level of fantasy. The themes present cruelty and harsh personal circumstances as potentially exciting because they are the subject of adventures. Equally important is the resolution: the way of dealing with the violence, cruelty and harsh circumstances. The theme which is present in these and all other stories in the two comics is selfless helpfulness. In the 'victim' stories the heroines carry on doing good deeds and accepting their fate in the most selfless manner. Indeed, the manner in which they do so is starkly contrasted by the villains of the stories, who may be other children or older relatives. These are shown as nasty, vicious and jealous: they wreak vengeance on the 'good' and selfless girls, who only respond to their torture by continued helpfulness, despite everything.

What seems to me important about this is that if cruelty is seen as exciting and works at the level of fantasy to romanticise difficult practical and emotional circumstances, this suggests a passive and not an active response to the violence (which in psycho-analysis would relate to the displacement of angry and hostile feelings onto others). It also provides the conditions for resolution: selflessness, even though it brings pain and suffering, brings its own rewards (knowledge of good deeds and righteousness). If the heroines are displayed as passive victims of circumstance, all bad and difficult actions and emotions are invested in others. The heroines suffer in silence: they display virtues of patience and forbearance and are rewarded for silence, for selflessness, for helpfulness. Any thought for the self, any wanting, longing, desire or anger is in this way produced within the texts as bad. This provides for the readers a value-system in which certain kinds of emotion are not acceptable, and a set of practices in which their suppression is rewarded by the provision of the longed-for happy family, the perfect bourgeois setting. So, bad and difficult circumstances are to be celebrated and triumphed over by the psychic organisation of emotions and the selfless production of good deeds. Through the narrative device of the inadequate or 'bad' family structure which is also the result of circumstance, not choice, the girls are shown themselves as being able to bring about by their own actions the conditions for the restoration of the *desired* family structure. The idealised family is the bourgeois and respectable nuclear family, shown as located in a desirable house with money and possessions. Class and gender relations are therefore dealt with by the idealisation of a certain kind of family, but also by the relations *within* the family, notably mother and father, and between siblings. Importantly these are always sisters: relationships with brothers are never explored. Paternal and maternal relations tend to be displaced on to adoptive parents, aunts and uncles, grandparents or simply evil couples, who, through various circumstances, have taken possession of the girl in question. Sibling rivalry and jealousy is a theme well explored, but it is always located in the anti-heroine or parent substitutes: the heroine rises above it. Critically then, certain material circumstances are presented as lived and worked through in various ways which lead to the presentation of the bourgeois individual, feminine and actively passive. So, while such selfless identities are not likely to be achieved by the readers, what I am suggesting is the possibility of the psychic *effect* of the resolution of conflict in which all features to do with anger and jealousy are displaced as bad.

This effectively means that girls are not presented with heroines who ever get angry. Their victory is in their very passivity and helpfulness. Selflessness is contrasted with selfishness, anger, greed and jealousy. So, for example, anger signifies as wholly negative, and is therefore never used in any positive way: it is never justified nor is rebellion ever sanctioned. This leads to the suppression of certain qualities as bad and therefore not to be displayed, or to be acknowledged at peril.[2]

It is in this way that girls become 'victims' – for example, angry and hostile feelings are projected on to the other and are suppressed in the self – passivity is thus *actively* produced as the result of an internal struggle. The overwhelming characteristic of the 'good' heroines is their selflessness. They do countless good deeds by helping others. Thus selflessness becomes a virtue and doing anything for oneself is by implication bad and selfish. Girls can, therefore, move mountains (metaphorically of course!) as long as they do it *for others*. This means that many acts are possible, but doing anything for one's own benefit is not. Girls in these comics are encouraged in a view of self which exists only *for* and through others. Such girls will always fail: how can they possibly be selfless enough? Another significant and perhaps surprising feature of the stories is the positive manner in which academic achievement is treated. Heroines are usually clever, and often at mathematics, the area in which girls are commonly supposed to fail (Walden and Walkerdine, 1982). Achievement brings parental pride. Academic achievement is thus acceptable; it is for others, for one's family or for the school. In the comics it is actually 'taken for granted' that girls are clever: it is certainly not presented as antithetical to femininity as some of the stereotyping arguments would suggest.

I have argued elsewhere (Walkerdine 1981) that it is precisely the slippage afforded in the term 'good girl' which allow girls to be good and helpful and like their mothers at home, and good and helpful and clever in the classroom. This fits with the studies which reveal that, relative to boys, girls' performance is extremely good in the primary school.

In one story the girl who is top of her class also looks the best in the school because she takes pride in her school uniform. When a friend says to her 'How do you manage to look so smart in our grotty school uniform? Mine hangs like an old potato sack!', our heroine replies: 'Well, you can improve it a bit by ironing and by taking in a stitch here and there. . . .' This signifying chain from neatness and helpfulness to academic attainment is really important in that there are no pejorative connotations attached to academic performance at this stage at all. However, there is a marked split between arts and sciences. Although heroines are often represented as good at maths and sciences, these are dull subjects: it is the arts which hold the romance and the excitement. In the story 'I Want to Dance', the heroine has won a scholarship to a prestigious boarding school in some science fiction setting in the future. Here the girls are called by numbers and not names are made to study even when asleep, and music is forbidden: indeed, the heroine destroys a precious tape recorder for fear of being expelled. We have, therefore, another example of textual splitting: romance and excitement are the order of the day. While it is taken for granted that girls are good at maths and sciences, it is in the arts that the key to romance lies. Thus attainment in the arts is posed as a positive and desirable goal. It is the investment of desire in the arts and the absence of desire from the sciences (I *want* to dance) which is crucial in the formation of semiotic chains. Arts are not posed, therefore, as potentially antithetical to other desirable outcomes, as is the case in *Jackie* where there is no place for any notion of educational achievement.

The preparation for the prince

The themes which appear in the comics act as powerful signifiers keying into struggles which are central to the production of femininity and female sexuality. Although there is little overtly sexual about the significations here, girls may be *prepared* in certain important ways for current adolescent heterosexual practices which appear to offer a way out, a resolution to their victimisation. That is, although heterosexuality is not an overt *issue*, the other features of femininity are so produced in the pages of the comics as to render 'getting a man' the 'natural' solution.

These 'regimes of meaning' are as follows. Girls are victims of cruelty but they rise above their circumstances by servicing and being sensitive to *others* – selflessness. The girl who services is like the beautiful girl whose rewards for her good deeds is to be taken out of her misery; she is freed by the prince. The semiotic chain slides into romance as the solution, with the prince as saviour. It is here that girls are produced as victims ready to be saved, prefiguring the heterosexual practices of *Jackie*. Cruelty and victimisation are the key features, but it is precisely those features which are salient in the production of women as passively sexual. Victimisation and martyrdom in Christian myth, for example Lacan's (1982) reference to the ecstasy of St Theresa, carry similar significations, in this case women giving themselves for and to Christ. In her article 'Sexual Violence and Sexuality' (1982) Rosalind Coward also analyses representations of female sexuality which suggest that women are the passive victims of violence. She gives examples of photographs of women in poses of passivity connoting sexual pleasure. In one of these the 'victim' appears dead. Coward's gloss to these photographs reads 'The representation of female sexual pleasure, submission and the ultimate passivity, death' (p. 19). She states:

> This leads on to the question of the code of submission, which is similarly problematic. This is the dominant code by which female sexual pleasure is represented as simultaneously languid and turbulent, the combination of orgasm and passionate death. The explicit association with death which is frequently seen is extremely disturbing: women are shown in passionate submission, their posture evoking at best romantic deaths, at worst sexual murders. This overlayed on the potentiality of photography unconsciously to suggest death, creates a regime of disturbing and erotic photographs. Not only do they reinforce ideologies of sexuality as female submission to male force, but they also powerfully re-circulate the connection between sexuality and death which is so cruelly played out in our society. (p. 18)

The circulation of this regime of definite meanings relates cruelty and sexual excitement. As Coward argues, this linkage is not confined to pornography: it is ubiquitous, and, I would argue further, relates clearly to the meanings which are circulated in the comics and which slide into those of the sexual representation of women. It is the relation between the representations at the level of fantasy and the production of meanings through which desire is understood and into which desire is invested which is important.

Fiction, fantasy and desire

I want to begin this section by outlining the romantic resolution of desire for adolescent girls by citing Angela McRobbie's analysis of romance in *Jackie* (1982a). She lists several points. The first is that romance and not sex is the key to sexuality: it is the moment of bliss as signified by the first kiss which is made predominant. Secondly, girls' lives are portrayed as dominated by their emotions: jealousy, possessiveness, and devotion. These spell out the conflicts which are produced between girls, making other girls into enemies, because the heroine has first to get a boy and then keep him. McRobbie demonstrated the contradiction (which is underplayed in the magazine) that while getting and keeping men is a constant struggle for girls the potential for romance is all over the place from the bus stop to the disco. In this sense then, what one girl can achieve in getting a man is constantly threatened by others with the same designs. In this way feelings of insecurity are constantly reproduced. The arrival of the prince is presented as the *final* solution which, of course, glosses over the problem that keeping a man is a serious threat to 'happiness ever after'. It is thus a fraught and fragile solution, but one that remains attractive precisely because it is the getting and keeping of the man which in a very basic and crucial way establishes that the girl is 'good enough' and 'can have what she wants'. It is because getting a man is identified as a central resolution to problems of female desire that it acts so powerfully.

The same fatalism which is apparent in the way in which girls in the pre-teen comics are supposed to suffer in silence is present in *Jackie* as a fatalism about *loss*: in this case the loss of a boy. Girls who lose their boyfriend to *another* are supposed to suffer in silence, certainly not make a fuss or get angry, and are supposed to work towards the next relationship in the hope of 'better luck next time'. The girl is therefore encouraged to put work into attracting the *next* boy rather than examining any aspects of the past relationship or for that matter, relationships in general: the next prince might after all be the 'real thing'.

If fiction therefore presents fantasies by the use of textual devices which engage with the desires of the reader, this would suggest a very different understanding of the development of gender than the one which is most commonly asserted. Those approaches stressing roles and stereotypes suggest a girl who is already rational, who takes in information, or takes on roles. By contrast, psychoanalysis offers a dynamic model in which there is no simple or static reality perceived by children. Central to psychoanalytic accounts is the production of complex and tortuous conscious and unconscious relations, centred upon the girl's relations with her family. The account psychoanalysis offers presents a subject both more resistant to change than a rationalist account might suggest and engaged in a struggle in relation to the achievement of femininity and heterosexuality.

Recent advances in the study of texts have made use of psychoanalysis in understanding the production of textual identities. They provide a potential way forward for exploring the cultural practices which produce fantasies and the relation of those to the development of sexuality.

Freud himself located the production of sexuality in the relations of the family. I have already mentioned some of the concepts he used, for example the way in which 'actual interactions' or family relations are lived by the participants through the framework of complex systems of psychic fantasy relations. Hence the importance of the working through in fantasy of certain wishes, particularly in relation to the mother. Freud insisted that the pain of separation from the maternal body experienced by the child pushes the infant into a struggle to possess the mother, to be dependent on her and yet to control her. The experience of psychic distress caused through the inevitable failure of the mother to meet the child's insatiable demands sets up a particular dynamic between them. Freud distinguished between need and wish (or desire). He recognised that the fantasy created in the gap between possession and loss was not made good by any 'meeting of needs' because the satisfaction would only be temporary and the object of desire would both constantly shift and be out of reach. The presence of siblings produced a rivalry in relation to the mother, setting up its own particular familial dynamic. However, the presence of the father, whose possession of the mother creates further rivalry is of *crucial* importance to Freud's account of the production of sexual differ- ence. Although the little boy struggles for possession of his mother, in competition therefore with the father, the little girl can never possess the mother. Freud therefore postulates the struggle for the transfer of desire from the mother to the father to account for female heterosexuality.

Subsequent schools of psychoanalysis (particularly Kleinian and Object Relations accounts) have tended to stress a difference from Freud along a variety of dimensions. The first one concerns the countering of the emphasis on Oedipal relations. Along with the stress on the mother in Object Relations accounts there is also the diminution of the emphasis on wish or desire. Such accounts move toward the possibility in practice of the adequate meeting of the child's needs by the mother.

The stress on the meeting of needs has been countered by the approach offered by Lacan. This has emphasised the gap between needs for bodily comfort and food, and the way in which demand always exceeds satisfaction. Freud demonstrated the way in which infants hallucinated the milk which had been withdrawn by the breast, or played games in which the presence and absence of the mother was controlled in fantasy. In this sense, Freud concentrated on the creation of fantasy in the gap between need and wish-fulfilment. Lacan developed this and argued that the satisfaction of need is an illusion and one sustained by practices which produce fantasy or imaginary resolutions. Although infants are clearly gratified by the mother, this gratification 'contains the loss within it'. The price paid for consciousness is the first recognition of the mother as Other, and therefore of the me/not me. Lacan uses the example of an infant's gaze at its own reflection in a mirror to stress the idea that singular identity is illusory. The infant is dependent and relatively powerless, but an illusion of unity and control is created by this mirroring. Lacan's account then stresses the importance of the acquisition of language by the child as the means for control over both the initial loss of the mother and the capacity for self-reference, the illusion of control. He uses two terms: the Imaginary and the Symbolic. The Imaginary relates to the imaged state of self-recognition in the mirror. The Imaginary is the location of fantasy-resolutions, the illusion of the meeting of needs. This is why the fantasies of completion and resolution of psychic conflicts offered in children's fiction are so important. They proffer possible resolutions, held out as the meeting of needs and fantasies of identity (wholeness). The Symbolic Order is the site of control in language, which fixes meaning. The fixing of meaning offers certainty and knowledge: the idea that we can have control over our loss by knowing the truth. This truth is identified not with a 'real father' as such but by what Lacan calls the 'paternal metaphor'. Lacan uses the term 'Phallus' to describe that in which the Symbolic is invested, the breaking of the mother-child dyad. If the child first imagines control through language, then it is the father, not as real father, but imagined guardian of 'the word' who holds the key to the Symbolic Order and thus to control.

The problem of sexual difference relates to the contradictory paternal and maternal identifications involved in being/having the mother, making good the loss, and having/being in control by having/being the Phallus. It is in this sense that sexual identity is taken never to be a secure achievement because there is no easy fitting into available roles. However, because language and fantasy play such a crucial part, identities created in the everyday locations the child enters, in schooling, in texts, and so forth, offer locations for imaginary closure. They engage with psychic conflicts, identifications and resolutions. They are therefore both crucial to change and yet problematic at the same time.

In the pages of the pre-teen girls' comics, the heroines convey an overwhelming sense of loss, which is resolved by its investment into the selfless service of others. As we have seen, difficult feelings about that loss are dealt with in these comics by locating them in the 'bad' characters. They are displaced. Such displacements in psychoanalysis are dealt with by the defences, which are unconscious, so no other fantasy engagement with loss is presented than its displacement and rechannelling into service. Anger and aggression are then not so much not dealt with but dealt with in specific and important ways.

As we have seen in relation to the comics, the loss is not so much buried and denied as, for example, Eichenbaum and Orbach claim, as dealt with in particular ways (1982, p. 362). There are good girls and bad girls, naughty and nice, kind and horrible and so forth. It is not so much the simple case of a repression or suppression, or inability to deal with loss (in pain, jealousy, anger, etc) but *how* and *where* it is dealt with. We are not all 'good girls' who are selfless, and who have repressed anger. Some of us are and were angry, jealous, horrid. But bad girls are punished, positioned in various ways. Identities are created to deal with those characteristics. Those identities are gender-specific. Being a naughty boy and a naughty girl is a very different matter (see Walkerdine 1984). So it is not the case that girls do not deal with loss or that the culture denies the loss. Perhaps it is more the case that certain ways of resolving the loss are sanctioned and others prohibited and punished. Such sanctions and resolutions are presented in the fantasies created in these comics. They are also created in the practices which make up the daily lives of the young girls. Thus comics do not 'tell it like it is', there is no psychic determinism which they represent. Their very groupings of meaning provide vehicles for the content of the gender differentiation and the resolution. If they did not do so they would not be successful as cultural products. This latter point is absolutely central to my argument. I am not arguing for a position in which psychoanalysis helps us to understand the internalisation of norms of femininity through processes of identification. This would be to operate as though girls, in identifying with the texts of comics or with the position of their mother, 'became feminine'. Rather, my argument is about how to understand the relation of cultural products and practices to the production of and the resolution of, desire. Such relations are not fitted easily on to girls but are struggled over. What I am trying to demonstrate therefore is the way in which that struggle is lived and the relation of content to the proffered solutions to psychic and material struggles. Rose says:

all this happens at a cost, and that cost is the concept of the unconscious. What distinguishes psychoanalysis from sociological accounts of gender (hence for me the fundamental impasse of Nancy Chodorow's work) is that whereas for the latter, the internalisation of norms is assumed roughly to work, the basic premise and indeed the starting point of psychoanalysis is that it does not. The unconscious constantly reveals the 'failure' of identity. Because there is no continuity of psychic life, so there is no stability of sexual identity, no position for women (or for men) which is ever simply achieved. Nor does psychoanalysis see such 'failure' as a special case in ability or an individual deviancy from the norm. 'Failure' is not a moment to be regretted in a process of adaptation, or development into normality, which ideally takes its course (some of the earliest critics of Freud, such as Ernest Jones did, however, give an account of development in just these terms). Instead 'failure' is something endlessly repeated and re-lived moment by moment throughout our individual histories. It appears not only in the symptoms, but also in dreams, in slips of the tongue and in forms of sexual pleasure which are pushed to the sidelines of the norm. Feminism's affinity with psychoanalysis rests above all, I would argue, with this recognition that there is a resistance to identity which lies at the very heart of psychic life. Viewed this way, psychoanalysis is no longer best understood as an account of how women are fitted into place (even this, note, is the charitable reading of Freud). Instead, psychoanalysis becomes one of the few places in our culture where it is recognised as more than a fact of individual pathology that most women do not painlessly slip into their roles as women, if, indeed, they do at all. (Rose, 1983, p. 9)

What seems to be at issue is not a series of roles or simple identities or images which are fitted on to girls. Nor is it a matter of certain behaviours being 'stereotypically feminine' and therefore allowed and others not. Rather, we need to understand the relationship between those practices which not only define correct femininity and masculinity but which produce it by creating positions to occupy. So it is not the case of unitary identities, but a question of those practices which channel psychic conflicts and contradictions in particular ways. 'Good girls' are not always good – but where and how is their badness lived? What is the struggle which results from the attempt to be or live a unitary identity? Much work is necessary to engage with such questions. But we might begin by exploring how different positions are produced and understood. In the comics good girls and bad girls are different personalities: they are mutually exclusive. So theories of 'personality' help to create a truth which informs those current practices which position girls in identity. Naughty girls might be maladjusted, or juvenile delinquents for example. In such practices relational dynamics and shifting identities are denied in favour of a fixed and measurable unitariness. Similarly, naughtiness in boys and girls is understood and lived in different ways. So, there is a complex and important relationship between theories and practices which produce truth and identities, and the contradictory, multiple positioning, of the little girls. I have examined one example of a practice: the fantasy of girls' comics. We might also look at the practices of schooling which produce positions for girls and claim to know the truth of such girls as singular beings: with personalities, intelligence and so on (Walden and Walkerdine, 1983; Walkerdine, 1984).

Towards the possibility of alternative practices

Finally then, if we want to understand the production of girls as subjects and the production of alternatives for girls, we must take account of desire and fantasy. It is no good resorting to a rationalist account which consists simply in changing images and attitudes. If new content in whatever form does not map on to the crucial issues around desire, then we should not be surprised if it fails as an intervention. Unfortunately, what happens when such interventions fail is that they leave the field wide open for reactionary explanations of femininity which after all 'must be true' if 'social conditioning' approaches fail to produce shifts in girls' actions and aspirations. Whatever we propose as alternatives, we have to recognise and deal with the production, fixing, and canalisation, of desire. Whether in this case we want to think about alternative cultural products or what form our intervention should take is an open question which must be urgently addressed.

Practices which put forward the possibility of alternative litera-ture and images for girls create a set of conflicts and contradictions for girls which often go unrecognised and may in fact make the struggle more difficult. For example, it is quite common in alternative or feminist literature for young children, to display women and girls engaged in activities traditionally undertaken by men. In psychoanalytic theory, one problem for girls in the struggle for femininity is the coming to terms with the recognition that the mother once considered all-powerful (the Phallic Mother) does not have the phallus. This becomes important in the move away from a simply located desire for the mother. Now, while shifts and transformations in practice mean that women can occupy positions which invest them with the phallus, they, too, are not coherent and non-contradictory identities. Just as Lacan has suggested that the 'phallus is a fraud' (that men also do not possess it, but rather struggle to achieve it) so women cannot be the Phallic Mother in any complete or total sense. This is not to suggest that those practices which position women are not important, nor that it is unimportant for girls to have powerful mothers. Rather it is suggested again that such a simple image or appropriation is more problematic and complex than it might at first appear. In one feminist reworking of a classic fairy tale the princess, instead of marrying the prince, goes off to be a feminist decorator in dungarees! What we need to ask here is how such texts operate at the level of fantasy. For some girls they might well provide the vehicle for an alternative vision, while for others they might, by stressing the one as alternative to the other, feed or fuel a resistance *to* the feminist alternative. We are only just beginning to explore such issues in relation to texts and readings.

We could ask, therefore, what exactly fiction, along with other cultural practices, produces for girls. And in examining current practices we can begin to explore the constitution of femininity and masculinity as not *fixed* or *appropriated*, but *struggled over* in a complex relational dynamic. The question of alternative fictions for girls might then engage with the relational dynamic. How might other kinds of fantasies be produced which deal differently with desires and conflicts? What other fantasy resolutions might be offered? What about characters who are not simply good or bad? Similarly, stories which engage with conflicts might relate to other kinds of resolution than a simple displacement to a future reward for present pain. It is not enough simply to present conflicts. If wish-fulfilment through fantasy is an important device for working through conflict, then resolutions will have to be engaged with, to create possible paths for action. By examining how present cultural practices deal with and offer resolutions to conflicts, we can understand both how they work and what they do and do not speak. By examining these alongside an understanding of the production of sexuality, we might begin to see what alternative fictions and fantasies could look like. If current fictions produce such powerful effects, such potent fantasies, we too must work on the production of other possible dreams and fantasies.

Notes

1. In psychoanalysis the term *phantasy* is classically used rather than *fantasy*. This is because the term is intended to be wider usage than simple imaginary production, but relates to the 'world of the imagination' (Laplanche and Pontalis, 1980, p. 314)
2. It is significant that when interviewing nine and ten year old girls as part of my current research, the girls gave me anger and selfishness as bad qualities in themselves, some to the extent that they could not claim to possess any qualities which they felt to be good.

8

Alice in the Consumer Wonderland: West German case studies in gender and consumer culture

Erica Carter

Changing gear: a reappraisal of the politics of style

People say ... well, what don't they say about teenagers?!
They start with the accusation that we have no manners or
sense of good behaviour, and that we're hopelessly lacking in
all religious belief. Then we are told off, either for dressing too
sloppily, or looking too old for our age ... 'Either', we are told,
'you run around like tramps in floppy jackets buttoned up at
the back and drainpipe trousers which are far too tight – or else
you slavishly follow the latest fashion trends'.
We would like for once to give our point of view ... We
teenagers have our own style. And that's what makes many
people see red.
(Advertisement for 'Triumph' underwear, *Bravo* magazine,
no. 42, 1958)

Since the beginning of the 1970s, theorists of youth subcultures in
Britain have appropriated the notion of 'style' from marketers of
teenage fashion commodities, and mobilised it for their studies of
oppositional subcultures in the post-war period. Recalling a tradition of cultural studies which reaches back to Richard Hoggart's
Uses of Literacy (Hoggart, 1958), early analysts of subcultural
deviance and opposition[1] seem implicitly to share his distaste for the
plastic glamour of commercialised youth culture; their gaze falls
rather on visible subversions of dominant forms. The discordant

notes sounded by Teds, rockers, mods, rastas or punks are seen to be pitched against the harmony of mass consumer culture; appropriating commodities from fashion, music and media industries, subcultural youths reassemble them into symbolic systems of their own which, if only at the moment of their birth, strike chords of disenchantment, rebellion and resistance. Like the phenomena which they examine, the analyses themselves are founded on a number of unspoken oppositions: conformity and resistance, harmony and rupture, passivity and activity, consumption and appropriation, femininity and masculinity.

In a discussion of sexism amongst the working-class lads of his 'Hammertown' study, Paul Willis finds himself slipping with ease into the discourse of consumerism.

> The male counter-school culture promotes its own sexism – even celebrates it as part of its overall confidence. Girls are pursued, sometimes roughly, for their sexual favours, often dropped and labelled 'loose' when they are given. Girls are asked to be sexy and inviting as well as pure and monogamous; to be consumed and not be consumed. (Willis, 1977, p. 146)

In a study from which girls are largely absent, the moment of their appearance is profoundly significant. Girls, it seems, are written into youth cultural theory in the language of consumption; initially – though not, as we shall see, of necessity – as objects for consumption by men. Under the regime of Althusserian structuralism in British cultural theory, this led to the perception of girls at best as an absence, a silence, a lack which could perhaps only be filled in some separate world of autonomous female culture. Ideology was an 'instance', consumption a 'sphere', severed from its tangled roots in the social institutions with which structuralism was primarily concerned – the family, ideology and the repressive State. Feminist researchers then turned towards the family as the pivotal point around which the existence of teenage girls revolved.

> If women are marginal to the male cultures of work (middle and working class) it is because they are central and pivotal to a subordinate area, which mirrors, but in a complementary and subordinate way, the 'dominant' masculine arenas. They are 'marginal' to work because they are central to the subordinate,

complementary sphere of the family. (McRobbie and Garber, 1976, p. 211)

Following working-class girls into the closed arena of the family allowed the researchers of female culture privileged insights into the possibilities of specifically female cultural forms. So-called 'bedroom culture' was analagous to male subcultures, in that here too dominant signs and symbols were appropriated, reassembled and reproduced in homology[2] with an already existing set of social relations. In male youth subcultures, these homologies existed between the lived culture of a subordinate *class* and the symbolic systems through which its members made that culture 'mean'. In bedroom culture, gender relations overlaid, overlapped and took precedence over relations of race and class.

Yet the search for autonomous female cultural forms in the bedroom hideaways of teenage girls has been consistently dogged by nagging doubts as to the creative, productive and potentially subversive power of this mode of femininity. The study of 'teeny bopper culture', for example, was recognised as a key which might unlock the potentialities of specifically female forms; on the other hand, teenage adulation of male pop idols remained a symbol of the 'future general subordination' of adolescent girls (McRobbie and Garber, 1976, p. 219). One problem with taking subculture theory as a starting point for studies of female culture was that the homologies which 'profane culture' moulded and shaped for itself were always preformed – and more readily reformed at the slightest hint of female autonomy – by an ever-watchful capitalist market.

The spectacle of working-class subcultures erupted into a yawning gap between class relations as they are lived by working-class youth, and the classless categories according to which capitalist markets are structured. Ever since Warner's classic study of social class in America (Warner, 1960) the marketing establishment has measured consumers against typological grids on which 'class' appears primarily as an attribute of personal status and income; working-class subcultures are, in part, a raucous rejection of a consumer culture which has continually repressed the seamier side of class subordination from view. Gender, on the other hand, operates as a dominant variable for the structuring of consumer groups. Thus not only have market researchers developed a vast apparatus of consumer surveillance which ensures the immediate recuperation and reassimilation of new – or hitherto unheeded – facets of femininity; the 'image industries' (fashion, cosmetics, the female mass media) have also consistently drawn on these marketing data to produce symbolic representations which fit skintight to female experiences. Hence the difference in mood, tone and resonance of masculine and feminine revolts into style. Male 'semiological guerillas' plunder the symbolic treasure chests of consumer culture, recreating their booty as signifiers of resistance whose signifier – the disaffection of subordinate class fractions – was until recently banished from the symbolic landscape of the teenage mass market. Conversely, even the unpleasures of femininity find continual, if oblique, reflection in commodities on the female market, from perfect cures for the imperfections of the female body (slimming pills, aerobic outfits, beauty aids), to more expensive, and correspondingly drastic remedies for the psychic ailments of the female condition – from nerve-tonics to psychoanalysis, with Babycham to add a touch of sparkle.

Deviance, resistance, autonomy, revolt: in the sociological tradition of the academic Left, these are located beyond the hostile walls of an impassive monolith – the Market. Analyses of subcultural style represented an attempt to freeze commodities-as-signifiers into fixed relations of subversive opposition; the (re)marketing of punk safety-pins and crazy-colour hairstyles was dubbed a 'recuperation' – silencing, defeat. The first punk safety-pin to spill off the end of the mass production line did indeed dislodge punk from its anchorage in the adolescent culture of the urban working classes; yet at the same time, it carried the meanings and values of punk into a wider field of teenage mass culture, where its progress has yet to be properly charted.

If subculture theory has traditionally remained standing somewhat suspiciously on the sidelines of commercial youth culture, the same has not always been true of research into girls' culture. Women researchers have had to plunge, head-on at times, into the seething morass of capital flows, emerging with a proliferation of critiques of the commodities which pattern the fabric of girls' lives: advertising images, fashionable clothes, mass magazines, popular ficiton. In feminist theory too, the theoretical terrain for a re-engagement with market mechanisms has been prepared since the beginning of the break with Althusser and structuralism. The market is not an institution with rigidly defined (if consistently subverted) hierarchies, structures, orders and conventions; neither is it a tightly-knit subculture whose practices and rituals can be traced onto frozen 'maps of meaning'. It is instead a vast machine for the regulation of interconnecting circulatory flows: the flow of capital and labour through the production process, the flows of money, commodities, visual and textual signifiers through the circuits of consumption unlocked by capital.

Recognising market practices as constant and unbroken flows demands a similarly supple set of categories for their analysis; the homologies and oppositions of structuralist symbolic deconstructions offer only one of many routes into the fragmented and splintered realities of female consumption. Shifting onto more fluid epistemological ground will not entail a feminist farewell to subcultures: charting the labyrinth of female market practices, we will be led to girls and women within *and* outside subcultures, all of whom participate in the regulation and organisation of market processes. The machine itself, if vast and apparently all-embracing, is never intrinsically monstrous; it is both manipulative and manipulated, controlled and controlling. Girls and women surface on a multitude of levels as both objects and agents of market processes: so, for example, the eighties boom in the second-hand rag trade owes its greatest debt to the 'nouvelle entrepreneuse' of New Wave subculture (and signals, incidentally, a successful attempt to divert fashion's commodity flows from their source in monopoly capitalist production).

An 'archaeology' of female consumption

Across the landscape of post-war mass markets, female consumers, too, emerge both as 'objects' (of market research, advertising campaigns, sexual consumption by men) and as active agents in consumption processes. The work presented in the following pages – studies of specific instances of female 'consumer culture' in post-war West Germany – represents a first step towards a latter-day 'archaeology' of female consumption; an attempt to grasp and represent aspects of female consumerism in all their myriad complexities; and an appeal for the postponement of premature outrage at the 'co-option', 'recuperation', 'objectification' of women and girls in post-war consumer culture.

The nascent Federal Republic of Germany may seem an unlikely point of departure. Yet the very distance between areas of study (in this case, both geographical and conceptual in nature) forces the disruption of established modes of understanding, pointing the way towards potentially more fertile theoretical terrain. In the first instance, looking at German attempts to build a new democracy out of the shattered ruins of Germany's Nazi past can shed light on processes which, in Britain, took on less visible forms. Germany in 1945 lacked the cosy security of the cultural institutions in which British democratic values were founded – from fair play in English cricket, to resonances of Empire in the British cup of tea. Analogous cultural forms and practices in post-war Germany resounded still with echoes of Nazism; meanwhile, the allied western powers demanded tangible evidence of a decisive break with the totalitarian past. The West German constitution of 1949, then was offered as an anchorage point for the fragile floating remnants of Weimar democracy; it contained, importantly, explicit guarantees of the equality of women and men before the law. The first section of the following study traces some of the processes whereby these constitutional promises came to be realised in the course of the 1950s. In practice, the explicit inscription of women as equal subjects in legal discourse was negotiated through their installation as consumers in a 'social market economy'; citizenship for women thus came to be defined through consumption on a capitalist mass market.

This, then, is a study of the ways in which the post-war market colonised and rooted itself in political discourses and institutions. The caesura of 1945 in Germany; attempts to suffocate a Nazi past under the cushion of consumer democracy; these may throw into sharper relief analogous developments in the consumerism of post-war Britain. Here as in Germany the middle-class housewife enacted her political enfranchisement through the exercise of economic rationality: choosing to buy or not to buy, to spend or to save, to covet or to shun.

Certainly in 1950s West Germany, this was part of the 'political' future to which teenage girls were widely urged to aspire; at the same time, the expanding market in teenage leisure commodities transported adolescent consumption into a separate dimension of 'symbolic' and 'hedonistic' pleasures (Woods, 1960). In the second section, then, I look at some aspects of fifties' leisure consumption for girls; at the symbolic systems of teenage lifestyles; and at one specific instance of female mass consumption: artificial 'silk' stockings for teenage girls. Heavily laden though nylons may be with predetermined 'sexist' meanings, a cool appraisal of the actual mode of their consumption reveals teenage girls engaged in the production of meanings and values more appropriate to their own needs. Nylon stockings, imported *en masse* from the USA, may appear simply as one of the more visible manifestations of American cultural hegemony. Yet a closer look at this one element in an emergent, and largely imported, teenage culture of consumption, points towards different questions to be asked of the process of consumption itself. Passive manipulation or active appropriation, escapist delusion or Utopian fantasy, consumerism can be all or none of these. The first step in its analysis is *rapprochement*, the dismantling of fronts in the youth cultural struggle, a recognition and reformulation of demands (our own included) for the pleasures which consumerism offers. 'Saying yes to the modern world is much more controversial and more provocative than saying no' (Freiwillige Selbstkontrolle, on West German rock).

Women and girls in the consumer public

The history of the public sphere in Germany has been documented in detail by Habermas in his *Structural Change in the Public Sphere*, first published in Germany in 1962. In it he traces the history of the transition in Germany from the 'representative public' of feudal times, marked, not by the later strict division between public and private spheres, but by the investment of public status in particular representative figures – the aristocracy, representatives of the Church and of the Crown. In the transition to bourgeois society, 'public' and 'private' came to be understood as distinct and separate spheres, the family and the workplace being primary sites of 'private' activity, against which the notion of a public sphere was defined. 'Offentlichkeit' (the public sphere) becomes the field of public discourse within institutions which understand themselves as bearers of a 'public opinion', a dominant consensus to which members of society purportedly subscribe.

From the eighteenth century onwards, the preferred institution of the bourgeois public, within which the interests of collectivities of individuals could find objective representation, was the press; and it is with the transformation of that institution through economic and technical innovation (primarily, through the increasing concentration of the press in late capitalism and the development of the electronic media) that a transformation of the bourgeois public also takes place. According to the liberal model of a free press, the medium retained its objective and unbiased character through its ownership by private individuals, who were by definition free from the partiality of State institutions. In the twentieth century, however, the increasing commercialisation of the press through its ever greater depenence on advertising revenue, as well as processes of economic and technological concentration, have called into question this equation of free speech with private ownership. Indeed, the legitimation crisis in the twentieth-century press is symptomatic of fundamental dislocations in the traditional bourgeois public. In an economic system founded on giant national and multinational corporations, economic power coalesces in ever larger blocks, opaque to the 'average' individual and clearly no longer always representative of her or his interests. Definitions of equality as equality in private ownership must, then, give way to new terms which reinvest power in the hands of the individual. In West Germany in the fifties precisely this shift took place, with the development of so-called 'consumer democracy'.

Ludwig Erhard, Minister for Economic Affairs under Adenauer, is remembered primarily as the prophet and founder of West Germany's social market economy. He defines the basic economic freedoms of the post-war German state in the following terms:

> by this is meant first and foremost the freedom of all citizens to shape their lives in a form adequate to the personal wishes and conceptions of the individual, within the framework of the financial means at their disposal. This *basic democratic right of consumer freedom* must find its logical counterpart in the freedom of the entrepreneur to produce or distribute whatever he thinks necessary and potentially successful in a given market context . . . Every citizen must be conscious of consumer freedom and the freedom of economic enterprise as basic and inalienable rights, whose violation should be punished as an assault on our social order. Democracy and a free economy belong as logically together as do dictatorship and a State economy. (Erhard, 1962, p. 10: author's emphasis)

Democracy realised, then, in the equality of producers and consumers as social partners striving towards a common goal: 'Wohlstand fur alle' (Prosperity for All). The rhetoric of consumer democracy borrows connotations of 'freedom', 'equality' and 'democratic rights' from classic notions of a critical and reasoning public, grafting these on to the concept of a mutual dependency between two equal partners, producer and consumer. The consumer public exercises its critical faculties in the 'rational' choice of those commodites which best correspond to its needs; power is invested in the hands of consumers, insofar as they may refuse products which fail to meet those needs.

If, in the fifties, consumer democracy became a byword of parliamentary rhetoric, then this was not simply the result of a single shift between two separate spheres, public and private. The 'public' is never unitary, always fragmentary; there is no unified public sphere, but instead an 'accumulation of public forms' (Bommes and Wright, 1982, p. 260) – television, the press, the educational apparatus, political parties, the army, church and legal establishment. Relations between public institutions and the organs of a monopoly capitalist economy are diverse; the managing director of a multinational company may be nominated for the post of government minister;[3] the same multinational may finance sports meetings or other cultural events; its sales director may frequent the same night club as well-known media magnates. Or those relations may be more ephemeral, locatable on the level of representation: the recurrence of single signifiers (freedom, humanity, femininity) across a range of discourses, and the associative chains thereby forged. Or again they may be rooted in interconnecting networks of finance; thus, for example, German marketing experts in the late 1950s advocated state financing of commercial market research, to be carried out by state educational institutions, universities and other research bodies, and used by commodity producers for forward planning. To study transformations in the public sphere is, then, both to examine specific sites on which a 'public' is constructed and, at the same time, to trace the wider network of relations through which these disparate elements are assembled into an ideological unity, the 'public sphere' at large. The notion of the 'rational consumer' slots in neatly here, as a link forged on a multiplicity of sites between the post-war state and an expanding capitalist economy. Capital was hungry for new markets, the

German nation for democracy. Conflating concepts of freedom and democracy with images of a critical consumer was an indispensable mechanism in the organisation of public consensus in the emergent social market economy. Thus Erhard, in a section of his book *Prosperity for all* entitled 'The Will to Consume', makes consumption the very foundation of liberation and human dignity.

> Only if the economy is subject to continuous pressure from the consumption sphere will the production sphere retain the strength and fluidity to accommodate increased demand and free the population from material deprivation and difficulty . . . Increased wealth . . . is the necessary basis for the liberation of human beings from primitive and purely materialist modes of thought. (Erhard, 1957, p. 134)

Women and citizenship

Within eighteenth and nineteenth-century political discourse, 'citizenship', though never marked as such, was in fact a masculine category; in state institutions which claimed to represent the interests of the collectivity at large, women's economic and political freedoms were severely curtailed, if not in some areas non-existent. Within 1950s definitions of the citizen-as-consumer, the position was reversed. The 'consumer', too, was a non-gendered category. Yet in relation to family consumption, it was women – specifically housewives – to whom it was applied. By the end of the fifties, the voices of official political and social scientific orthodoxy in West Germany were proclaiming that patriarchy was dead. Anchored in Article III of the constitution, women's formal equality was seen to have been realised in the gradual restructuring of gender relations at work and in the home, according to an overriding principle of 'equality in difference'. Equal rights legislation passed in 1957 outlined the practical effects of Article III ('Men and Women are equal') for the private lives of married couples. Wife and husband were to be mutually responsible for all decisions relating to their life together; the one significant exception to this rule was Paragraph 1356, which began: 'The wife carries sole responsibility for the running of the household'. Domestic labour remained in law the exclusive province of the married women; legally, the assumption of this housewifely role was defined at one and the same time as a woman's right and as her duty, both to her husband and to the community at large.

In this sense, women could be seen to be fulfilling a public role in performing the daily tasks of domestic labour. Yet it was not enough for women to continue practising traditional forms of childcare, cookery, shopping and cleaning; as Erhard had emphasised, true integration into the democratic public demanded more sophisticated modes of consumption, which alone could fuel the economy on which democracy depended. More importantly, equating the rights of citizenship with women's right to consume allowed a neat integration of women's demands for equality into a consumer-oriented economy. Thus it was as consumers that women were called upon by public institutions to work for the good of the community at large. Housewives' organisations were regularly called in by government bodies for advice and information on consumer affairs. In 1956, the Adenauer government passed a bill revising and expanding Federal regulations on food standards and labelling. Not only had the bill been drafted almost exclusively by fifty-two female members of the Bundestag; the campaign for the revision of existing regulations had also been carried by women's organisations, who had worked together with nutritional scientists and consumer pressure groups.

The 7 per cent of the female population organised in housewives' associations constituted a powerful pressure group in itself; at the same time, the non-organised housewife was commonly depicted as having similar power to influence state legislation and market trends. One such grandiose claim was made by consumer expert Ingrid Landgrebe-Wolff on behalf of the American housewife, whom she saw in 1957 as actively participating in the development of world food markets, in ways as yet unfamiliar to German women. She cites as a classic example the coffee market of the mid-1950s, when demand fell rapidly as a result of rising prices. Even for a beverage so central to the diet of the average American, housewives were unwilling to pay the exorbitant prices demanded. They turned instead to tea, milk or malt drinks, leaving coffee companies in despair over mounting stockpiles. The housewife demanded cheaper coffee, and in the end not only packaging companies, but also growers of coffee for the international market, were forced to comply. World prices sank, breathing new life into the American home market. 'Thus', concludes Landgrebe-Wolff, 'the American housewife finally had her way' (Landgrebe-Wolff, 1957, p. 56).

Teenage girls in the consumer public

There are no simple connections to be made between women's position within relations of consumption for the fifties family, and the situation of adolescent girls as consumers on a mass teenage market. On the one hand, it was clearly the case that women taking up their new position of equality were seen to be lacking in the qualities necessary for democratic citizenship. Since women's assumed tendency to be over-emotional was said to hamper them in the exercise of rational consumer choice, it became the task of both state and private institutions (centrally, of course, the advertising establishment) to educate women into the required patterns of consumption.

There is, then, indeed a sense in which drives towards the end of the decade to initiate girls into new modes of consumption were simply preparing them for their entry into an adult female world. On the other hand, teenage consumption, revolving as it did around leisure commodities, was clearly distinct from that practised by housewives. Why, after all, should girls with a well-trained eye for fashionable colour combinations – the right shade of lipstick to set off matching gloves and shoes – necessarily be similarly adept at differentiating between an increasingly confusing variety of washing-powder brands?

Yet via the notion of the 'public', there are crucial links to be made. For the fifties housewives, one component of domestic labour – shopping – was lifted out of the enclaves of home and the local street, and transferred to the 'public' terrain of the supermarket and the neighbourhood or regional shopping centre. Abstract promises of a public identity for women as consumers took concrete form in the reorganisation of public space around centralised loci of commodity exchange. Shops and stores gradually abandoned earlier styles of personal service, in favour of more up-to-date self-service methods. A number of stores introduced the so-called 'Kiebitz' system, displaying placards or badges which invited the customer to 'come in and look around', with no obligation to buy. Shop displays were reordered accordingly, with an emphasis on the commodity as image and spectacle; at the same time, posters and labels on or near individual articles drew the customers' attention to their particular advantages. Firms originally specialising in mail-order delivery expanded their department store chains; in urban centres in particular, specialist shops began to lose custom to larger department stores and supermarkets.

Developments in town planning further accelerated the centralisation of the consumption process. West Berlin was particularly interesting in this respect; having sustained heavy bombing in the Second World War, the city centre was a blank page across which architects and town planners would write the forms of their social Utopias. In 1946, a town planning collective under the directorship of Hans Scharoun opened debates on the future of the city with an exhibition, 'Berlin plant' (Berlin plans). They proposed using the wide-open spaces left by bomb damage to break with previous traditions of high-density housing and closed communities in which living, sometimes also working-space had been integrated with leisure facilities – the obligatory 'Eckkneipe' (local bar) – and other points of commodity exchange: the equally indispensable 'Tante-Emma-Laden' ('Aunt Emma's corner shop'). The post-war Berlin of Scharoun was to draw sharp boundaries between these diverse spheres of city life; strips of parkland and fast, wide roads were to divide off residential areas from commercial quarters, and from sites of work and leisure – including centralised shopping areas.

Through their integration into an expanding teenage market, adolescent girls were drawn in increasing numbers into this new public space. The new generation of young consumers were particularly attracted to self-service and department stores, where they were free to look, compare and admire at their leisure, with no immediate compulsion to buy. A 1957 Intermarket survey of West German consumer habits records the preference of teenagers for these more impersonal stores, as well as their predilection for the 'Americanised' off-the-peg fashions still regarded with suspicion by their older compatriots.

If girls are absent from subcultures, then, they become visible at the point of consumption. Working-class girls in particular have never been entirely absent from the street, the cinema or the dancehall; they have not lived a life of seclusion away from the eyes of predatory men. A favourite occupation of young female factory workers in 1950s West Germany was an evening stroll along main streets, in search of excitement and the company of contemporaries. Again, it was shopping which drew them onto the street and into public life. In a series of sociological monographs published in 1958 (Wurzbacher and Jaide, 1958, pp. 169–70), Bärbel – fifteen-years-old at the time of the study, and employed since leaving school in a knitwear factory – relates how she is sent out every evening to fetch milk for the family (a duty she is only too happy to perform, since the dairy is a favourite meeting place for a large proportion of the local village youth).

Here new films and the latest fashions are discussed. The boys at first set themselves a little apart, in order to be able to pass comment on the girls; later they make attempts to pick them up. This is a place for young people to talk together; this is the place where dates are made. There is always something going on at the dairy.

If the market offers itself to women and girls as a stage for the production of themselves as public beings, then it does so on particularly unfavourable terms. Bärbel's dairy was a meeting place for separate groups of boys and girls: the girls, whatever their own motives for assembling there, found themselves on display to boys angling for a date – or something more. It is this overwhelming power of men to position women as sexual prey that has made the feminist search for autonomous female subcultures so consistently difficult. Doubtless, though, the difficulty resides equally in the subculturalists' choice of object, cultural resistance being located chiefly in formal innovations by an adolescent avant-garde. If anything is to be learned about the lived realities of consumption, then we must shift the terms of the youth culture debate, looking first at the dominant forms of a supposedly conformist culture of consumerism (as well as its everyday subversions). One route into this project is the examination of teenage lifestyles: of their assemblage on the production line of commodities for the teenage market, and their deconstruction, appropriation, subversion and reassemblage by teenage girls themselves.

Girls in West Germany and the teenage dream

The word teenager first entered the German language in the 1950s, imported like chewing gum and Coca-Cola from the USA, and vibrant with connotations of crazy styles, zany humour, rock'n'roll parties, Elvis, James Dean, loud music and soft park-bench romance. Its partner, the 'Twen', arrived around the same time and is of somewhat more dubious origin. Signifying 'young people in their twenties', it relied on associations of Americanness ('false' ones, insofar as the 'Twen' does not exist outside Germany) to construct an image of the older, more responsible, but nonetheless fun-loving party-going free-spending twenty-year-old. The average marital age in late 1950s Germany was twenty-six, and the relatively high disposable income of unmarried 'Twens' made them particularly attractive to producers of consumer goods in the upper price range of the leisure market. A survey carried out by the DIVO Market Research Institute in 1961 estimated the disposable income of twenty-one to twenty-four-year-olds by 1960 at DM192 per month for men (compared with DM91 for seventeen to twenty-year-olds), and DM180 per month for women (compared with DM100 for their seventeen- to twenty-year-old counterparts).

It was on the teenage market, then, that girls represented a particularly attractive target group for the leisure industries. During their late teens (from the age of fifteen onwards) girls in general drew a higher income than boys, but dropped back below their male contemporaries on reaching the age of twenty. In part, this resulted from their greater store of 'cultural capital' (Bourdieu, 1967); girls leaving school in their mid-teens were likely to be initially better qualified for jobs requiring school certificates (Volks-schulabschlüsse), while boys tended to make up for their lack of academic qualifications by entering an initially lower-paid appren-ticeship or trainee post. The most lucrative section of the female market, then, was the group of 'Angestellte' (clerical and secretarial workers); their disposable income amounted to three or four times that of their grammar school and college counterparts, or of working-class girls in unskilled factory work. Girls on the margins of the middle income bracket were, in a sense, the deviants of marketing discourse, and 'Angestellte' the norm against which teenage market potential was measured.

To the marketing establishment, it was clear that the golden egg of the female market had to be cracked with care. The male leisure market offered no adequate model for marketing to girls for whom leisure and pleasure were elastic and unstable terms. Female consumption constantly slipped between the grey world of work on the one hand and, on the other, the glittering but (above all sexually) dangerous domain of unbounded hedonism. The leisure commodities favoured by boys offered pathways to present and immediate pleasures; for girls, on the other hand so-called 'leisure' commodities embodied their more sober demands for future security in a precarious world. Girls in the middle to higher income brackets spent a significant portion of their income as unmarried females on collecting objects for their bottom drawer. This traditional feminine institution, having gone into decline in the austerity years of the forties and early fifties, celebrated its comeback towards the end of the decade, when girls began once again to collect bedclothes, table linen, crockery, cutlery, glasswear – the accoutrements of the bourgeois domestic idyll. Teenage boys and young men, meanwhile, were busily buying motor-bikes, cars, cameras, sports equipment and other consumer durables: the only piece of technical equipment more highly favoured by female consumers was the typewriter (Scharmann, 1965, pp. 33–8). Like the bottom drawer (which raised women's value on the marriage market) the typewriter represented an investment in a comfortable future, girls' production of themselves as desirable commodities on a competitive job market, and a key to the door of future financial security.

Private faces in public places

As girls and women entered the post-war market place, whole new areas of their lives began to become the 'public' property of marketing institutions. Modern surveillance systems were installed in shops and supermarkets for the observation and control of consumer behaviour: consumer panels were constituted as a source of information on attitudes to specific commodities and brands: 'in-depth' psychological testing came into vogue with the rise of

Housewife. Berliner Morgenpost, 26th Feb. 1961. "Women as consumers play an important role in today's economic life. As managers of the household budget, they exert a considerable influence on the market as a whole".

Berliner Morgenpost, 18th Nov. 1962. "On the control stand of a large supermarket. Equipped with a TV screen and loudspeakers, supermarket managers will in future watch over the shopping process. In the United States, this equipment is said to have brought positive results. . . . The manager can contact each shop-assistant by telephone. But the television eye does not only control the sales personnel. Light-fingered shoppers, too, who take 'self-service' all too literally, are no longer quite so unobserved as they perhaps feel".

Berliner Morgenpost, Cyd Charisse and Fred Astaire in *Silk Stockings*. 13th Feb. 1957. "After the fashion of so-called 'drain-pipe' trousers had come into vogue in girls' schools . . . the school authorities decided to put a stop to this indecency and recommended the girls to change into more 'seemly' attire. Now only the afternoons after school remain for them to take a walk with their 'drain-pipes'".

motivation research. Investigations into consumer behaviour required a massive apparatus for the gathering and processing of data on consumer habits, preference, tastes and whims; hence the post-war boom in market research, when the five major West German institutes (DIVO, EMNID, GfM, IFD, INFRATEST) were founded in the space of as many years, between 1945 and 1950. The unifying principle of diverse market research techniques was the regulation of information flows, which were to proceed in one direction only: from the consumer upwards to the institutions of the image production industries. Here, data on consumers would be 'reprocessed', before being returned to them in the shape of commodity representations: product design, packaging, advertising, public relations. Until reaching the stage of its reproduction in these more palatable forms, knowledge of the consumer was channelled through scientific discourses within which she was placed only as object, never as subject of the consumption process. In commodity representations the situation was reversed. The same knowledge was used by the image industries to construct image commodities-as-symbols, from advertising images to fashionable clothes for a teenage mass market. First however, it had to be 'translated' from the terms of social science into those of what may be called the 'commodity aesthetic' within which, importantly, consumers were replaced as subjects of consumption practices.

Since the second half of the nineteenth century, the proliferation and increasing differentiation of public images of and for women has been intimately bound up with their role as consumers. The effects of market research have been visible for almost a century in the newspaper industry; as early as the 1890s in America, newspapers began to extend society news and entertainment sections, after they discovered that women – the audience at whom these features were primarily aimed – carried the greatest potential as a future consumer market (Noelle, 1940, p. 92). Yet it was not until well into the 1950s that market research in Germany first turned its attention to the younger generation of female consumers. In 1959, the Gesellschaft für Marktforschung carried out a survey of 1500 male and female teenagers between the ages of fourteen and nineteen. The study was supplemented by further investigations in 1960, which aimed both 'to re-examine certain findings of the previous year' and 'to gain further basic insights into this important consumer group' (Scharmann, 1965, p. 17). While sociological and media research carried out earlier in the decade had confined itself to quantitative studies of adolescent leisure pursuits the GfM study was the first to focus specifically on the teenager as consumer and to attempt a broad sociometric analysis of teenage habits, preference and tastes.

In 1961, DIVO followed the GfM lead with a report commissioned by the advertising editors of *Bravo* magazine, a music, film, television, fashion and fiction teenage weekly which had been launched five years previously in 1956. By the early sixties, *Bravo* had already established itself as a leading light on the developing market for magazines aimed at a specifically teenage (male and female) readership. The 1961 survey aimed to spotlight the potential of the teenage market for the advertisers on whose revenue the magazine increasingly depended. *Bravo*, they argued, could operate as a bridge to span the gap between commodity producers, advertisers and consumers; its potential for success lay in its proven ability to capture and sustain a loyal readership amongst young people between the ages of twelve and twenty-four. In offering advertising space to the producers of commodities for a teenage market, it could ensure the dissemination of commodity representations amongst a teenage public constituted as such primarily through their role as consumers. *Bravo* readers, the publishers claim, are to be 'taken seriously' as consumers; for it is as such, they say, that teenagers primarily understand themselves.

> Confronted daily with literally hundreds of magazines and newspapers, young people may, it is true, pick up any one of them at any given time. Yet the only medium which will truly appeal to them is one which they feel is meant for and aimed only at them. They want, rightly, to be taken seriously enough for efforts to be made directly on their behalf. This is why *Bravo* has to be the way it is. (DIVO, 1961)

In the face of moral outrage on the part of teachers, parents, academics and other guardians of Culture, Decency and Good Taste, *Bravo* was out to legitimise its own innovations in the field of popular taste. If teenagers were to assert themselves in a hostile world, they needed, it was argued, a mouthpiece through which their grievances could be aired, and it was in this capacity that *Bravo* offered its services, claiming itself to be the only forum in which teenage protest could – and should – find expression. The mode of teenage rebellion was to be, not 'political', but aesthetic: 'We teenagers have our own style. And that's just what makes so many people see red' (Triumph advertisement, 1958). In the opening pages of the DIVO survey, *Bravo* then offered its services as an open site on which new teenage forms could be built and subsequently assembled into smoothly polished consumer lifestyles.

Girls in teenage lifestyle

The discourse of marketing defines lifestyles in terms of the specific configurations of commodity ownership which characterise particular consumer groups. In Germany, the Nürnberg Gesellschaft für Marktforschung was the first marketing institute to develop its own theory of lifestyle; it was not until the mid-fifties that other market research establishments began to look in earnest to sources outside classical economics for more finely differentiated analyses of potential target groups. Taking up the work of Thorstein Veblen, Margaret Mead, Freud, Jung and others, consumption theorists now set about recuperating information gathered in the academic disciplines of cultural anthropology, sociology and psychology to feed the data banks of the capitalist market. Classical political economy had tended to neglect the consumer, or to consider consumption only in relation to the economics of commodity production and distribution. In opposition to this, the new wave of consumption theorists, with Bengler and Vershofen in Nürnberg as their avant-garde, argued consistently for a more sophisticated awareness of the social and aesthetic dimensions of commodity use. Wilhelm Vershofen proposed that the concept of commodity use value should be broken down into three analytical components: basic, or original use value; and social use value, measured against variables such as social prestige; and aesthetic use value, measured against given standards of social taste (Vershofen, 1954, p. 12). Members of the artistic and literary establishment were taken to task for their confinement of Culture to a discrete and autonomous sphere, floating freely above the colourless wasteland of everyday life. The mutual dependence of economy and culture was seen by Vershofen to take active form in the daily exercise of consumer choice, determined as much by aesthetic as by economic or socio-psychological considerations.

The aesthetic principle regulating consumer lifestyles was a unity of form which bound the separate elements through which they were constructed. Part of the function of teenage commodities was to provide aesthetic forms for a cultural 'space' (adolescent leisure culture) which was differently inhabited by female and male consumers. For middle-class and working-class girls, home, the workplace and the street, where they shopped in the daytime and strolled by night, were always simultaneously sites of labour and of leisure. For the female consumer, the focal point of leisure, pleasure and personal freedom is not traditionally any fixed geographical location, but the female body itself. It was therefore the 'image industries' – the female mass media, and fashion and cosmetics industries – which constituted the largest sector of the post-war market in leisure commodities for girls.

The unity of post-war consumer lifestyles demanded new forms, too, for the feminine woman, produced in part on the production lines of the fashion, cosmetics and beauty-care industries. A glance at 1950s fashion images shows designers engaged in the business of sculpting, shaping and moulding ever more imaginative feminine forms: in 1954, the H-line, in spring 1955, the A-line, Dior's 'sack' in 1957, the trapeze line in spring 1958, into 1959 with the Empire line. At the same time, rigorous beauty-care regimes ensured that female bodies slipped smoothly into these new forms. Young girls turning for advice to *Bravo*'s beauty-care columnist were taught techniques of body culture and maintenance whereby each part of the body could be separately shaped and trained. When skirts hems rose to just above the knee, attention was focused on the female leg:

> From Paris comes the news that skirts are getting shorter – and short skirts show more leg! Are your legs in a fit state for public display? Nylon stockings show up every little blemish: do your stockings highlight the soft sheen of your well-cared-for skin . . . or is it the hard rough patches on thighs and knees which show up most? If it is, then something must be done at all costs! (*Bravo*, no. 10, 1958)

Tips on leg maintenance in *Bravo* between 1957 and 1959 included regular gymnastics, massage with 'slimming cream' (sic), visits to the chiropodist for sufferers from flat feet, lukewarm saltwater compresses for fat thighs, cycling for thin legs, trips to the doctor for red and inflamed skin. In conjunction with the beauty column, representations of women in the popular cultural discourses which traversed the pages of *Bravo* (film, television, fashion, rock and pop music and so on) reproduced certain common conventions of pose, gesture and body shape. For the perfect female leg, the general emphasis was on long, sweeping lines, further accentuated by high-heeled shoes tapering down to a pointed toe. Perfection was seen as embodied in particular representative female figures; Marlene Dietrich's legs, like Sophia Loren's hips and Brigitte Bardot's curves, were the talk of fifties beauty columns. Yet *Bravo* did not offer film star pin-ups as models of an ideal to which teenage girls should necessarily aspire; the ideal was displaced from visual representations, and located instead in the masculine gaze. 'Fashion has made skirts shorter', said the *Bravo* beauty tip in March 1958, 'More than ever, eyes are drawn to your legs'. That these were the eyes of men had been made clear in the same column in an earlier edition of the magazine, which sounded the following note of comfort for girls whose legs, despite hours of tortured beauty treatment, remained stubbornly inelegant.

A lot of men – for whose sake, after all, we go to all this trouble – don't have anything against legs that are a little stocky. A true man doesn't fall in love with external appearances. And if he does, he's the wrong one for you!' (*Bravo*, no. 44, 1957)

On the one hand, girls were exhorted to invest time and energy into the labour of body maintenance, grooming and careful dressing; on the other, the desired product of their labours remained persistently out of reach. The 'perfect female self' to which girls were urged to aspire was mirrored in the gaze of the men and boys with whom they shared their everyday lives; thus it remained unknowable, not signified in visual or textual representations, but in the ambiguous amorous attentions of men.

'Bravo girls' were offered one route out of this predicament; it led, not directly towards, but around and between the images of women which peopled the pages of the magazine. Mass media icons (film stars, fashion models, pop idols) were mediated to female readers by authoritative experts on fashion and beauty care – 'Ilse' in Triumph underwear advertisements, or 'Trixi' in *Bravo*'s own fashion column. The information they filtered down to the female reader concerned, not *what* she should look like, but instructions on *how* to make the best of her own resources. They celebrated, not any single image of femininity, but a set of aesthetic principles as possible instruments for the construction of a more beautiful self. Tailored to the modest resources of the 'Angestellte' who were *Bravo*'s most lucrative market, the mode of aesthetic production propagated here was rule by principles of sobriety, discretion, restraint, moderation and self-control.

> Our 'style' may perhaps tend at times to copy adult fashions. But in general it is still *more restrained, less changeable and less expensive* . . . Slaves to fashion? We're convinced . . . and we hope you are too – that that's the last thing we want to be. (*Triumph* advertisement, *Bravo*, no. 42, 1958; author's emphasis.)

'Consumption' as cultural practice

In the preceding sections of this survey of fifties consumer culture, I have outlined some of the ways in which capital organised commodity markets to expand the boundaries of female consumption. From this analysis of dominant forms, perspectives for future work on gender and consumption now begin to emerge. In the first instance, it is capital which dictates the forms which commodity consumption takes; yet the market remains dependent on the development by the female consumer of specific sets of social competences and skills: from the rational decision-making of the thrifty housewife, to teenage girls' production of themselves as aesthetic objects in the symbolic configurations of teenage life-styles. The category of 'consumption' covers a multitude of sins: symbolic readings of commodity representations, processes of sensual gratification, practices of economic and cultural exchange. The so-called 'sphere' of consumption can thus be dismantled into a multiplicity of complex forms, relations and practices, which operate on diverse and discrete market sites. On each of these 'levels' of consumption, female consumers engage differently with the market machine, activating multiple sets of functions, meanings

and values in the commodities they consume. Rules and conventions governing these consumer practices are laid down in consumer
law, advice and information; thus we have seen *Bravo*'s fashion
advisors setting out implicit and explicit rules for the production of
teenage style through the consumption of fashion commodities.

Analyses of these rules and conventions are indispensable to, yet
at the same time inadequate for feminist research into female
practices of consumption. Highlighting the mechanisms of control
which capital deploys, they fail to grasp the experiential quality of
consumer culture for women and girls. Biographical narratives offer
one way of bridging this gap, by tracing the paths whereby social
subjects negotiate dominant forms; thus I have chosen to end this
series of case studies in gender and consumer culture with two short
narratives: a fictional filmic narrative, and a biography taken from
an account of ethnographic field-work in the fifties. Positioned
within radically different contexts, their common feature is the
central significance accorded to one commodity: stockings. By
1961, nylons had swamped the young female market in West
Germany; *Bravo*'s DIVO survey shows 85 per cent of 'Bravo girls'
between the ages of twelve and twenty-four (compared with 80 per
cent of non-readers in the same age group) to be wearing seamless
stockings; the percentage of female *Bravo* readers who did not
possess either Perlon or nylon stockings was nil (DIVO 1961,
p. 137). These figures can neither be read as indicators of girls'
blind submission to the dictates of the market, nor do they signify
female capitulation to fetishistic 'male' fantasy. The all-
pervasiveness of synthetic silk stockings begs different questions:
what were the sources of their popularity, and how were they
actually 'consumed'?

Ninotchka

In the late fifties, *Bravo* ran a series of half-page advertisements for
'Opal' seamless stockings, depicting crossed female legs, long and
sophisticated, emerging from the folds of an elegant black dress.
Parallel to the 'Opal' campaign, the magazine carried reports on
Silk Stockings, Cole Porter's musical remake of Ernst Lubitsch's
Ninotchka (1939). In the fifties' musical, Wim Sonneveld plays a
Russian people's representative in Paris, whose loyalty to the Party

is beginning to fade. Three Soviet commissars are ordered from Moscow to Paris: their mission – to rescue their colleague from the clutches of that decadent capital. When they in turn disappear, super-activist Ninotchka (Cyd Charisse) is sent on their trail. She soon recognises the American, Edwin Canfield (Fred Astaire), as her main adversary; he meanwhile, is amused, fascinated, but never convinced, by her fervent defence of socialism and the Soviet way of life. He guides her instead down the boulevards of Paris, knowing that no woman – 'above all no woman with the charms of Ninotchka' – can withstand the 'democratic temptations' of their dazzling window displays. The 'fortress Ninotchka' finally falls; she succumbs to the charms of Edwin, and of the Western world he represents.

> Moscow – and politics – have lost Ninotschka for ever. Silk stockings may be thin, but in the end and above all, they are more attractive than the best of political convictions. (Bravo, no. 4, 1958)

Consumers of 'symbolic commodities' have preferred textual sources from which they draw the meanings with which those commodites are invested. *Bravo* is one such source for teenage consumers, and in 1958 it offered its readers a range of texts ('Opal' advertisements, fashion and beauty tips, reviews of *Silk Stockings*) in which synthetic silk (nylon or Perlon) stockings were encoded into new configurations of meaning. In part, these were drawn from the symbolic field of meanings around genuine silk, with its traditional associations of exoticism, sensuality, luxury and mystery: the legend of the Chinese princess said to have discovered the secret of the silkworm more than five thousand years ago: or the two sixth-century monks reputed to have smuggled the eggs of the silkworm out of China to the court of the Byzantine Emperor Justinian. But the additional glamour of the American nylon has specific origins elsewhere. On post-1945 black markets, American soldiers were well known as the main purveyors of nylon stockings; by the 1950s, poster graphics were using images of stockinged female legs for comparative representations of rising productivity rates in European countries. In popular representations of the Cold War period, the stocking became a dominant signifier of freedom, democracy and the American way of life; the musical *Silk Stockings* was Hollywood's contribution to this modern myth. In the *Silk Stockings* narrative, real anxieties over a simmering East-West conflict are played out in fantastic form across the female body. Ninotchka first becomes a 'true' woman through romantic association with a Western man – and through her consumption of fashion commodities for the feminine woman. In *Bravo*'s review, the resolution of the romantic narrative is couched in terms of military defeat ('the fortress Ninotchka . . . falls'); in the person of Edwin Canfield, America emerges victorious, not only over Ninotchka herself, but over the red threat she represents.

Reconstructing the *Silk Stockings* narrative, *Bravo*'s review becomes instrumental in the production of a store of meanings around synthetic silk hose, from which teenage consumers might potentially have drawn. Those meanings cannot, however, simply be read off the *Bravo* text. Post-structuralist studies of narrative as complexly codified systems of representations (Barthes, 1975) have shown meaning to be the product of relationships between reader and text, and thus not an intrinsic characteristic of the narrative itself. In order to make sense of any given narrative, the reader engages differently with each of its multiple 'codes', reproducing in her/his signifying practices the relations of tension and contradiction which exist between those codes. In *Bravo*'s *Silk Stockings* review, the so-called 'hermeneutic' and 'cultural' codes may be seen to produce just such contradictory meanings and values. The 'hermeneutic code' is the one which poses the central questions of the narrative, delaying the answers until the final moment of narrative resolution. The enigma of Ninotchka's narrative is the question of her possible transformation into a 'true' woman – a question answered at the end of the narrative in the language of female submission. Ninotchka capitulates to imperialist drives to colonise enemy continents, drives which are encapsulated here in the sexual passion of Edwin Canfield.

According to Barthes' definition in *S/Z*, the 'cultural code' of narrative refers the reader to meanings and values in the social world beyond the text. The social meaning of synthetic silk stockings is not exhausted in the *Bravo* narrative alone; indeed, connotations from other sources may badly disfigure the patterns of meaning constructed by 'internal' narrative codes (which are, in Barthesian terms, the hermeneutic and the semic codes). The following example of a second 1950s 'stocking narrative' shows one of the forms which these potentially oppositional meanings might take.

Annette

Between 1955 and 1957, a West German social worker, Renate Wald, put together a collection of biographical monographs of working-class factory girls, which were later published in Wurzbacher's *Die junge Arbeiterin* (1958). She drew on a pool of ethnographic research conducted by a team of participant observers, all of whom had lived and worked as factory employees for a number of months or years.

One of the girls, Annette, works with her mother in a textile factory; an only child, she spends much of her 'leisure time' at home with the family, helping her mother around the house, or enjoying precious moments of lazy conversation when the chores are finally done. Annette's mother, wary of the dangers of possible sexual adventures, is unwilling to allow her to develop close friendships with young people of either sex; even female friendships, she fears would ultimately lead to perilous encounters with the opposite sex. At the age of fifteen, Annette still amicably complies with her mother's wishes, remaining a model daughter in almost all respects. Even her taste in clothes is dictated by her mother's preferences for careful but unobtrusive dressing:

> She wears plain . . . dark clothes; although she uses powder and lipstick, she does so with care and in moderation; her hair is well-groomed and simply styled. She has an air, not so much of homeliness, as of exceptional respectability. (Wald, in Wurzbacher, 1958, p. 161)

Although mother and daughter rarely clash, there is one niggling point of conflict. The Perlon stockings which Annette wears to work every day cannot stand the rigours of shopfloor labour; inevitably, she wears out two or three pairs a week. Since Annette spends her weekly pocket money on biscuits and sweets, her mother has constantly to replenish her stock of nylons out of the housekeeping money. Her acid comment on her daughter's prodigality: 'She oughtn't to spend so much on titbits to eat. There's plenty of fruit and sweets to be had at home' (Wald, in Wurzbacher, 1958, p. 150). A striking characteristic of Annette's biography is the dreary regularity of her everyday life. Up at six in the morning to snatch a quick breakfast, stack the washing up, air the bedrooms and make the beds before setting out for work: nine hours at the production line: arriving back home at six-thirty in the evening to dust the rooms and clean the stairs before sitting down to eat with the family: retiring to bed by ten o'clock at the latest to recoup energy for the day ahead. Both at home and at the workplace, time, space, experience and action are regulated for Annette by institutions and agents of social control – the family and parents, the factory, overseers and management. In this context, Annette's conflict with her mother over stockings becomes more than a whimsical and inconsequential detail. A moment of disorder and disruption, it marks the displacement of potentially more grandiose demands for self-determination onto the only site where they may realistically be met. Annette is financially and emotionally dependent on the security of family life; she cannot allow herself prolonged struggles over points of generational difference. Repressed from the placid routine of everyday family life, these (inevitable) differences find expression in tangential conflicts and struggles.

It has been suggested that similar processes of displacement were in play in the formation of post-war youth subcultures (Cohen, 1972, p. 26). Yet subcultural resistance was no solution for Annette; isolated as she was from her contemporaries, her struggles necessarily took more minutely personal forms. Her conflicts with her mother centred on practices of day-to-day consumption – the money she wasted on frivolous treats, and her (mis)use of Perlon stockings. Perlon is made to be used and thrown away; mending stocking ladders is difficult, and diminishes aesthetic appeal. The 'built-in obsolescence' of Perlon stockings allowed Annette to use them to express an aberrant disregard for her mother's principle of moderation in all things, a principle to which she otherwise strictly adhered. Mass commodities demand to be consumed to excess: Annette, unconsciously perhaps, took them at their word.

Conclusion

As work on male youth subcultures has traced the 'hidden

contradictions' which they 'magically resolve' (Hebdige 1979, p. 18), so Annette's biography can shed light on some of the ways in which girls may live out the contradictions of their lives through an everyday culture of consumption. Her individual reformulation of the logic of built-in obsolescence took place *within* a teenage consumer culture; for her, hedonic consumption itself became a practice of refusal *vis-à-vis* dominant codes of social taste.

Feminists have commonly represented the 1950s as an age of repressive quiescence, in which women's disaffection with their feminine lot was successfully obscured and silenced. Since Betty Friedan's *Feminine Mystique* (1963), the blame for a widespread fifties' female malaise has been laid predominantly at the door of capitalist marketeers, to whom is ascribed the ability to dupe and seduce women into slavish submission to the authority of the market. But was 'consumerism' an adequate name for the problems of the female condition? Is there a hidden history of authentic female experience to be unearthed from beneath the glossy façade of fifties' femininity? Or could it not equally be the case that the façade itself 'speaks' the problems (and the delights) of the female condition? Consumerism not only offers, but also continually fulfils its promise of everyday solutions – albeit limited and partial ones – to problems whose origins may lie elsewhere. In post-war West Germany, women were constrained to search beyond national boundaries for female cultural forms untainted by aftertastes of Nazism. To don the accoutrements of an American female ideal – nylon stockings, scarlet lipstick, narrow skirts and high-heeled shoes – was in part to register a public disavowal of fascist images of femininity: scrubbed faces shining with health, sturdy child-bearing hips sporting seamed stockings and sensible shoes. Fifties consumerism, while it held many traps for women, nonetheless offered ways and means of negotiating a cultural history of militaristic discipline and rigorous control. Female 'resistance' of the period was perhaps not so much silenced, as pitched at a different level from earlier campaigns for women's equality (which in the fifties was proclaimed to have been achieved) or later feminist struggles against women's commoditisation and objectification on a capitalist market. At specific moments in post-war history, the market has become a target for the rhetoric of a necessary and well-founded feminist opposition; yet in relation to the fifties – and possibly in the eighties too – there was, and is, little to be gained from 'opposi-tional' postures of aloof distaste.

> For me, the eighties are more than this: love the things that bring you down. I can't change things, I can't think plastic out of my world, so I try to turn the tables on it and see what's actually good about it. Do you see . . . I can drape myself with as much silk and linen as I want, and the plastic still won't go away. So I try to look at it differently. Love the things that bring you down. (Annette Humpe, Ideal)

My thanks are due to Brigit Cramon-Daiber, Ryszard Gagola, Angela McRobbie, and Maureen McNeil, whose critical comments and eminently helpful suggestions have been incorporated at various stages in the writing of this article.

Notes

1. The seminal work in this field was Phil Cohen's 1972 study of 'Subcultural Conflict and Working-class Community' (Birmingham 1972). Other works to which both explicit and implicit reference will be made in the following pages include Hall and Jefferson (1976), Hebdige, (1979) and Willis (1977).
2. The term 'homology' is used in subcultural theory to describe the 'degree of fit' between the structure of group experience and the cultural forms through which that experience is expressed. Thus for example in Paul Willis's studies of hippy and bike-boy culture, the music of each group was seen to exist in a relationship of 'homology' with its lifestyle and values. 'The preferred music must have the potential, at least in its formal structure, to express meanings which resonate with other aspects of group life.' (Willis, 'The Cultural Meaning of drug use', in Hall and Jefferson, 1976, p. 106)
3. A recent case in point was the so-called Schwarz-Schilling affair in West Germany in the winter of 1982–83. Christian Schwarz-Schilling, the new telecommunications minister in the Kohl cabinet, came under attack for his plans to inject at least DM1 billion of state money into cable TV projects, after it had become known that he himself had private interests in the cable industry.

Bibliography

Alderson, C. (1968) *Magazines Teenagers Read* (Oxford: Pergamon).

Allen, H. (1982) 'Political Lesbianism and Feminism – Space for a Sexual Politics?', *m/f*, no. 7.

Bailey, R. and M. Brake (1975) *Radical Social Work* (London: Edward Arnold).

Bandura, A. (1964) 'The Stormy Decade: Fact or Fiction', *Psychology in the Schools*, pp. 224–31.

Barrett, M. *et al.* (eds) (1979) *Ideology and Cultural Production* (London: Croom Helm).

Barrett, M. (1980) *Women's Oppression Today* (London: Verso).

Barthes, Roland, (1970) *S/Z* (London: Jonathan Cape).

Bernstein, B. (1977) *Class, Codes and Control, vol. 3: Towards a Theory of Educational Transmissions* (London: Routledge & Kegan Paul).

Blanch, M. (1979) 'Imperialism, Nationalism and Organised Youth', in J. Clarke, C. Critcher and R. Johnson (eds), *Working-Class Culture* (London: Hutchinson).

Bommes, M. and P. Wright (1982) 'Charms of residence: the public and the past', in R. Johnson, G. McLennan, B. Schwarz and D. Sutton (eds), *Making Histories: Studies in History-Writing and Politics* (London: Hutchinson).

Bone, A. (1983) *Girls and Girls-only Schools* (Manchester: Equal Opportunities Commission).

Bourdieu, P. (1967) 'Systems of Education and Systems of Thought', *International Social Science Journal*, vol. XIX, no. 3.

Brunsdon, C. (1981) 'Crossroads: Notes on Soap Opera', *Screen*, vol. 22, no. 4.

Burke, P. (1978) *Popular Culture in Early Modern Europe* (London: Temple Smith).

Califia, P. (1981) 'Man/Boy Love and the Lesbian/Gay Movement', in D. Tsang (ed.), *The Age Taboo: Gay Male Sexuality, Power and Consent* (London: Gay Men's Press).

Camden Area Youth Committee Report (1982) *'Out of Sight' A report on how the ILEA Youth Service in the Camden area is meeting the needs of girls and young women.*

Campbell, B. (1980) 'Sugan 'n Spice 'n Nice 'n Angry', *Time Out*, 25 Jul.

Clarke, J. *et al*. (eds) (1979) *Working Class Culture* (London: Hutchinson).

Cockburn, C. (1981) 'The Material of Male Power', *Feminist Review*, no. 9.

Cohen, P. (1972) 'Subcultural Conflict and Working-class Community', *Working Papers in Cultural Studies*, no. 2, Spring.

Cohen, P. (1982) 'Schooling for the Dole', *New Socialist*, no. 3.

Cooper, D. (1971) *The Death of the Family* (London: Allen Lane).

Corrigan, P. (1979) *Schooling the Smash Street Kids* (London: Macmillan).

Coward, R. and W.A.V.A.W. (1982) 'What is Pornography? Two Opposing Feminist Viewpoints' in *Spare Rib* 119.

Coward, R. (1982) 'Sexual Violence and Sexuality', *Feminist Review*, no. 11.

Cowie, C. and S. Lees (1981) 'Slags or Drags', *Feminist Review*, no. 9.

Davies, B. (1981) 'Social Education and Political Education: In Search of Integration', *Schooling and Culture*, no. 9.

Davin, A. (1978) 'Imperialism and Motherhood', *History Workshop*, no. 5.

Deaux, K. (1976) *The Behaviour of Women and Men* (Belmont, California: Wadsworth).

Deem, R. (1980) *Schooling for Women's Work* (London: Routledge & Kegan Paul).

Delamont, S. (1978) 'The Contradictions in Ladies' Education', in S. Delamont and L. Duffin (eds), *The Nineteenth-Century Woman* (London: Croom Helm).

Delphy, C. (1981) 'Women in Stratification Studies' in H. Roberts (ed.), *Doing Feminist Research* (London: Routledge & Kegan Paul).

DIVO/Kindler und Schiermeyer Verlag AG (eds) (1961) *Bravo-Leser stellen sich vor* (Munich: Kindler und Schiermeyer).

Dixon, B. (1977) *Catching Them Young: Race, Sex and Class in Children's Fiction* (London: Pluto).

Dworkin, A. (1981) *Pornography: Men Possessing Women* (London: Women's Press).

Dyer, R. (1982) 'Entertainment and Utopia' in R. Altman (ed.), *Genre: The Musical* (London: British Film Institute).

Dyhouse, C. (1981) *Girls Growing Up in Late Victorian and Edwardian England* (London: Routledge & Kegan Paul).

Eichenbaum, L. and S. Orbach (1982) *Outside In, Inside Out* (Harmondsworth: Penguin).

Ellis, J. (1982) *Visible Fictions* (London: Routledge & Kegan Paul).

Eppel, M. and E. M. Eppel (1966) *Adolescents and Morality* (London: Routledge & Kegan Paul).

Erhard, L. (1962) *Wohlstand für alle* (Gütersloh: Signum).

Farrell, W. (1974) *The Liberated Man* (New York: Random House).

Fernbach, D. (1980) 'Ten Years of Gay Liberation', in *Politics and Power 2* (London: Routledge & Kegan Paul).

Finn, D., N. Grant and R. Johnson (1977) 'Social Democracy, Education and the Crisis', in *Working Papers in Cultural Studies* no. 10 (Centre for Contemporary Cultural Studies, University of Birmingham).

Fisher, L. and M. Landy (1982) 'The Eyes of Laura Mars: A Binocular Critique', *Screen*, vol. 23, no. 3/4.

Foucault, M. (1972) *The Archaeology of Knowledge* trans. Alan Sheridan (London: Tavistock). (First published in French, 1969.)

Foucault, M. (1973) *The Birth of the Clinic*, trans. Alan Sheridan (London: Tavistock).

Foucault, M. (1977) *Discipline and Punish*, trans. Alan Sheridan (London: Allen Lane).

Foucault, M. (1979) *The History of Sexuality*, Vol. 1 (London, Allen Lane).

Freud, S. (1908) 'Family Romances', in *Standard Edition of the Complete Psychological Works of Sigmund Freud*, vol. IX (London: Hogarth Press and the Institute of Psychoanalysis).

Freud, S. (1933) 'Femininity', *Standard Edition of the Complete Psychological Works of Sigmund Freud*, vol. xii (London: Hogarth Press and the Institute of Psychoanalysis).

Frith, G. (1985) 'The Time of Your Life! The Meaning of the School Story' in C. Steedman, C. Urwin and V. Walkerdine (eds), *Language, Gender and Childhood*, (London: Routledge & Kegan Paul).

Frith, S. (1978) *The Sociology of Rock* (London: Constable).

Frith, S. (1981) 'Youth in the Eighties: A Dispossessed Generation', *Marxism Today*, vol. 25, no. 11.

Garnsey, E. (1978) 'Women's Work and Theories of Class Stratification', *Sociology*, vol. 12, no. 2.

Gay Left Collective (1981) 'Happy Families? Paedophilia Examined', in D. Tsang (ed.), *The Age Taboo: Gay Male Sexuality, Power and Consent* (London: Gay Men's Press).

Gillis, J. R. (1974) *Youth and History* (London: Academic Press).

Goldthorpe, J. H. (1980) *Social Mobility and Class Structure in Modern Britain* (Oxford University Press).

Gordon, L. and E. Dubois (1983) 'Seeking Ecstasy on the Battlefield: Danger and Pleasure in Nineteenth-Century Feminist Sexual Thought', *Feminist Review*, no. 13.

Habermas, J. (1962) *Strukturwandel der Öffentlichkeit* (Darmstadt und Neuwied: Luchterhand).

Hall, S. and T. Jefferson (eds) (1976) *Resistance Through Rituals: Youth Subcultures in Post-War Britain* (London: Hutchinson).

Halsey, A. H., A. F. Heath and J. M. Ridge (1980) *Origins and*

Destinations: Family, Class and Education in Modern Britain (Oxford: Clarendon Press).

Hamblin, A. and R. Bowen (1981) 'Sexual Abuse of Children', *Spare Rib*, no. 106.

Hansen, S. and J. Jensen (1971) *The Little Red Schoolbook* (London: Stage 1).

Heath, A. (1981) *Social Mobility* (London: Fontana).

Hebdige, D. (1979) *Subcultures: The Meaning of Style* (London: Methuen).

Hebdige, D. (1982) 'Hiding in the Light', *Ten. 8*, no. 9.

Henriques, J., W. Hollway, C. Urwin, C. Venn and V. Walkerdine (1984) *Changing the Subject: Psychology, Social Regulation and Subjectivity* (London: Routledge & Kegan Paul).

HMSO (1960) *The Youth Service in England and Wales* (The Albermarle Report).

HMSO (1969) *Youth and Community Work in the Seventies*.

HMSO (1982) *Experience and Participation: Report of the Review Group on the Youth Service in England* (The Thompson Report).

Hobson, D. (1978) 'Housewives: Isolation as Oppression', in Women's Studies Group (ed.), *Women Take Issue* (London: Hutchinson).

Hoggart, R. (1957) *The Uses of Literacy* (Harmondsworth: Penguin).

Hudson, A. (1983) 'The Welfare State and Adolescent Femininity', *Youth and Policy*, vol. 2, no. 1.

Hutter, B. and G. Williams (1981) *Controlling Women* (London: Croom Helm).

Inner London Education Authority (1981) *Youth Service Provision for Girls*.

Intermarket Gesellschaft für Internationale Markt- und Meinungsforschung (1957) *Das Verhalten des Verbrauchers* (Düsseldorf: Intermarket).

Jephcott, P. (1954) *Some Young People* (London: George Allen & Unwin).

Kitwood, T. (1981) *Disclosures to a Stranger* (London: Routledge & Kegan Paul).

Lacan, J. (1977) *Ecrits: A Selection* (London: Tavistock).

Landgrebe-Wolff, I. and AID (Land- und hauswirtschaftlicher Auswertungs- und Informationsdienst e.V.) (eds) (1957) *Mehr Käuferbewusstsein! Verbrauchererziehung und Ernährungsberatung in den USA, mit Anregungen fur Deutschland* (Frankfurt-am-Main: Kommentator).

Laplanche, J. and J. B. Pontalis (1973) *The Language of Psychoanalysis* (London: Hogarth Press and the Institute of Psychoanalysis).

Larner, C. (1981) 'Male Feminism and the Future Perfect' *New Society*, 9 April.

Lasch, C. (1982) *The Culture of Narcissism* (New York: Sphere).
Lee, C. and R. S. Stewart (1976) *Sex Differences, Cultural And Developmental Dimensions* (New York: Urizen Books).
Lobban, G. (1975) 'Sex-Roles in Reading Schemes', *Educational Review*, vol. 27, no. 3.
Loftus, M. (1974) 'Learning Sexism and Femininity', in Allen, S., L. Saunders, and J. Wallis (eds) *Conditions of Illusion: Papers from the Women's Movement* (Leeds: Feminist Books).
McRobbie, A. (1978) 'Working Class Girls and the Culture of Femininity', in Women's Studies Group (eds), *Women Take Issue* (London: Hutchinson).
McRobbie, A. (1980) 'Settling Accounts With Subcultures', *Screen Education*, no. 34.
McRobbie, A. (1981) 'Just Like a *Jackie* Story', in A. McRobbie and T. McCabe (eds), *Feminism For Girls* (London: Routledge & Kegan Paul).
McRobbie, A. (1982a) 'Jackie: an Ideology of Adolescent Femininity', in *Popular Culture: Past and Present*, ed. Waites, B., Bennet, T. and Martin, G. (London: Croom Helm and The Open University Press).
McRobbie, A. (1982b) 'The Politics of Feminist Research: Between Talk, Text and Action', *Feminist Review*, no. 12.
McRobbie, A. and J. Garber (1976) 'Girls and Subcultures', in: S. Hall and T. Jefferson (eds), *Resistance Through Rituals: Youth Subcultures in Post-War Britain* (London: Hutchinson).
Marchant, H. and H. Smith (1977) *Adolescent Girls at Risk* (London: Pergamon).
Mayhew, H. (1968 edition) *London Labour and the London Poor* (New York: Dover).
Millett, K. and M. Blasius (1981) 'Sexual Revolution and the Liberation of Children', in D. Tsang (ed.), *The Age Taboo: Gay Male Sexuality, Power and Consent* (London: Gay Men's Press).
Mitchell, J. (1980) 'On the Differences Between Men and Women', *New Society*, 12 June.
Moody, R. (1980) *Indecent Assault* (London: Word is Out/Peace News).
Moody, R. (1981) 'Man/Boy Love and the Left', in D. Tsang (ed.), *The Age Taboo: Gay Male Sexuality, Power and Consent* (London: Gay Men's Press).
Morley, D. (1981) 'The Nationwide Audience, A Postscript' *Screen Education*, no. 39.
Mulvey, L. (1981) 'Visual Pleasure in Narrative Cinema', in T. Bennett *et al.* (eds), *Popular Television and Film* (London: British Film Institute).
Mungham, G. and G. Pearson (1976) *Working Class Youth Cultures* (London: Routledge & Kegan Paul).
Musgrove, F. (1964) *Youth and the Social Order* (London: Routledge & Kegan Paul).

Musgrove, F. (1969) 'The problem of youth and the structure of society in England', *Youth and Society*, vol. 1, no. 1.

Nava, M. (1980) 'Gender and Education', *Feminist Review*, no. 5.

Nava, M. (1982) 'Everybody's Views Were Just Broadened: A Girls' Project and Some Responses to Lesbianism', *Feminist Review*, no. 10.

Nava, M. (1983) 'From Utopian to Scientific Feminism? Early Feminist Critiques of the Family', in L. Segal (ed.), *What is To Be Done About the Family* (Harmondsworth: Penguin).

Nava, M. (1984) 'The Urban, The Domestic and Education for Girls: An Examination of their Relationship in Victorian and Edwardian England', in G. Grace (ed.) *Education and the City* (London: Routledge & Kegan Paul).

Noelle, E. (1940) *Massenbefragungen über Politik und Presse in USA* (Frankfurt-am-Main: Diesterweg).

Oakley, Ann (1972) *Sex, Gender and Society* (London: Temple-Smith).

Oakley, Ann (1977) *Housewife* (Harmondsworth: Penguin).

Pearson, G. (1983) *Hooligan: a History of Respectable Fears* (London: Macmillan).

Perkins, T. E. (1979) 'Rethinking Stereotypes', in Barrett *et al.* (eds), *Ideology and Cultural Production* (London: Croom Helm).

Phillips, A. (1981) 'Marxism and Feminism', in Feminist Anthology Collective (ed.), *No Turning Back* (London: Women's Press).

Pinkerton, G. (1982) 'Challenging Sex Stereotypes: Ideas For the Class-room', *Contact*, 12 Nov. (Inner London Education Authority).

Prendergast, S. and A. Prout (1980) 'What Will I Do . . .? Teenage Girls and the Construction of Motherhood', *Sociological Review*, vol. 28, no. 3, pp. 517–35.

Presland, E. (1981) 'Whose Power? Whose Consent?, in D. Tsang (ed.), *The Age Taboo: Gay Male Sexuality, Power and Consent* (London: Gay Men's Press).

Roberts, R. (1971) *The Classic Slum* (Harmondsworth: Penguin).

Robins, D. and P. Cohen (1978) *Knuckle Sandwich* (Harmondsworth: Penguin).

Rose, J. (1983) 'Femininity and Its Discontents', *Feminist Review*, no. 14.

Rubin, G. (1981) 'Sexual Politics, the New Right and the Sexual Fringe', in D. Tsang (ed.), *The Age Taboo: Gay Male Sexuality, Power and Consent* (London: Gay Men's Press).

Scharmann, D-L. (1965) *Das Konsumverhalten von Jugendlichen* (Munich: Juventa).

Schofield, M. (1968) *The Sexual Behaviour of Young People* (Harmondsworth: Penguin).

Segal, L. (1983) '"Smash the Family?" Recalling the 1960s', in L. Segal (ed.), *What is To Be Done About the Family?* (Harmondsworth: Penguin).

Segal, L. (ed.) (1983) *What is To Be Done About the Family?* (Harmondsworth: Penguin).

Shacklady-Smith, L. (1978) 'Sexist Assumptions and Female Delinquency, an Empirical Investigation', in C. Smart and B. Smart (eds), *Women, Sexuality and Social Control* (London: Routledge & Kegan Paul).

Shaw, J. (1980) 'Education and the Individual: Schooling for Girls, or Mixed Schooling – a Mixed Blessing?', in R. Deem (ed.) *Schooling for Women's Work* (London: Routledge & Kegan Paul).

Simon, B. (1974) *Education and the Labour Movement 1870–1920* (London: Lawrence and Wishart).

Smart, C. and B. Smart (eds) (1978) *Women, Sexuality and Social Control* (London: Routledge & Kegan Paul).

Smith, M. and T. Taylor (1983) 'The Problem of Men: Sexism and the Male Trainer', *Working With Girls Newsletter*, no. 14.

Spender, D. and E. Sarah (eds) (1980) *Learning to Lose: Sexism and Education* (London: The Women's Press).

Stedman Jones, G. (1976) *Outcast London* (Harmondsworth: Penguin).

Steedman, C., C. Urwin and V. Walkerdine (eds) (1984) *Language, Gender and Childhood* (London: Routledge & Kegan Paul).

Thomas, W. I. (1967) *The Unadjusted Girl* (New York: Harper and Row). (First published 1928.)

Thompson, P. (1975) 'The War With Adults', *Oral History* vol. 3, no. 2.

Tolson, A. (1977) *The Limits to Masculinity* (London: Tavistock).

Tsang, D. (ed.) (1981) *The Age Taboo: Gay Male Sexuality, Power and Consent* (London: Gay Men's Press).

Vershofen, W. (1954) 'Rationalisierung vom Verbraucher her', *Deutsche Wirtschaft im Querschnitt* (Beilage zu *Der Volkswirt*) no. 28.

Walden, R. and V. Walkerdine (1982) *Girls and Mathematics: The Early Years*, Bedford Way Papers, (London: Heinemann).

Walden, R. and V. Walkerdine (1983) *Girls and Mathematics: From Primary to Secondary Schooling*, University of London Institute of Education mimeo.

Walkerdine, V. (1981) 'Sex, Power and Pedagogics', *Screen Education*, no. 38.

Walkerdine, V. (1984) 'Power, Gender, Resistance', in C. Steedman, C. Urwin and V. Walkerdine (eds), *Language, Gender and Childhood* (London: Routledge & Kegan Paul).

Walvin, J. (1982) *A Child's World* (Harmondsworth: Penguin).

Warner, W. L. (1960) *Social Class in America* (Evanston, Illinois: Harper and Row).

Webster, P. (1981) 'Pornography and Pleasure', *Heresies*, no. 12.

Willis, P. (1977) *Learning to Labour: How Working Class Kids get Working Class Jobs* (London: Saxon House).

Willis, P. (1979): 'Shop-floor Culture, Masculinity, and the Wage Form' in J. Clarke *et al*. (eds) *Working-Class Culture* (London: Hutchinson).

Wilmott, P. (1966) *Adolescent Boys of East London* (London: Routledge & Kegan Paul).

Wilson, D. (1978) 'Sexual Codes and Conduct: A Study of Teenage Girls', in C. Smart and B. Smart (eds), *Women, Sexuality and Social Control* (London: Routledge & Kegan Paul).

Wilson, E. (1983a) *What Is To Be Done About Violence Against Women?* (Harmondsworth: Penguin).

Wilson, E. (1983b) 'The Context of "Between Pleasure and Danger"': The Barnard Conference on Sexuality', *Feminist Review*, no. 13.

Wolpe, Ann-Marie (1977) *Some Processes in Sexist Education* (London: Women's Research and Resources Centre).

Women's Studies Group, Centre for Contemporary Cultural Studies (eds) (1978) *Women Take Issue* (London: Hutchinson).

Woods, W. (1960) 'Psychological Dimensions of Consumer Decision', *Journal of Marketing*, vol. 24, no. 3.

Working with Girls National Association of Youth Clubs (NAYC) Leicester.

Wurzbacher, G. and W. Jaide (eds) (1958) *Die junge Arbeiterin: Beiträge zur Sozialkunde und Jugendarbeit* (Munich: Juventa).

Index